CITY OF PROMISE

CITY OF PROMISE

RACE & HISTORICAL CHANGE IN LOS ANGELES

Edited by

Martin Schiesl

Mark Morrall Dodge

Regina Books

Claremont, California

Book design: Regina Books
Cover design: Mary Stoddard

ISBN 1-930053-42-8 paperback

Regina Books
Post Office Box 280
Claremont, California 91711
Tel: (909) 624-8466 / Fax (909) 626-1345

Manufactured in the United States of America

CONTENTS

DEDICATION

We dedicate this book to our colleague Nadine Ishitani Hata—a scholar, teacher, and senior administrator, and a tenacious advocate of civil rights and educational causes—who died at her home on February 25, 2005, after a long struggle with breast cancer. She was 63.

Her research, publications and public service were often in collaboration with her historian husband, Donald Teruo Hata.

Preface

In 1900 Los Angeles boosters, despite Mexican cultural traditions that extended back to the eighteenth century, celebrated the city's Anglo values and institutions. The years from 1910 to 1945 saw the influx of many African Americans, migrants from Mexico, and Asian and Pacific immigrants into the city. Larger numbers of these groups entered Los Angeles in the postwar decades. By the end of the century, the city had become the biggest multicultural center in the nation boasting an extraordinary racial diversity.

Inspired by the reception of *20th Century Los Angeles: Power, Promotion, and Social Conflict* (1990), the authors of the essays in *City of Promise* have drawn upon a wide range of primary and secondary materials to provide a rich description and discussion. They show that nonwhite newcomers withstood much discrimination, formed a variety of cultural and social institutions, established permanent communities, and gained political power. The result is a very important addition to the understanding of the history of race and race relations in Los Angeles and the urban American West.

The editors are indebted to many people. We thank all our contributors for their cooperation as we prepared the volume for publication. We thank David Deis who produced the maps on Los Angeles' racial composition in 2000. We also received help from library archivists in securing photographs for this book. Our publisher, Richard Dean Burns, shepherded the volume through its various stages with much attention and care. Finally, Martin Schiesl deeply thanks his wife, Sharon, for her constant encouragement and support.

Martin Schiesl
Mark Morrall Dodge

INTRODUCTION

Ali Modarres

*C*ity of Promise offers an interpretation of Los Angeles through the eyes of its minority population. Of course, this does not mean that all voices are or can be included. Even within Latino, African-American, and Asian communities, which the authors of this book discuss, there exists a multiplicity of voices that cannot be fully addressed in one volume. Guatemalans, Salvadorans, Colombians, and many other sub-ethnic categories of the Latino population will have their individual stories to tell, as will Koreans, Vietnamese, Thai, and many other Asian sub-ethnic and linguistic groups. Los Angeles also has a rich history of various White ethnic communities that can give us unique understandings of how the area may have been imagined by its diverse residents. This introductory chapter cannot address what is not in the present book, but it can acknowledge the value of including the missing voices in other stories on Los Angeles. After all, every story has its own message and purpose. It is for that reason that storytellers can continue to chronicle the past anew in varying narrations.

It is within the narrow scope of situating the book and its contents that this introductory chapter provides readers with the logic and interpretive quality of the book. How minorities came to see the city and experience it is a story worth telling in multiple variations. This is the task this book undertakes and its authors tell us how specific historical narrations (i.e., as interpreted by them) help us deconstruct the city. Even though the authors may appear to adopt a structuralist approach to interpreting the city, readers may be surprised by the level of attention afforded to human agency and its role in resisting the forces of inequity.

City of Promise is logically divided into two sections, discussing the city before and after WWII. The war was pivotal to the history of Los Angeles: the city was re-shaped due to the economic boom it experienced in the war years, during which time it attracted a large number of laborers, including members of several racial/ethnic groups. In the period of 1900-1945, Los Angeles was a refuge for African-Americans who escaped oppressive conditions in the south and the emerging industrial northwest, while Mexican-Americans left the revolutionary and poverty-stricken conditions of their homeland, and Asians congregated in a few neighborhoods to escape the xenophobic conditions in other regions of the country. The period since 1945 has seen further population growth of Mexican-Americans and Asians as a direct result of the Bracero Program, the 1965 Immigration Act, and other immigration (or anti-immigration) policies that have shaped Los Angeles into its emerging status as the Ellis Island of the west. Los Angeles, before and after 1945, was qualitatively and quantitatively two different cities. Not only did immigration reshape the city, but so did its economic position, political relevance, and an urban growth that was fueled by the expanding economic opportunities in the region. This prosperity was, unfortunately, not shared equally by the whole city, and the chapters in this book reflect the growing pains of the region and its landscape of inequities.

The book opens with a chapter on Mexican immigrant families and their conditions in the pre-war era. Focusing on the factors that pushed these immigrants out of their homeland and into an immigrant's life, Gloria Miranda provides us with an interesting glimpse into the social construction of Mexican-American identity and its embedded social, political, and economic inequities. In evoking the strong image of "refugees," the author sets the stage for a narrative of economic challenges, assimilative forces, and community formation processes. The journey for many of those who immigrated before 1945 was a rural to urban migration, albeit across an international boundary, promoted by revolution and economic stagnation. Miranda points to a number of communities in Los Angeles that suggest at inter-group, as well as within group struggles. Mexican immigrants were not necessarily welcomed by those already living in Los Angeles. The Mexican-American identity thus bore the stamp of temporality, mapped against the geography of segregation. What made the deplorable social conditions bearable were the urbanity of Los Angeles and whatever opportunities were available. These spaces of hope were intermittently closed shut by anti-immigration movements, the worst of which occurred in the 1920s, culminating in the tragedy of Mexican repatriation.

Donald and Nadine Hata tell the familiar Asian story in two acts, separated along the temporal division of the book. Chapter 2 begins with a rarely told narrative of Asian immigration to Mexico, which extended geographically to the Philippines during the Spanish colonial period. This opening lends itself to the history of the Asian presence in California and Los Angeles, especially the Chinese and Japanese, during the 18th and 19th centuries. The narrative is familiar to those knowledgeable about the history of Asian immigration and their treatment, socially and politically, at the hands of Anglo society. The Chinese Exclusion Act of 1882 was the singular precedent for exclusionary immigration policies that culminated in the 1924 Immigration Act. The authors relate the struggle, survival, and community building among Chinese and later Japanese immigrants with clarity, illustrating a promise created through the discovery of gold that transformed into hardship and an abusive social environment in California, and how the community fought the alienating forces of xenophobia and racialization. Chinese merchants, fishermen, and farmers played a significant role in building the Los Angeles of the late 19th century; however, overwhelmed by the hostile policy environment that excluded the Chinese from immigration to the U.S. and attacks on their community, their numbers declined. This population was soon replaced by Japanese immigrants, who in turn faced discriminatory practices and the eventual hardship of internment camps that fell upon them with WWII and the Japanese army's attack on Pearl Harbor.

Chapter 2 does not stop at telling the stories of the Chinese and Japanese, which are often narrated as a part of the racial and ethnic history of Los Angeles. An interesting contribution to this chapter is its brief history of the South Asian community at the beginning of the 20th century. This narration allows the authors to crystallize their views regarding race relations in Los Angeles during its formative years. By expanding the discussion to a number of ethno-national Asian subgroups, Donald and Nadine Hata expose the fragmentary nature of the "Asian/Pacific Islander" identities, on the one hand, and on the other, illustrate the collective historical treatment of these groups nationally and locally. This historical analysis allows us to explore, once again, the importance of the American sociopolitical context in ethno-genesis. The treatment of the Japanese in the U.S. during WWII reminds us that Japanese identity in the U.S. is significantly different from being Japanese from Japan. Embedded in the Japanese-American identity is a history of victimization and mistreatment unknown to people from their ancestral land.

Chapter 4, "Into the Mainstream," picks up the story from WWII and narrates the era of Asian "arrival"—socially and otherwise. The years before and after the 1965 Immigration Act were uniquely affective in shaping the Asian-American identity through population growth, fueled by immigration and paths forged to economic, political, and social inclusion. Although Asian-Americans faced multiple challenges, the rise of the Pacific Rim after WWII, in terms of its economy and geopolitics, meant that conditions were present for higher possibilities of inclusion and empowerment. To be sure, the new and old Asian populations were not the same. Chapter 4 uniquely unfolds the observed differences between these two groups before and after 1965. However, the authors illustrate that despite the apparent cultural and socioeconomic differences and the fact that the newer Asian immigrants had their own challenges to face, it is their marginalization that unites them with their older Asian-American counterparts. In fact, to the extent possible, the authors narrate the experience of a plurality that makes the Asian-American community in Los Angeles. In both the second and the fourth chapters, we can clearly see the importance of activism and the role that individuals can play in promoting and achieving empowerment. As the authors argue, by challenging the sociopolitical structures that promote exclusionary practices and by building institutions around which community-based activism can occur, the Asian community, collectively and individually, has been able to "move from the margins into the mainstream." This move, however, has been neither comprehensive nor complete.

If the Asian and Latino communities can point to success stories and failures, African-American communities provide us with some of the most disheartening failures of the *City of Promise* as well as illustrating some of its progress. Chapters 3 and 5 deal with the hopes and desires of a marginalized population that sought to escape the racial hardships of the South and the industrial northwest. Though for a fleeting moment it appeared that a window of opportunity was open for them, the exclusionary treatment followed them to the land of sunshine and abundance. The "Simple Quest for Dignity" is a reverberating theme that runs through both chapters.

Delores Nason McBroome tells us the story of pre-WWII Los Angeles from the perspective of individual African-Americans as well as the larger group. Even though African-American migration to Los Angeles was indeed an escape from racial practices elsewhere, Jim Crow segregation followed them in the 1920s. The author tells us about a few visionaries, lost opportunities, and the failure of an imagined promise. These are exemplified by the stories of Jefferson L. Edmonds, Robert C. Owens, Reverend J.E. Edwards, Frederick Roberts, Phillip Randolph, and Hugh Macbeth, which show us the history of African-American communities prior to the 1920s, especially the formation of advocacy organizations such as the Los Angeles Forum and the African-American press prior to the WW II era. These hopeful voices of this era promoted empowerment through collective efforts and self-help. Theirs was a utopian dream of becoming productive and equal members of society. Ideas such as the "back-to-the-soil movement" may have brought African-Americans to Southern and Baja California, but it was not enough to create the much needed level playing field. If "hope" was the common factor that held the African American population together, it was collective marginalization that bounded their socio-political space. From the 1912 Shenk Rule to the national security paranoia of WWI, the Red Scare of 1919 and 1920, and the Ku Klux Klan activities of the 1920s in Los Angeles, African-Americans and their leaders found their civil liberties systematically ignored and their opportunities in their newfound home gradually eroded.

Josh Sides tells us that the fundamental purpose for African-American migration was to shed the "mask" of racial inferiority assigned to them in the South. But what attracted them to Los Angeles was the possibility of homeownership, the main pillar of the American Dream. The rise of industrial Los Angeles and its

job opportunities made this promise even more achievable. Sides
maps the political economy of migration onto the landscape of race
relations, individual agency, and the regional economy to situate
his narrative within a complex era in the experience of a diverse
African-American population. Uneven terrains of power, tensions
created between democratic aspirations and the reality of a capitalist
economy, and the overwhelming forces of racist ideologies create
an apt background against which the African-American experience
since 1945 can be understood. While the author documents the
hardships faced by this population into the 1970s and beyond, he
also casts an occasionally positive light on what has been achieved,
in terms of economic and political empowerments. Sides' detailed
focus on the geography of African Americans and their relationships
with other racial and ethnic groups allows us to see a more
comprehensive image of the city and its changes during the last few
decades. It is in telling this story of spatialized inter-group relations
that we discover the author lamenting the death of the California
Dream for African-Americans, beginning in the 1980s. This is
attributed to increased ethnic competition, especially with Latinos.
An important and sensitive topic, especially when we consider that
African-Americans are currently the third largest racial minority
group in the County, the issue of inter-group competition naturally
culminates in possibilities for collaboration. Sides points aptly to
such a possibility in the last few pages, resurrecting the era of
Edward Roybal and Kenneth Hahn. This topic is analyzed and
discussed by Kenneth Burt in the last chapter of the book.

Before the historical narration of collaborations and struggles
for political empowerment, Martin Schiesl, in chapter 6, tells us
about the importance of understanding the role of institutional
racism, exemplified in the day-to-day operations of the Los Angeles
Police Department (LAPD), in creating and further exacerbating
the disempowered position of minorities. In "Behind the Shield,"
the author tells the story of the LAPD from the perspective of
Latinos and African Americans, reminding us of the brutality with
which this organization played the march of racism. Schiesl's cast
of characters does not include the activists whose names remind
us of how power was attained one district at a time. They are
typically police chiefs and their allies who come across as icons
of the racist past. Watts and the 1992 riots are used as backdrops
against which the behavior of the police department is examined.

The author also reviews African-American activism and the role played by organizations such as the Black Panthers in resisting systematic harassment by police. Schiesl's unique contribution in this chapter goes beyond relating how African Americans were treated by the police. He includes the experience of Latinos with the police to show how unequal treatment is pervasive. The growth of the Latino population in the 1960s made it necessary for this group to mobilize and seek justice. Schiesl documents the roles played by a number of individuals and institutions in this process and highlights how we may have to reassess the conditions that helped produce a number of street gangs in the Latino and African American communities alike. The identity of these groups and their membership was influenced as much by their sociocultural characteristics as it was formed by their experiences with the police. This chapter reminds readers of the events of the post-WWII era and what role inter-group collaborations could and will have to play in creating more hopeful and dignified living conditions for minorities in Los Angeles.

In this political spirit, the last chapter appropriately ends the book with a rich commentary on coalition building efforts in the years immediately after WWII. Though focused on Latinos and some of the individuals who shaped efforts toward achieving higher levels of political representation, Kenneth Burt reminds the reader about the importance of inter- and intra-group coalition building, as well as labor- and minority-friendly policy making. The author points to voter registration and political participation as perhaps the most important factor in minority empowerment.

Burt begins his chapter with the promise of comparing the political activism of the 1940s and 1990 and provides much to think about on that topic. The chapter centers on the political life of Edward R. Roybal, but the author gives us a wide view of the sociopolitical conditions that brought Roybal to power. Burt's narration points to the importance of catalysts in mobilizing the population. Roybal's 1947 campaign is compared with that of 1949, when he was successfully elected to the City Council, illustrating that it took coalition-building, the support of labor, organizational assistance from the Community Services Organization (CSO), and aggressive voter registration to gain the sought after political access. Burt's rich history of behind-the-scene activities in the Latino communities of Los Angeles from the late 1940s to the 1960s informs us about the cast of characters and the institutions that they built and supported to create the political landscape many take for granted today. The fight for empowerment was fought on many fronts in order to improve access to resources and enable Latinos to have an improved chance for success. The "Latino Political Machine" and its rise to power is seen as a testimony to structural solutions to structural problems and the subtext that rights are rarely given, but are always taken. The author, however, cautions against the emerging distinction between multigenerational Latinos and recent immigrants and argues that in order for Latinos to maintain and expand their political position, the drive for voter registration and political participation must be relentless. Proposition 187 was a reminder that exclusionary forces remain in operation: coalition building remains a necessary instrument to counter those forces. The empowerment of Latinos will rely partly on their ability to see the anti-immigration and anti-Latino voices as one and the same. The doubling of voter registration among Latinos from the passage of 187 to 2000 indicates that the importance of political participation by all Latinos is not lost on the group. The election of Mayor Antonio Villaraigosa is a signal that the Latino Political Machine needs to be inclusive and build bridges across multiple racial and ethnic groups. The Latino mayor of the 21st century represents a multicultural group that has been made more complex by immigration, politics, and a post-industrial economy.

As the chapters in this book illustrate, to be a minority is to be disempowered and excluded. Race is the excuse used by colonialism, imperialism, and capitalism in exercising exclusionary practices. In the U.S., minority status was created and maintained through a racial discourse and the establishment of institutions and structures that enabled them to perpetuate differences in favor of the powerful. This book offers a historical interpretation of how such systems were created, operated, and maintained in Los Angeles—albeit through the perspective of three racial/ethnic groups. It also tells us about how this abusive system was resisted by various minority groups. The lesson learned is that in the years to come, we will have to continue dismantling the relics of inequitable structures built in the previous centuries, even as the White population continues to decline in numbers.

PART ONE

1900-1945

Chapter I

MEXICAN IMMIGRANT FAMILIES
CULTURAL CONFLICT, SOCIOECONOMIC SURVIVAL, AND THE FORMATION OF COMMUNITY IN LOS ANGELES, 1900-1945

Gloria E. Miranda

The 1910 Mexican Revolution and the Cristero Rebellion of the 1920s greatly stimulated the growth of the Mexican population in the United States. Over one million inhabitants fled the political and social upheaval that raged in their homeland during the first decades of the twentieth century. These refugees entered the United States seeking jobs and a temporary place to relocate their uprooted families until civil strife subsided in Mexico. The geographical proximity and historical affinity of the cultural landscape of the southwestern United States attracted the majority of migrating Mexicans who settled in rural and urban communities throughout the region. In this setting, immigrant families mingled with Mexican American residents and noticeably contributed to the expansion of the historical Hispano-Mexican culture of the Southwest. The demographic transformation of the vast landscape by these immigrants contributed to a distinctive pattern of community formation in the first half of the twentieth century.

THE MEXICAN RETURN TO LOS ANGELES

For a variety of reasons, Los Angeles was selected as one of the more popular final destinations of immigrant Mexicans traveling north across the border. The city's expanding economic growth and development meant diverse employment opportunities for individuals desperately seeking to feed and clothe their families. Southern California represented both a fertile agricultural region and an expanding urban and industrial center in pre-World War II times. In particular, the rapid growth of agribusiness necessitated an aggressive recruitment effort directed at employment of a work force willing to labor in the fields. With the passage of hostile anti-Asian legislation at the turn of the century, the Japanese lost their primacy in the fields. Agribusiness turned to Mexican campesinos (farm workers) who, arriving in large numbers during World War I, rapidly emerged as the principal labor force in Southern California agriculture.[1] In addition, plentiful opportunities on the railroads and in local industries such as canning, garment and gas works also proved appealing to many unskilled and semi-skilled immigrants.

Proximity to the border and a familiar cultural environment similarly enhanced the appeal of Los Angeles as a resettlement site for displaced Mexicans.[2] The Mexicans who migrated north during this tumultuous era generally brought their relatives along. In some cases, single and married men journeyed north to the United States without their families, but women rarely traveled by themselves.[3] Mexican migrants who arrived in Los Angeles at the turn of the century discovered that the former Mexican cultural dominance had been substantially altered by the large numbers of non-Mexicans who had settled in Southern California during the last quarter of the nineteenth century.

By 1890, the once numerous native-born Spanish speaking community comprised a mere ten percent of the region's total population. At the onset of statehood forty years before, the new community of Mexican American citizens had represented over ninety percent of the inhabitants of Los Angeles. One of the primary reasons for this population shift was the expansion of the railroads into the southland. Transplanted Easterners and Midwesterners along with new European immigrants took advantage of the transportation expansion to the Pacific Coast to move to the City of the Angels.

The majority of Mexican Americans no longer lived in a manner resembling the pre-American social setting of California. Only a minority of professional or middle class Californio families had succeeded in gaining acceptance into the dominant Caucasian mainstream. These clans made inroads by claiming Spanish ancestry. In contrast, at the beginning of the twentieth century, most brown Americans of Mexican descent could be found living in segregated downtown Los Angeles barrios such as Sonoratown and the adjacent Plaza district. These isolated enclaves were destined to become the home of many new immigrant Mexican arrivals for several reasons. First, the barrios represented already established communities within Los Angeles with a vibrant Mexican cultural core. Second, the downtown area offered the immigrants affordable housing. And third, the homes in this sector were but a short distance from the workplace for most residents.

These recent immigrants lived side by side with Mexican American families in these enclaves during the pre-World War II era. Both groups experienced devastating racial discrimination, cultural disdain, inferior educational opportunities and economic impoverishment. The general prevalent pattern of anti-Mexicanism in Los Angeles assumed various forms during the first four decades of this century.[4] In the period before the Second World War, nativist sentiment, coupled with Social Darwinist propaganda, incited a campaign in the 1920s to restrict Mexican immigration into this country. A subsequent national deportation program during the Great Depression in the following decade escalated these virulent attitudes into a concerted repatriation program.

At the same time, Americanization efforts engendered by local Protestant churches aimed at winning Mexican converts away from Catholicism had escalated with the arrival of the immigrants. This aggressive proselytism paralleled Americanization programs in public schools aimed at transforming Mexicans into productive workers. At best, the Americanization campaign (really de-Mexicanization) succeeded at marginalizing and alienating some second generation youngsters of this era. However, the tragic legacy of Americanization rested on the failure of the public school system to guide brown youngsters to a successful completion of their education.[5] In this unsettling climate, the family surfaced as a critical cultural force to combat the negative consequences of publicly championed de-Mexicanization efforts. Indeed, immigrant and second generation families proved to be resilient and instrumental in the group's ability to withstand the onslaught of the sometimes inflammatory anti-Mexican climate of the 1920s and 1930s in Southern California.

Scholars generally have lumped together in their assessment the social and political experiences in this country of Mexican immigrant and native-born Mexican American families primarily because of their shared Mexican culture and community life. It is a well-documented fact that a major breach in that connection in Los Angeles emerged with the demographic realignment of southland enclaves during and after World War II. This population dispersal out of the barrio would signal intense assimilation efforts by Mexican Americans hoping to be received into the American mainstream on the merits of their wartime heroic activities. Until then, the traditional cultural basis of family life for both groups, retained compatibility in terms of language, religion, traditions, gender and parental roles until the mass exodus out of numerous Los Angeles area barrios which was directed by the brown American G.I. generation.

The Formation of Barrio Life and Cultural Solidarity

The growing influx of immigrants into downtown Los Angeles at the turn of the century impacted traditional residential life as the city's original Sonoratown and Plaza district barrios became quickly overcrowded with newcomers. As the influx continued over the next decade, the Plaza district's numbers swelled to 50,000 residents—some forty percent of the city's total Mexican and Mexican American population.[6] This overcrowding stimulated the first of several exoduses as the new arrivals were forced to relocate elsewhere. Soon, many began moving eastward across the Los Angeles river, while others followed the railroad tracks southward toward Watts and beyond into adjacent communities. Other families moved into the eastern San Fernando Valley, some into older existing Mexican American enclaves. For many Mexicans, the new barrios they established, generally signaled their first opportunity to live in an urban setting because the majority of them came from rural areas in Mexico.[7] Their unsophisticated appearance stemmed from the hardships of life in their homeland. Mainly impoverished and illiterate, these recent arrivals to Los Angeles, lacked the social refinements considered essential to sophisticated city dwellers. Tragically, the immigrants' lowly class status created social tensions between themselves and Mexican Americans.

To the native-born, the immigrant did not appear sophisticated enough to be accepted as a social equal. To emphasize their case, in some Mexican American barrios, residents began characterizing immigrant newcomers as *cholos* (low class), *chuntaros* (stupid), *zurumatos* (dumb), or other equally demeaning terms. In self-defense, Mexicans considered their United States born and socialized counterparts aliens to their cultural heritage. The immigrants labeled them *pochos* (faded Mexicans).[8] How extensive this pattern of name calling developed in Los Angeles barrios has yet to be fully assessed, but similar friction prevailed in other pre-World War II southwestern barrios.

Despite these socioeconomic class biases, the two groups typically socialized within the context of barrio life. At this juncture in the Chicano experience within the United States, both pre-World War II groups considered themselves to be culturally as one. Their clannishness bonded the barrio residents while affording immigrants and the American-raised Mexican greater opportunities to celebrate their common cultural affinity than those occasions when verbal sparring marred barrio solidarity. Both spoke Spanish as their primary language in the home and identified with their Mexican Catholic faith, customs and cultural celebrations. To immigrant and Mexican American alike, the integrity of family life had to be sustained if children were to remain faithful to their heritage. Furthermore, in the 1920s and 1930s the frequency of intermarriage between the two groups was greater than with non-Mexicans.[9] Marital bonds strengthened and unified barrio enclaves in Los Angeles irregardless of the general poverty and squalor found in these communities.

SOCIOECONOMIC PLIGHT

The economic impoverishment of early twentieth century barrios did not evade the notice of local officials. Mexican families that inhabited the downtown Plaza area in the first fifteen years of the century lived in overcrowded slum conditions. The one and two room shacks (called *jacales* in Spanish) were without adequate running water, heating or lighting. A number of Los Angeles' reform-minded Progressive residents considered these residences to be the city's most disgraceful houses. The Progressives contended that the horrendous living standards of immigrant families were a blemish on the community's reputation.[10] The Los Angeles Housing Commission, founded in 1906 largely to solve this urban crisis, two years later surveyed the extent of the housing shortage. The commission's official report revealed that the Plaza district was indeed an eyesore.

> Here we found filth and squalor on every hand. Miserably constructed houses, made of scrap sheet iron, old bagging and sections of dry goods boxes, were huddled together without any attempt at proper construction or order...The more Mexicans to the lot, the more money for the owner.[11]

The commission also noted that generally most of the sector's families had four or more members living with them in the congested shacks.

City officials hesitated for a few years before deciding to condemn and demolish these slums. However, in arriving at this decision the housing commissioners were guided less by humanitarian factors than by the business sector's demand for more city land upon which to construct commercial buildings since the growing business district was adjacent to the barrio.

Consequently, the displaced residents dispersed in different directions, but a significant number of them moved east of the Plaza across the Los Angeles River lured there by employment opportunities and inexpensive housing. This relocation resulted in the emergence of one of the largest brown communities of the Los Angeles region.[12] By the end of the 1920s, the community of Belvedere numbered in excess of 30,000 residents. Reverend Robert McLean, a Protestant proselytizer and Americanization proponent working among Mexican immigrants, marveled at their ingenuity in developing Belvedere.

> Just outside the city limits a real estate company secured possession of some rolling acres which had formerly been used as pasture land for a dairy. This was divided into fifty-foot lots, and sold out to the

Mexicans on small payments. There were no sewers, no sidewalks, no playgrounds; and the only restriction as to the number of houses which could be built upon a single lot was the size of the lot. In a few short months a miraculous change took place. Mexicans bought property, lost it through the failure to make payments, and then bought again. They built their houses out of second-hand lumber—"jacales" they call them—and in some cases roofed them over with tin cut from Standard oil cans. Two, four, five, and sometimes six little shacks were built on a single lot. It seemed as if all Mexico were moving to Belvedere. A public school which was opened with a few hundred pupils, had reached an enrollment of eighteen hundred in less than five years. Everywhere there were the usual evidences of overcrowding and inadequate housing, for the families were not only large, but were augmented by the aunts and uncles and cousins coming from Mexico who, with ready hospitality were entertained until they could build for themselves.[13]

Other Southern California barrios experienced similar phases of growth and development much like Belvedere.

The emergence of these pocket settlements, like Chavez Ravine north of the downtown center, resembled Belvedere in character. According to Carey McWilliams, another observant local analyst of the pre-war era, in Chavez Ravine which was located in the hills between Elysian Park and North Broadway, "shacks cling precariously to the hillsides and are bunched in clusters in the bottom of the ravine." McWilliams noted that the city generally neglected this area and offered the ravine's residents little or no municipal services.

At various points in the ravine, one can still see large boards on which are tacked the rural mail-boxes of the residents—as though they were living, not in the heart of a great city, but in some small rural village in the Southwest. Goats, staked out on picket lines, can be seen on the hillsides; and most of the homes have chicken pens and fences. The streets are unpaved; really trails packed hard by years of travel. Garbage is usually collected from a central point, when it is collected, and the service is not equal to that which can be obtained in Anglo districts bordering the ravine. The houses are old shacks, unpainted and weatherbeaten.[14]

Yet in spite of the isolated and neglected condition of these barrios, newly arrived immigrants in the 1920s marveled about urban life. For this reason, they bestowed the nickname of *Maravilla* (wonderful) on the cow pasture of Belvedere. This influx to alluring Los Angeles tripled the size of the eastside communities and gained for the city by 1930 the title of "Mexican capital of the United States."[15]

In the evolving social and cultural milieu of these barrios, immigrants physically succumbed to the tragic consequences of their impoverished lives. Illness and disease plagued them incessantly since they resided in areas with as inadequate facilities as those in the older downtown slums. In due time, Los Angeles County health officials became alarmed by the extremely high incidence of communicable disease prevalent among the Mexicans. Respiratory ailments like pneumonia and tuberculosis, influenza and even meningitis swept through barrio enclaves. In the mid 1920s the local health department reported that one-sixth of all tuberculosis cases and one-fourth of all such deaths in Los Angeles occurred in barrios. The children were the most vulnerable. Statistics on infant mortality revealed that two to eight times more Mexican and Mexican American babies died than Caucasian newborn.[16]

Noticeably alarmed, health officials in 1921 launched a campaign to reduce infant mortality rates throughout the county. Within less than ten years, infant fatalities declined by one-half in Southern California, but the rate in the Mexican community still remained one-third higher. At a loss to explain the disparity, local health authorities concluded that the inferior genetic makeup of Mexicans was to blame.[17] The socioeconomic conditions of barrio life for families trapped in the vicious cycle of miserable poverty eluded the officials in their assessments.

Predictably, family sizes suffered because of the mortality rate. Between 1918 and 1927 the average number of children for Los Angeles Mexican and Mexican American couples was 4.3. Families exceeded this average in actuality but statistics reveal a significant number averaged less than three children. However, given the fact that the brown populace of the 1920s experienced the highest birthrate of any group resident in Los Angeles, the fatality rate clearly impacted family size.[18]

Male heads of families who sought employment to support their spouses and offspring discovered that widespread job discrimination meant either low status and low paying jobs insufficient to feed their families, or unemployment. Those who found work labored mainly in agriculture, on local railroad lines and in manufacturing plants. In most instances, job opportunities in the urban sector became scarce, forcing the "Mexicans" (both immigrant and native-born) to leave the city in search of seasonal employment. Emory Bogardus, the distinguished sociologist who researched the status of Mexican immigrants in the 1920s, lamented the deplorable circumstances which uprooted already impoverished families.

> The Mexican has been a victim of the seasonal labor situation. In order to make a living he has piled his family into "the old Ford" and almost become a transient in seeking out the widely separated seasonal labor fields.[19]

Bogardus also decried the consequence of seasonal employment which aggravated housing patterns. "Migratory labor conditions beget deplorable housing accommodations, and the Mexican and his family have suffered," he observed.[20] Statistics underscore the depth of socioeconomic dispair of families: only six percent of male wage earners were classified as professionals or skilled laborers.

Out of sheer necessity, Mexican women—mothers, daughters and other relatives—joined the labor force. The women found employment in service related jobs and in manufacturing. In the 1930s the city's garment industry relied extensively on these females.[21] Others found work in the food processing sector which employed "more Mexican women than did any other local industry, including the apparel firms." In Los Angeles County, "88.8 percent of Mexican food processing workers were women."[22] They generally suffered similar job discrimination as Mexican males endured and frequently were "assigned the least skilled and most routine tasks, such as packing lemons or washing peaches."[23]

Confined to low status employment and equally low wages, most Mexican and Mexican American families could not measurably improve their standard of living. In the 1930s Bogardus surmised that even if the Mexican immigrant became a citizen, improved his skills and salary and sought to enhance his life in Los Angeles, he would be rebuffed. According to Bogardus, when the immigrant selected a home in a better neighborhood, the "neighbors... opposed...him" and "threaten if he moves in."[24]

NATIVISTS, AMERICANIZATION, AND THE MEXICAN PROBLEM

Struggling to survive, the immigrant family's adjustment to living in the United States became increasingly complicated by rising nationwide neo-nativist anti-Mexican campaigns that increased in momentum after World War I. The reactionary posture of racial supremacists toward Mexicans gave local impetus to the notion that the United States had a serious "Mexican problem." Staunch nativists depicted the issue in simple economic terms. Immigrants took jobs from citizens. However, the real issue was more profound. Social Darwinists considered the Mexicans racially and culturally inferior to Caucasians and thus unassimilable. One social commentator who considered all Mexicans to be peons described them as "among the most unassimilable of all immigrants." The nativist's greatest fear was articulated in racial terms as the xenophobics underscored their aversion to miscegenation. "Ultimately his descendants will be our descendants, and 'gringo' and 'greaser' will be one," argued one nativist.[25] Others feared that uncontrolled immigration from Mexico would ultimately lead to a general disintegration of the more superior "American way of life." Even Robert McLean, who worked among the Mexican people, theorized that they posed a major challenge to the W.A.S.P.—White, Anglo-Saxon, Protestant—ethos because their culture was based on an Indian racial, and Catholic, value system. McLean cautioned that the Mexican way of life, as imported by immigrant families, had the potential to destroy the nation's way of life. He explained the crisis in the following colorful manner:

> Fifty and one hundred years ago Uncle Sam accomplished some remarkable digestive feats. Gastronomically he was a marvel. He was not particularly choosy! Dark meat from the borders of the Mediterranean, or light meat from the Baltic, equally suited him, for promptly he was able to assimilate both, turning them into bone of his bone, and flesh of his flesh—But this *chili con carne*! Always it seems to give Uncle Samuel the heartburn; and the older he gets, the less he seems to be able to assimilate it. Indeed, it is a question whether *chili* is not a condiment to be taken in small quantities rather than a regular article of diet. And upon this conviction ought to stand all the law and prophets as far as the Mexican immigrant is concerned.[26]

In other words, the assimilation of the distinctive Mexican would not resolve the "Mexican problem."

Yet other southland nativists in the 1920s claimed, almost hysterically, that Mexicans were "diseased of body, subnormal intellectually and moral morons of the most hopeless type."[27] Conversely, few sympathetic assessments of Mexican cultural traits appeared in print. Reverent Vernon McCombs, a contemporary of McLean's, took exception to the popular commentary. McCombs praised the spiritual depth of Mexican character when he remarked that they were "self-forgetful and generous beyond all measure—or even common cause. They share their last crust [of bread] with each other. Sacrifices of life itself are not uncommon."[28] Unfortunately, the content of their character mattered very little to critics who concerned themselves solely with the burden immigrants placed on the local economy.

Widespread discrimination increased in these years and impeded the immigrant's struggle for dignified social treatment. Extensive segregation practices in many southland areas resurfaced as recreational facilities, business establishments, schools and even churches were guilty of anti-Mexicanism. Los Angeles schools practiced widespread and insidious segregation sanctioned by local educators who gave approval of such practices as separate graduation ceremonies at centers where Anglos attended classes with Mexican youngsters. Indeed, the ideal of Americanization introduced into the public school system in the 1920s was at odds with this segregation stance. After all, if assimilation was the aim of Americanization, why then treat Mexican youth as separate and inferior?[29]

Ironically, Protestant groups who eagerly sought converts to their respective denominations, failed to convince the majority of Mexicans that American Christianity was color blind. Protestant churches in greater Los Angeles reportedly championed segregation by denying their brown membership the right to worship alongside Caucasian co-religionists.[30] Discriminatory treatment of this magnitude emphatically created serious barriers for immigrants seeking to gain acceptance in American society through conversion to Protestant Christianity.

For the family, the greatest challenge in this period of Americanization concentrated on insuring the retention of traditional family values. For the majority of Mexican immigrants, Caucasian American society was comprised of pronounced secular and materialistic traits. Conversely, whites generally viewed Mexican culture through a narrow and supremacist lens. The earliest sociological and anthropological studies on Mexican family life depicted this institution as monolithic and patriarchal. To the avid nativist, the Mexican family's sole function centered on "excessive breeding." During the peak years of the restrictionist crusade to halt the free flow of Mexican immigration, supporters of closing the border vehemently argued that Mexicans, because of their prolific fecundity would eventually outnumber the nation's white population if immigration continued unchecked by legislation.[31] Others feared that Mexicans might intermarry with whites, thereby tainting the genetic superiority of Caucasians. Even sympathetic statements that Mexicans did not practice racial miscegenation from public officials like George P. Clements of the Los Angeles Chamber of Commerce Agricultural Department, did not deter the clamor of restrictionist proponents.[32]

Emotionally charged impressions of Mexican culture heightened further the already volatile climate of the latter 1920s. Nativists failed, however, to realistically assess the actual circumstances surrounding the Mexican immigrant's lowly status in the United States. In the first place, many of them came from rural regions in Mexico with deeply rooted cultural traditions and provincial attitudes toward religion and family life. Second, these rural areas represented pre-industrial and staunchly patriarchal communities where the family exercised a preeminent place in society. In contrast to the average American counterpart, the immigrant family lacked secular, material or individual attributes found typically in industrialized societies.

Ignoring these circumstances, nativists in the 1920s continued to clamor for legislation to restrict migration across the border into the United States. Disappointed when Congress failed to enact laws to stop Mexican immigration, they delighted when the Great Depression reopened the issue and offered a solution to the long-standing "Mexican problem."

REPATRIATION AND THE ASSAULT ON THE COMMUNITY

In 1931, the federal government launched a national repatriation campaign to deport Mexican nationals living in the United States without proper credentials. By the end of the decade, when the campaign had subsided, one third of the officially listed Mexican population of this country had been deported south across the border.

In Los Angeles, federal and local agencies quickly began conducting raids of public places and private residences. The government willingly sponsored the shipment of many of the deportees. But other families, fearing they would never be allowed to remain in the area, left of their own volition. Frequently, wives and husbands did not travel together, so the County offered to pay the way for women in order that they rejoin repatriated spouses already in Mexico.

In the city's barrios, the Mexican Consulate and other community organizations offered assistance to those families whose sudden dislocation interrupted their efforts to join the American society.[33] They provided both official and moral support to the repatriates in an effort to minimize the trauma of readjustment to life in Mexico. Many of the repatriated Mexicans had been longtime residents of Southern California with children accustomed to life in the United States. Other children were born in this country and had never visited Mexico. In the course of repatriation, an unknown number of families experienced painful separations when youngsters remained in the care of relatives who escaped deportation. In other instances, the children accompanied their parents to a land they considered a foreign country.[34] In some cases, children who saw themselves as Americans, ran away from home rather than accompany their parents to Mexico.[35]

Callous Los Angeles County officials added to the trauma of families in this era by encouraging mentally ill, bedridden and terminally ill patients to join the mass exodus. The family of Petra Sanchez Rocha were convinced by officials that joining the repatriates heading to Mexico offered her only hope for recovery from a nervous breakdown. County-sponsored orphanages also shipped children, even American-born, across the border under the premise that their deportation would reduce expenses.[36] Clearly, the solution of the "Mexican problem" precluded a humanitarian spirit among the city's health caregivers. Thereby, contributing to the anguish in the barrios of southern California.

Even though the repatriation campaign diminished after the mid-1930s, Mexican nationals and Mexican Americans understandably remained bitter long afterwards. They had been singled out for deportation by a society that had ignored their contributions to the local, state and national economy and to the growth and expansion of the American West. Nonetheless, the cultural instincts of those who avoided repatriation, served to aid the survival of the family as the repository of Mexican values.

CULTURAL AND GENERATIONAL CONFLICTS

Longtime immigrant residents in Los Angeles concluded that American family life, which included the belief that a greater degree of individuality, freedom and independence, was a threat to the stability of their cultural ethic. Customarily, Mexican culture placed a greater value on family solidarity, good manners and respect for parents. Retention of these traits posed dilemmas for Mexican immigrant parents since many of their adolescent offspring favored the more relaxed urban social environment of Los Angeles. Parents who responded by reasserting their parental authority soon found a clash of cultures within their families.

In the 1920s and 1930s, Bogardus studied the culture conflict experienced by immigrant and native-born families, and recorded numerous comments made by Mexican parents. He particularly noted that Mexican mothers agonized over the affects of the social freedoms on their daughters. One mother interviewed by the sociologist lamented that she could "never get used to it...the freedom which our women enjoy. She cannot understand how women can go unaccompanied on the street, or how they can go about to and from their homes and their work alone." The woman added:

> It is because they can run around so much and be so free, that our Mexican girls do not know how to act. So many girls run away and get married. This terrible freedom in this United States. The Mexican girls seeing American girls with freedom, they want it too, so they go where they like. They do not mind their parents; this terrible freedom. But what can Mexican mothers do? It is the custom, and we cannot change it, but it is bad. I do not have to worry because I have no daughters, but the poor *senoras* with many girls, they worry. I only have three sons; they are gone now, they have been dead many years.[37]

Parents attempted to restrict their children's' freedom through curfews in an attempt to protect them from discrimination, which as heads of households, they had frequently experienced living in the hostile setting of the early 1900s. Some parents believed that reinvigorating the custom of chaperoning young females seemed to be a reasonable way to handle the problems posed by urban living. Elena Torres de Acosta, an immigrant from Guadalajara, Jalisco, recalled that in the 1920s she never went out alone in Los Angeles. "I always went out with the lady [her landlord] or with her daughters."[38]

Many adolescent girls disapproved of the practice of chaperoning because it seemed out of place in an urban setting. Going on a date to a movie, dance or even a church social traditionally called for supervision by a godparent or relative. Thus, as young women gained a taste of social life—Anglo-American style—they felt their parents "old fashioned" and not "liberal" like Americans" for sticking to these customs. Some young women chafed against these family norms but realized that if they breached family role-playing etiquette, their family might suffer. One adolescent of this era recalled that, "I fought with my parents...but didn't try to sneak out because I didn't want our neighbors to talk about me the way they talked about some other girls. That kind of *chisme* would hurt my family."[39] Consequently, joining the work force offered the daughters of Mexican immigrants opportunities for greater independence from the confines of the home. In the process, they supplemented their family's income and afforded themselves the financial resources to purchase tickets to local movie houses or other luxuries they never knew in Mexico, such as cosmetics and the latest in dress fashions.

Historian Vicki Ruiz has analyzed at length the social impact of American fashions on immigrant girls, noting that Southern California barrio residents succumbed to the consumerism epidemic of the 1920s. Ruiz observed that even the Spanish-language newspaper of Los Angeles, *La Opinion*, provided readers with information on the latest in fashions, cosmetics, hairstyles and Hollywood gossip. In addition, the popular barrio-style beauty contests sponsored by various community organizations, also contributed to popularizing American fashion and beauty among second generation females.[40] And, while immigrant parents voiced their disdain of American consumerism's impact on their daughters expectations, some became more acutely distressed when a daughter sought employment exclusively as a ticket out of the home. In general though, most women who sought employment in local industries receptive to them, fortified rather than disrupted the solidarity of the Mexican family. Not only daughters, but mothers, aunts and other female relatives joined the labor force in garment or food processing work.[41] The ability to enhance a family's income while at the same time maintaining links to one's relatives and barrio friends proved a boon to Mexican culture in Los Angeles.

As a consequence, generational parent-daughter conflicts only occasionally prompted a small number of daughters to declare they would never marry a Mexican man. These declarations more directly reflected the social impact of de-Mexicanization on the thinking of second generation barrio females exposed to the Anglo-American way of life through newspapers, movies, and work. Nonetheless, judging from the statistics on racial intermarriage in Los Angeles during the 1920s and 1930s, these emotional threats never amounted to much. Many women wed at a young age, but they married men with a similar cultural ancestry. Early marriage offered a compromise solution to fleeing parental authority.[42] But for most Mexican American women, disobedience or defiance was unthinkable and showed extreme disregard for their family.

But the fears of Mexican parents were not totally unfounded. In the course of his field work, Bogardus interviewed women who lamented that excessive independence in the United States led to the disintegration of family life. One Mexican mother observed the process first hand.

> The thing that shocked me most about the United States was the lack of solidarity in the home. The American children do not have much regard for their parents. I was renting in an American home where there were four daughters from nine to sixteen years of age and every one of them was out until three o'clock at night. Their parents had no control over them. In Mexico I had to be in at eight o'clock with my father and mother. But here it is different. Of course it makes for individuality and independence. They learn to think for themselves, but experiences teach wonderful lessons, and they refuse to use or accept the lesson which the

broader experiences of their parents have taught them. The freedom and independence in this country bring the children into conflict with their parents. They learn nicer ways, learn about the outside world, learn how to speak English, and then they become ashamed of their parents who brought them up here that they might have better advantages.[43]

Immigrant parents in local barrios held almost universally, similar views of Anglo-American behavior and family mores. Understandably, the majority of them rejected exaggerated freedom for children in favor of retaining their own customs. Elisa Silva, another transplanted Angelino, put it succinctly: "Of the customs of this country I only like the ones about work. The others aren't anything compared to those of Mexico." Silva felt that people were kinder in Mexico than in the United States, and "less ambitious about money."[44] Another immigrant, Fernando Sanchez, supported this sentiment. "I follow my Mexican customs and I won't change them for anything in the world. I haven't let my sisters cut their hair or go around like the girls here with all kinds of boys and I have also accustomed my sons to respect me in every way."[45]

As attractive as the more liberal social mores and customs of the United States were to the adolescents, they never seriously jeopardized the preeminence of family and community norms. Barrio life revolved around activities such as religious fiestas, patriotic Mexican celebrations or even community beauty contests. Parents encouraged children to participate in these events which included Cinco de Mayo, Mexican Independence on the Sixteenth of September, and the feast of the Virgin of Guadalupe. The latter event received official sanction as an archdiocesan sponsored procession in 1928 when Bishop John Cantwell agreed to review the parade and officiate at the benediction service.[46] At these various celebrations, the Spanish language, Mexican food and music prevailed as indicators of the vitality of culture that staunch proponents of Americanization hoped to uproot.[47]

FAILURE OF THE AMERICAN SCHOOL SYSTEM

In spite of the typical Mexican immigrant disapproval of the secular and individualized dimension of Anglo-American culture, parents wholeheartedly supported the value of the educational system of this country. In the 1920s Mexican and Mexican American

Shades of L.A. Archives, Los Angeles Public Library

The September 16 parade in 1938 at Brooklyn and Ford Streets in East Los Angeles celebrating Mexican Independence Day

children accounted for 17.1 percent of the total elementary school enrollment in the city and 13.5 percent of the county total.[48]

More than eighty percent of these youngsters attended segregated schools which were popularly called "Mexican schools." These schools scarcely provided the sons and daughters of immigrants the same educational opportunities that Caucasian youngsters received in the more affluent communities of greater Los Angeles.

Educators rationalized that school segregation practices provided a more effective learning environment for Spanish speaking children in need of mastering English. Other more outspoken officials even went so far as to suggest that segregation was crucial to the safety of the larger student body of the city because of the "Mexican temperament, the high percentage of juvenile arrests among Mexicans, the nature of the offenses committed and their low moral standards."[49]

Only a small minority within the Caucasian community of Los Angeles expressed genuine sympathy and motivation for educating immigrants on a fair and equal level. Social workers and clergymen generally backed an Americanization program of instruction as the means of integrating Mexicans into the dominant society. As a rule, however, Americanization schools concentrated on vocational training and English language instruction. In the chauvinistic and ethnocentric educational climate of the 1920s and 1930s, few educators championed a curriculum aimed at preparing Mexican and Mexican American youngsters for a college education. Instead, Americanization efforts only underscored the point that "Mexicans were intended only to assimilate into the bottom segment of the American work force as low-paid, yet loyal, workers."[50] Without an educated professional base upon which to build savvy political leadership, second generation Mexican Americans had little hope for a better life in these two decades. Indeed, education ended abruptly for most brown youngsters before they left the junior high school level.[51] This educational pattern prevailed into the 1940s. Los Angeles County Superintendent C. C. Trillingham in 1943 charged that secondary school principals supported the practice which denied children of Mexican ancestry the opportunity to enter the tenth grade.[52]

The consequences of such an educational policy that assailed the Mexican's heritage traumatized many children to the point that they left school prematurely before reaching the senior high level. In Los Angeles schools, corporal punishment for speaking Spanish on school grounds, bestowing callously Anglo sounding reidentification of children's names, omission in class studies of positive Mexican role models and ignoring the historical contributions of Mexicans to North American history created considerable cultural conflict and bitter disillusionment for brown children. Superintendent Trillingham, observing the state of local education as it related to the brown youngsters, confirmed that these classroom practices seriously impeded any opportunity they might ever have for any success and mobility in the mainstream society. Trillingham proposed a corrective solution. The superintendent's "good neighbor policy," as he called it, was a master plan to introduce a culturally pluralistic curriculum into Los Angeles classrooms. The "good neighbor" approach which included community involvement was a forerunner of more recent Los Angeles Unified City School District bilingual-bicultural programs.[53]

The well-intentioned superintendent was astute enough to conclude that a culturally sensitive educational policy would serve as a deterrent to culture conflict. For too long, Mexican

American children, eager to master the skills necessary for success in American society, had discovered that the secular, material and individualized focus of the American way of life depreciated their culture by demeaning their heritage of service and devotion to family, community and religious convictions.

The real conflict took place in the classroom where teachers failed to strike a meaningful balance when evaluating the merits of the American way of life over the assumed demerits of Mexican culture. For most adolescents, leaving school prematurely proved the only way to avoid the unsettling affects of alienation that psychologically and culturally demoralized other non-whites. Even though most youth left school to enter the work force, the majority of them dropped out of school before permanent emotional anguish undermined their sense of self-worth. By World War II, most of them had come to recognize the futility of seeking a high school education in the hostile and indifferent environment of the Los Angeles educational system.[54]

For a minority of the adolescents, lowered self-esteem, distorted self-images and generalized insecurity produced a major crisis of racial and ethnic identity. While the alienated second generation adolescent lost touch with his or her heritage, they also realized that Caucasian society rejected them because they were "Mexican." In response to this dilemma, these adolescents created their own distinctive but nonetheless subcultural lifestyle. Deviation from the general cultural values of their parents peaked by World War II when they became known locally as Pachucos and Pachucas.

Their mannerisms, tough demeanor, flashy zoot suits and peculiar speech pattern or argot (called *calo*) easily distinguished them in the barrios where they continued to reside. Since they no longer emulated positive Mexican role models, these Pachucos and their female admirers adopted new ones as surrogate examples of defiance like the fictional 1930s villains of the cinema, Humphrey Bogart, James Cagney and the "Dead-End Kids." And as they linked up with other disoriented adolescents, the Pachucos organized the first major barrio gangs in Los Angeles.[55]

Most families were unfamiliar with marginal behavior among their children so they did not share in the personal bewilderment and apprehension of the few parents whose offspring had become

Los Angele Times photo

World War II saw considerable tention between Anglos and minorities. Looking for Mexican American youths wearing Zoot Suits, rioting military personnel stop a streetcar at Main and 3rd in downtown Los Angeles. June, 1943

alienated from their roots. Statistically, only a small percentage of Mexican American youth joined these neighborhood gangs in Los Angeles.[56] Yet concerned experts believed that this minority segment in the barrios could be assisted in containing the confusing and demoralizing affects of cultural alienation through social service assistance to the parents of gang affiliated youngsters. Bogardus, for one, believed that minimizing cultural conflict aided successful assimilation of the United States born generation.

> Too many of these parents are at a loss to know how to help their children to make adjustments as bicultural human beings. The trained welfare worker is needed to carry into the homes of Mexican-American children a scientific knowledge of parent-child relations, especially where two cultures are in contrast and in conflict. Social workers need a training, which most do not have, whereby they can interpret the immigrants parents' culture to the children, and also the parents' problems in our country to the children. The youth also needed greatly the skillful assistance of the social worker who is trained in the social psychology of leadership and who thereby can help immigrant children to see and to assume their responsibilities in helping their parents to become culturally assimilated. Thousands of homes need the social worker who is versed in the nature and methods of cultural assimilation.[57]

Unfortunately, few agencies cared enough to respond to Bogardus' challenge. Instead, the hostile resurgence of the earlier prewar nativist engendered perspective of the "Mexican problem" flared anew in Los Angeles during World War II, culminating in the tragic race riots of June 1943. The violent unrest, popularly labeled the Pachuco or Zoot Suit Riots, were perpetrated mainly by local servicemen on a minority community they perceived to be un-American and criminally prone. A preponderance of scholarly studies have documented extensively the causes and consequences of the servicemen's riots, acknowledging that the Los Angeles press inflamed and distorted adolescent life in the Chicano barrios of this era.[58] In truth, only a minority of second generation youngsters were hard-core and culturally marginalized Pachucos. What was overlooked by the hostile anti-Mexican elements in the city was the depths of frustration and resentment that Mexican and Chicano families felt at the injustice inflicted on their offspring. An overwhelming number of barrio residents displayed patriotic fervor and contributed much service to the country during the war.

THE WAR YEARS

The attention given by the local press and law enforcement agencies to the pattern of juvenile delinquency among some second-generation barrio adolescents obscured the impact that the Second World War had on the notion of patriotism and civic duty on immigrant and native-born Mexican American families. The war initiated socioeconomic changes to family and barrio community life that altered self-images, self-expectations, cultural solidarity and aspirations among second-generation brown Angelinos by the postwar period.

Nationally, Mexican Americans participated in record numbers in the armed forces with Los Angeles contributing the largest percentage of recruits and draftees than any other community.[59] Representing ten percent of the city's population, the group numbered one-fifth of all casualties reported in local newspapers and earned record numbers of citations for valor in combat. As the second generation reached maturity, their parents yielded control of the city's barrio enclaves to their bilingual offspring. Their children succumbed as adults to the American way of life in its material and political manifestations more intimately than had immigrants a few decades before. For one, employment opportunities dramatically increased with the demands of the war effort. Mexican American women found employment in various wartime industries and white-collar occupations previously closed to them. In particular, the departure overseas of enlisted men including many barrio males, allowed Chicanas to seek jobs in various defense industries across the southland. Working alongside other men and women of diverse backgrounds exposed them to mainstream values, gave them earning power to improve their living standards, and allowed them more social mobility than possible in the past. Local resident Alicia Mendeola Shelit financed her first home while working for Douglas Aircraft during the war. She recalled that she was able to "bring the money in to feed my kids, like a man."[60]

Typically, wartime Los Angeles barrios reflected increasingly the imprimatur of the second generation as English language, American music, dance, food, movies and fashions took root and set in motion the intellectual reshaping of the immigrant community. Mexican culture would be replaced in the postwar period by a Chicano counter-culture which was a composite of Mexican intellectual and American political and social values. In addition, the influx of Mexican Americans from other regions of the Southwest to Los Angeles exposed barrio residents simultaneously to both provincial sentiments and other urban attitudes among New Mexicans, Tejanos and other Chicanos and Chicanas. Finally, the returning war veterans put a new face on the future of the barrios. Serving their country alongside Caucasian soldiers had given them the confidence that they were full-fledged Americans, too. The war veteran reacted strongly to the blatant wartime discrimination directed at their barrio compatriots, particularly during the 1942 Sleepy Lagoon case trial and the subsequent servicemen's riots. At the same time, they were determined to confront and eradicate the pattern of prejudice and injustice that still stymied Mexican Americans in Los Angeles. The establishment of postwar civil rights political organizations such as the Community Service Organization and the emergence of leaders like Edward Roybal marked a significant new direction for the future.

More significantly for family life, the war had ushered in some changes in gender roles and socioeconomic conditions and intruded American material customs into the internal structure of daily living. Nonetheless, the traditional cultural clannishness still influenced barrio residents. But no longer would the barrio remain as insular as it had in the years prior to World War II. In the prewar period, racial and ethnic pride, Spanish linguistic solidarity and community social involvement were hallmarks of the family's sphere in these enclaves. By the end of the war, greater social mobility, bilingual skill among children, and fascination with American fads and fashions governed the new interests of the evolving Chicano generation. With the war veteran's return, the realization of the "American dream" seemed within reach. To achieve this goal, the brown veterans led the first significant exodus of Mexican Americans out of the barrios throughout the Los Angeles area. Their parents generally remained in the older isolated enclaves. In the post-war decades the formation of new communities outside of the barrio signaled the emergence of a more diverse and less traditional Chicano family life in greater Los Angeles.

NOTES

[1] Mark Reisler, *By the Sweat of Their Brow, Mexican Immigrant Labor in the United States, 1900-1940* (Wesport, CT: Greenwood, 1976), p. 25.

[2] Ricardo Romo, *East Los Angeles, History of a Barrio* (Austin: University of Texas Press, 1983), p. 59.

[3] *Ibid.*, p. 54.

[4] For an insightful study of the national climate of the 1920s and the rise of anti-Mexicanism in the United States, see Reisler, pp. 151-183.

[5] George J. Sanchez, *Becoming Mexican American: Ethnicity, Culture and Identity in Chicano Los Angeles, 1900-1945* (New York: Oxford Press, 1993), p. 257.

[6] Alberto Camarillo, *Chicanos in a Changing Society, From Mexican Pueblos to American Barrios in Santa Barbara and Southern California, 1848-1930* (Cambridge,MA: Harvard University Press, 1979), p. 205.

[7] Manuel Gamio, *Mexican Immigration to the United States, A Study of Human Migration and Adjustment* (New York: Dover,1971), pp. 13-23; Romo, pp. 33-40.

[8] Gamio, p. 129; E.C. Orozco, *Republican Protestantism in Aztlan* (Glendale, CA: Petereins Press, 1980), p. 242.

[9] Constantine Panunzio, "Intermarriage in Los Angeles, 1924-1933," *Journal of Sociology*, 47 (March 1942): 692.

[10] Romo, p. 9.

[11] Camarillo, p. 203.

[12] Romo, pp. 78-79.

[13] Robert McLean, *That Mexican! As He Really Is, North and South of th Rio Grande* (New York: Fleming H. Revell, 1928), pp. 146-147.

[14] Carey McWilliams, *North From Mexico: The Spanish-Speaking People of the UnitedStates* (Westport, CT: Greenwood, 1968), p. 224.

[15] Antonio Rios-Bustamante and Pedro Castillo, *An Illustrated History of Mexican Los Angeles, 1781-1985* (Los Angeles: Chicano Studies Research Center, University of California, Los Angeles, 1986), p. 130.

[16] "Health, Relief and Delinquency Conditions among the Mexicans of California," in Manuel P. Servin, ed., *An Awakened Minority: The Mexican Americans*, 2nd Ed. (Beverly Hills: Glencoe Press, 1974), p. 72.

[17] *Ibid.*, p. 73.

[18] *Ibid.*, p. 70.

[19] Emory Bogardus, "Current Problems of Mexican Imigrants," *Sociology and Social Research*, 25 (1940):170.

[20] *Ibid.*

[21] Rosalinda M. Gonzalez, "Chicanas and Mexican Immigrant Families, 1920-1940: Women's Subordination and Family Exploitation," in Lois Scharf and Joan M. Jensen,eds., *Decades of Discontent: The Women's Movement, 1920-1940* (Westport, CT: Greenwood, l983), p. 70.

[22] Vicki L. Ruiz, *Cannery Women, Cannery Lives: Mexican Women, Unionization, and the California Food Processing Industry, 1930-1950* (Albuquerque: University of New Mexico Press, 1987), p. 14.

[23] *Ibid.*, p. 168.

[24] Bogardus, p. 168.

[25] Glenn E. Hoover, "Our Mexican Immigrants," *Foreign Affairs* (1929):103-104.

[26] McLean, pp. 162-163.

[27] Reisler, p. 161.

[28] Vernon McCombs, *From Over the Border, A Study of the Mexicans in the United States* (New York: Council of Women for Home Missions and Missionary Education Movement, 1925), p. 61.

[29] Beatrice Griffith, *American Me* (Westport, CT: Greenwood, 1973), pp. 191-192; Romo, pp. 139-140.

[30] Griffith, pp. 191-192.

[31] Reisler, pp. 155,157.

[32] Camille Guerin-Gonzales, *Mexican Workers and American Dreams: Immigration, Repatriation, and California Farm Labor, 1900-1939* (New Brunswick, NJ: Rutgers University Press, 1994), p.68.

[33] *Ibid.*, p. 86; Francisco Balderrama, *In Defense of La Raza: The Los Angeles Mexican Consulate and the Mexican Community, 1929 to 1936* (Tucson: University of Arizona Press, 1974), p. 146.

[34] Abraham Hoffman, *Unwanted Mexican Americans in the Great Depression: Repatriation Pressures, 1929-1939* (Tucson: University of Arizona Press, 1974), p. 146.

[35] Francisco E. Balderrama and Raymond Rodriguez, *Decade of Betrayal: Mexican Repatriation in the 1930s* (Albuquerque: University of New Mexico Press, 1995), pp. 105-106.

[36] *Ibid.*, p. 107, pp. 109-110.

[37] Emory S. Bogardus, *The Mexican Immigrant in the United States* (New York: Arno Press, 1982), p. 28.

[38] Manuel Gamio, *The Life Story of the Mexican Immigrant: Autobiographical Documents* (New York: Dover, 1971), p. 239.

[39] Ruiz, pp.11-12.

[40] Vicki L. Ruiz, *From Out of the Shadows: Mexican Women in Twentieth-Century America* (New York: Oxford University Press, 1998), pp. 55-57.

[41] Ruiz, *Cannery Women, Cannery Lives*, pp.14, 19.

[42] Ruiz, *From Out of the Shadows*, p. 60.

[43] Bogardus, *The Mexican Immigrant in the United States*, p. 29.

[44] Gamio, p. 161.

[45] *Ibid.*, p. 68.

[46] Balderrama, *In Defense of La Raza*, p. 77.

[47] Balderrama and Rodriguez, *Decade of Betrayal*, pp. 38-39; George J. Sanchez, "Go After the Women": Americanization and the Mexican Immigrant Woman, 1915-1929," in Vicki L. Ruiz and Ellen C. DuBois,

eds., *Unequal Sisters: A Multicultural Reader in U.S. Women's History* (New York: Routledge, 1994), p. 291.

[48] Balderrama, *In Defense of La Raza*, p. 55.

[49] *Ibid.*, p. 56.

[50] Sanchez, *Becoming Mexican American*, p. 167.

[51] *Ibid.*, p. 266; Edward McDonagh, "Status Levels of Mexicans," *Sociology and Social Research*, 33 (1949):451; Ruiz, *Out of the Shadows*, p. 63.

[52] C.C. Trillingham and Marie M. Hughes, "A Good Neighbor Policy for Los Angeles County," *California Journal of Secondary Education*, 18 (1943):343.

[53] *Ibid.*, pp. 343-346.

[54] Emory S. Bogardus, "Gangs of Mexican American Youth," *Sociology and Social Research*, 28 (1943):61.

[55] Bogardus, pp. 54-58, 61.

[56] McDonagh, p. 451.

[57] Bogardus, p. 65.

[58] Edward J. Escobar, "Zoot Suiters and Cops: Chicano Youth and the Los Angeles Police Department During World War II," in Lewis A. Erenberg and Susan E. Hirsch, eds., *The War in American Culture: Society and Consciousness during World War II* (Chicago: University of Chicago Press, 1996), p. 291; Ruiz, From *Out of the Shadows*, p. 83.

[59] Romo, p. 165.

[60] Ruiz, p. 82.

Chapter 2

INDISPENSABLE SCAPEGOATS
Asians & Pacific Islanders
in Pre-1945 Los Angeles

Donald and Nadine Hata

Asians and Pacific Islanders resided in Mexico more than a century before the founding of Los Angeles. Filipinos had settled in Acapulco and a Chinese merchant enclave was firmly established in Mexico City. Most arrived as crew and passengers aboard the fabled Manila Galleons that connected Spain's colonies in the Philippines and Mexico as early as 1565.[1] Twelve families (*Pobladores*) were recruited in Mexico for the trek north to establish a settlement at Los Angeles in 1781, but only eleven arrived. Antonio Miranda Rodriguez, one of the original Pobladores and described as a Chino in the census of 1781, might have been the first Filipino in Los Angeles had he not stayed behind to care for a sick daughter.[2] Almost a century passed before a significant Asian presence emerged in the form of Los Angeles' first Chinatown near the site of what is now El Pueblo State Historic Park.[3]

Chinese and Japanese Pioneers

Responding to the discovery of gold and railroad jobs in the northern part of the state, thousands of Chinese came to California in the 1850s. Most were from small villages around the port city of Canton in southern China. After working on the western portion of the trans-continental railroad, many moved south. By July 1876 Chinese comprised two-thirds of the 1,500 workers on the strategic San Fernando Tunnel that linked Los Angeles by rail to San Francisco. Chinese workers followed the Southern Pacific into Arizona, New Mexico, and Texas. Others constructed the great aqueduct which brought water to the parched Los Angeles basin. They looked to Chinatown for refuge between seasonal employment, and many remained to operate restaurants, laundries, and other small businesses. Community associations arbitrated disputes between members, loaned money, and provided social services. The associations were organized around villages and districts, clans and families, benevolent services, businesses and professions, and secret societies.

By the early 1860s Chinese entrepreneurs participated in the development of a diverse local economy. Merchants set up shop along Calle de Los Negros ("Negro Alley") near the Garnier Building on Los Angeles Street. As early as March 1860, fishermen in Los Angeles found themselves competing with a Chinese company. Chinese comprised an estimated one-third of the county's abalone fishermen in the 1870s and 1880s. Chinese tenant farmers in Southern California planted vegetable crops. During the 1880s, Chinese from the northern mining regions began to move into the San Joaquin Valley and Los Angeles, where opportunities in agriculture beckoned. Los Angeles County s Chinese population swelled from 1,169 in 1880 to 4,424 in 1890. They were tenacious and by 1880 no less than 88.9 percent of the county's 234 truck gardeners were Chinese.[4]

The ability of the Chinese to work and survive in towns and fields under wretched conditions made them a threat to organized labor and nativist-racist groups. The early Chinese in Los Angeles, as elsewhere throughout the West, became convenient and indispensable scapegoats for problems ranging from unemployment to outbreaks of epidemics. Beginning with the arrival of Chinese during the Gold Rush, California lawmakers and judges promoted an anti-Chinese climate. In 1854 the California State Supreme Court ruled that Chinese could not testify against Caucasians in the courts. An 1858 law prohibited Chinese from landing "upon the Pacific Coast except when driven by stress of weather." When unemployment rose after the completion of the trans-continental railroad in 1869, labor unions and a converging coalition of racists, nativists and xenophobes in San Francisco accused Chinese of taking jobs away from "native" Americans. Ironically, the mobs were exhorted by Denis Kearney, an Irish immigrant who bypassed the East Coast where nativists despised Irish immigrants. Kearney represented a uniquely Western mutation of nativism when Irish Catholics joined White Protestants to demand that "the Chinese must go!"[5] The anti-Chinese movement spread south to Los Angeles where a mob invaded Chinatown in October 1871, killed 19 Chinese, looted shops, burned homes, and demonstrated that the anti-Chinese movement was not limited to mere rhetoric.[6]

Federal officials endorsed California's anti-Chinese xenophobia. The official status of Chinese was defined in the phrase "aliens ineligible to citizenship," a category created by excluding Asians from the naturalization provision in the Fourteenth Amendment to the U.S. Constitution. Citizenship via naturalization was defined as limited to Whites and Africans, and Asians were not even allowed the opportunity to take the naturalization tests. In 1882 Congress banned immigration from China for 10 years. The successful drive to renew the law focused on allegations that Chinese were a threat to White "racial purity" and "Western civilization." After 1892, the accusation of unfair competition from "cheap coolie labor" was overshadowed by allegations that all "Orientals" were "undesirables," the sinister vanguard of a "Yellow Peril," and unsuitable for acculturation or racial assimilation.

The early Chinese community in Los Angeles, as elsewhere, was dominated by single males who were sojourners or "birds of passage" seeking jobs. Federal legislation prohibited the entry of brides and families from China after 1882, and anti-miscegenation laws forbade them to marry non-Chinese. The inhumane laws were ruthlessly enforced. At the turn of the century, there were barely 60 families among the 2,000 Chinese in Los Angeles. By 1900 the Chinese population in California dropped to 45,753 from an earlier high of 75,132 in 1880.[7] With the permanent enactment of the federal Chinese Exclusion Law in 1904, the status of Asians was aptly summarized by the cruel cliche in Bret Harte's novels of the West: "You don't have a Chinaman's chance."

The cheap labor vacuum created by Chinese exclusion was largely filled by Issei ("first generation") Japanese emigrants. Most arrived in San Francisco, with only a handful settling in Los Angeles prior to 1900. The devastating 1906 San Francisco earthquake, combined with the anti-Chinese environment in the north, led many Japanese to seek opportunities in Southern California.[8] Issei farm laborers saved funds to purchase or lease farming lands for vegetable, berry and flower crops. Truck farms were scattered from the Palos Verdes Peninsula, Moneta-Gardena, Bellflower and Beverly Hills, to the San Gabriel and San Fernando valleys. Japanese entered the wholesale produce and flower markets.[9] Other Issei settled along the coast, in East San Pedro, Santa Monica, and Oxnard. In 1901, Japanese fishermen discovered abalone at White's Point in San Pedro, and began to ship their dried catch to Japan. Driven out by hostile neighbors, they moved to Terminal Island where their ability to bargain collectively with White cannery owners made them a significant force in the local commercial fishing industry.

The successes of Japanese emigrants, coupled with Imperial Japan's growing strength in Asia, reinforced xenophobic and nativist warnings that they threatened the state's economy and the nation's security. Imperial Japan's unexpected victory in the Russo-Japanese War (1904-1905) resulted in a dramatic shift in the Pacific balance of power and fueled fears that Japanese residing on the Pacific Coast were a "Yellow Peril." Labor unions felt threatened by the entry of Japanese workers into areas such as logging, mining, fishing, canneries, and railroad work. They saw the Japanese as "scabs" like the Chinese before them, and 67 labor organizations met in San Francisco in 1905 to form the Asiatic Exclusion League. A year later the San Francisco School Board bowed to the League's pressure and banned all Japanese and Koreans from attending integrated schools. Tokyo officially protested, but it also feared the growing anti-Japanese mood and approved the 1908 Gentlemen's Agreement which banned emigration of unskilled laborers from Japan to the United States. The Japanese government strictly enforced the new policy, causing a major shift of migrant laborers to destinations in Latin America.[10]

The Gentlemen s Agreement transformed the Japanese American population by permitting passports to be issued to the "parents,

Courtesy of the Seaver Center for Western History Research, Natural History Museum of Los Angeles County

A parade on Marchessault Street in Chinatown, about 1900

wives and children of laborers already resident" in the United States. Los Angeles soon became the largest concentration of Japanese on the U.S. mainland. The arrival of thousands of "picture brides" created families and produced children, the Nisei ("second generation") Japanese Americans who were U.S. citizens by birthright. Nativists and xenophobes were outraged by the growth of Japanese immigrant families, and by 1913 they engineered the enactment of state alien land laws banning the sale or lease of land to "aliens ineligible to citizenship," a euphemism for Asians. California's alien land laws were soon emulated by other West Coast states.

In 1924 a nationwide nativist coalition pressured Congress to pass an immigration law (the National Origins Act) which established permanent restrictive quotas on immigrants from areas outside northwestern Europe. Free immigration of Chinese had been banned by earlier federal legislation, and the 1924 law added a special provision for the total exclusion of Japanese. Immigration from Asia virtually stopped until after World War II. While cruel to individuals and families, the isolation from ancestral homelands accelerated the Americanization of Japanese and other Asians. The children of immigrant families were U.S. citizens by birthright, attended public schools, spoke English as their native tongue, and had few contacts with traditional languages and cultural values outside their homes. Asian first names were modified to sound more American, and popular American culture was mimicked. Traditional institutions and customs were forced to adapt or die. The Americanization of Japanese Buddhism was apparent in the holding of services on Sunday, the adoption of "church" for "temple," and the singing of "Buddha loves me, this I know . . ." to the tune of "Jesus loves me . . . ."

DEFIANCE AND ACCOMMODATION: RESPONSES TO OPPRESSION

Asians and Pacific Islanders fearlessly stood up for their rights and challenged their oppressors. Workers protested unequal pay, miserable working conditions, and physical abuse. During the winter of 1878-79, Chinese vegetable peddlers in Los Angeles went on strike for several weeks to protest restrictive ordinances aimed at their businesses. Asian laborers organized labor unions and sometimes joined with other groups in common cause. In 1903 Mexican and Japanese sugar beet workers in Oxnard formed a unique example of inter-ethnic cooperation when, instead of competing against each other, they formed the Japanese-Mexican Labor Association. Their meetings included simultaneous translations into Spanish, Japanese and English, and they succeeded in striking for better wages and working conditions.[11] Others united to oppose discriminatory legislation. An effort to pass an anti-alien fishing bill in the State Legislature was defeated in 1923 because Japanese fishermen in Los Angeles were well-integrated into the industry and because of "their close relationship to the large American canneries." [12] They used the courts to fight immigration exclusion and to secure naturalization and citizenship rights, but with little success. In the landmark case of *Takao Ozawa* v. *U.S.* (1922) the U.S. Supreme Court confirmed that aliens of Japanese ancestry were "ineligible to citizenship" via naturalization because they were neither White nor Black. It made no difference that Ozawa had spent most of his life in the United States, spoke English in his home, graduated from Berkeley High School, and attended the University of California. The pursuit of racial equality by Asian Indians was similarly rejected in *U.S.* v. *Bhagat Singh Thind* (1923).

Sikhs from the Punjab region of the Indian subcontinent were the majority of some 5,800 emigrants who arrived between 1900-1911. They started in railroad and lumber jobs, quickly shifted to agriculture, and established communities in the Sacramento and Imperial Valley regions. Asian Indian women were extremely scarce, and 80 percent of marriages were with women from Mexican migrant labor families.[13] Many Asian Indians supported nationalist movements until 1947, when British India dissolved into two independent nations, India and Pakistan.[14]

Women were outnumbered amidst the male laborers who dominated early Asian immigrants, but they played diverse and important roles in the development of families and a social infrastructure for permanent immigrant communities. Some of the earliest Asian women arrived as prostitutes, but others worked as domestic servants and migrant laborers in addition to their roles as wives and mothers. Often oppressed at home and on the job, the lives of many immigrant women were harsh and cruel, but their struggles and sacrifices were essential to the emergence and survival of families in which their children were U.S. citizens by birthright.[15]

While many immigrants struggled to merely survive, others succeeded in moving from unskilled jobs on farms and in towns and became farmers and shopkeepers. Small and medium sized entrepreneurs formed the core of early enclaves, and some went on to become wealthy and powerful voices in their communities. In Little Tokyo, Benjamin Bungaro Mori built his Asia Company, a general store that included a post office, into the largest and wealthiest Japanese-owned business in Los Angeles in the 1920s. Early Korean entrepreneur Leo C. Song established a wholesale fruit and vegetable company in Los Angeles, K & S Jobbers, and popularized the nectarine.

Los Angeles's Chinatown and Little Tokyo evolved into shops, restaurants and services catering to outsiders and tourists in addition to their own residents. A metamorphosis occurred in both enclaves as merchants assumed leadership, controlled contacts with public officials and the outside community, and sanitized the public image from vice dens to "all American" tourist attractions.[16] On January 25, 1924, the Chinese Chamber of Commerce published the following resolution in the *Los Angeles Times*:

> Whereas, Chinatown has been made to suffer in the past because of the bad name generally applied to this district, the same being no fault of the Chinese residents,
>
> Be it resolved:
>
> First, that we the merchants of Chinatown, use every opportunity to induce white people of the city and tourists to visit Chinatown; that we extend to visitors every courtesy on visiting our shops and places of interest.
>
> Second, that we . . . spread the word that Chinatown is a safe place for women to come to, whether escorted or alone.
>
> Third, that we . . . suppress rowdyism among the lower classes of white people visiting Chinatown . . . .
>
> Fourth, that we extend Los Angeles an invitation to visit Chinatown on the celebration of the New Year and see for themselves the conditions that prevail . . . .

Amidst the public image makeover, however, the original site and structures of Chinatown were systematically and deliberately obliterated by outside forces. The process began in late 1920 when Chinese residents were evicted from the Plaza area to permit a romanticized and commercial reconstruction of Olvera Street. In 1933, the decision to build a new Union Station required the condemnation, evacuation and demolition of all that remained of the original Chinese residences and businesses in the area. But the Chinese business community was resilient. By 1938 they constructed two complementary projects north of El Pueblo and the new Union Station: New Chinatown and China City.[17]

By 1910, a cluster of shops and residences known as Little Tokyo rose next to Chinatown. Little Tokyo followed the Chinatown model and transformed itself from an isolated ethnic enclave to a tourist attraction. Issei shop owners hired acculturated Nisei to deal with English-speaking customers. During the Great Depression, Nisei Week was created as an annual festival to revitalize small businesses by attracting Nisei and outsiders. Japanese American women played indispensable roles as volunteers and performers and "were dangled as bait for consumers, [but] were excluded from the highest levels of decision-making."[18] By 1940, there were 36,866 Japanese in Los Angeles County, two-thirds of whom lived in the inner city.

Aside from a few political exiles who came to the continental U.S. as early as 1885, there was little Korean emigration until 1903-1905. Imperial Japan's annexation of their homeland in 1910 created an ironic identity problem for Koreans in Southern California. In 1913, Korean fruit pickers in Hemet were attacked by a White mob who had mistaken the Koreans for Japanese. Insult was added to injury when the Japanese Consul General in Los Angeles intervened on behalf of the Koreans, an offer rejected by the Southern California Korean National Association. Political exiles, many of whom were students, sought refuge here and organized movements to liberate their homeland from Japan.[19] The early Korean community included few wives and was dominated by single males who were denied intermarriage by anti-miscegenation laws. The 2,000 Koreans in the 1930 census were concentrated in California, with the majority of those drawn to the Los Angeles area by railroad and farming jobs. A major source of strength for Los Angeles' Koreans lay in the strong network of Korean Christian churches which served as centers of political and social cohesion. The churches helped the community to survive the grim Depression decade of the 1930s. On the eve of World War II, a small but hardy core of Korean businesses included "thirty fruit and vegetable stands, nine groceries, eight laundries, six trucking companies, five wholesalers, five restaurants, three drug stores, two hat shops, one employment agency, and one rooming house."[20]

Pacific Islanders and Filipinos were the only groups untouched by the 1924 federal immigration law's exclusion of Asians. Small numbers of Pacific Islanders were present in California before the Gold Rush. Native Hawaiians, for example, were brought by John Sutter to build a fort in the Sacramento Valley. Samoans and Guamanians arrived aboard fishing and merchant vessels and settled in Long Beach, Wilmington and San Pedro. While few Pacific Islanders settled in California until after World War II, large numbers of Filipinos began to arrive in the 1920s. Some were students, but most were domestic servants and unskilled workers, many of whom moved to the West Coast from Hawaiian sugar plantations. The 1924 exclusion of Japanese created a cheap labor vacuum on the West Coast, and large farmers saw Filipinos as replacements. As "nationals," neither citizen nor alien, they were exempt from federal immigration quotas. This designation permitted their unlimited recruitment as cheap labor. Seasonal farm workers sought fishing and domestic jobs in towns and cities, and Little Manilas were established in Los Angeles and Long Beach. By 1928, competition for scarce jobs led to race riots against Filipino laborers. Filipino old timers recalled those years with bitterness:

> The lives of Filipinos were cheaper than those of dogs. They were forcibly shoved off the streets when they showed resistance. The sentiment against them was accelerated by the marriage of a Filipino to a girl of the Caucasian race in Pasadena. The case was tried in court . . . to degrade the lineage and character of the Filipino people.[21]

Nativists saw Filipinos as a "third wave of Oriental immigration" that had to be halted. But the Philippines were American territory and, as a cynical solution, it was decided that future Philippine independence would settle the issue. After all, Filipinos would be citizens of a sovereign foreign nation, and therefore subject to laws against the immigration and settlement of aliens in America. Thus, observed Carey McWilliams, "those who sought to bar Filipino immigration suddenly became partisans of Philippine independence."[22]

Asian names and faces as stars of blockbuster motion pictures are taken for granted today. But long before the martial arts exploits of Bruce Lee, Jackie Chan or Lucy Liu, early pioneers of the movie industry included Japanese and Chinese silent screen actors Sessue Hayakawa and Anna Mae Wong. They, along with other peoples of color, disappeared from leading roles in the 1930s as racist and escapist images of Anglo supremacy took over the casting and script priorities of Tinseltown. Keye Luke was one of super-sleuth Charlie Chan's numerous sons, but the role of the erudite Chan was never given to an Asian actor. Unknown to the general public, but respected by his professional peers, was the keen eye of innovative cinema cameraman James Wong Howe. For Korean actor, Philip Ahn, the Depression years were lean: "I ate steamed cabbage for breakfast and potato for supper . . . all day I wandered looking for a job."[23]

By 1940, on the eve of World War II, America's Asians and Pacific Islanders were a heterogeneous and minuscule portion—489,984 or 0.4 percent—of the total population. The Asian and Pacific dimensions of the war would juxtapose the explicitly racist realities of American society against Imperial Japanese propaganda that promised to liberate Asia from White European and American colonial masters. Tokyo's wartime propaganda condemned the long history of America's official endorsement of segregation and exclusion of peoples of color, including Asians and Pacific Islanders. A series of Japanese victories in the first six months of the war caused hysteria in the Pentagon and the White House, and resulted in the mass removal and incarceration of Japanese Americans. Other Asian Pacific Americans benefitted from the government's need to court those who had been suspected, scorned, or simply ignored before the war.

MASS REMOVAL OF JAPANESE AMERICANS IN WORLD WAR II

At sunrise on December 7, 1941, prior to an official declaration of war, the Empire of Japan launched an audacious naval air attack on U.S. military installations at Pearl Harbor, Hawaii. President Franklin D. Roosevelt declared it "a day that will live in infamy."[24] The attack directly affected Japanese Americans on February 19, 1942, when Roosevelt signed Executive Order 9066, authorizing and directing the U.S. Army to identify "areas . . . from which any or all persons may be excluded . . . ." The United States was also at war with Nazi Germany and Fascist Italy, but only Americans of Japanese ancestry were subjected to mass evacuation and incarceration. In the interval between Pearl Harbor and the president's decision, a climate of hysteria and paranoia was created by local newspapers and radio commentators. On January 16, 1942, a *Palos Verdes News* editorial complained that "we still have the Japanese farmers here cultivating the land immediately adjoining the ocean and military objectives . . . the Japanese are everywhere." Some 40 Japanese who farmed 500 acres on the Palos Verdes peninsula had their leases abruptly cancelled on February 13. California Governor Culbert Olson inflamed suspicions about Japanese American loyalty in a broadcast on February 4. The next day Los Angeles Mayor Fletcher Bowron further fueled hysteria with the warning that "right here in my own city are those who may spring to action at an appointed time in accordance with a prearranged plan wherein each of our little Japanese friends will know his part in the event of any possible invasion or air raid."[25]

Contrary to the unfounded charges, Japanese Americans, both citizen and alien, committed no acts of sabotage. But even after weeks had passed without evidence of their disloyalty, Earl Warren, at that time California Attorney General and a gubernatorial candidate, testified to an investigative committee chaired by California Congressman John Tolan on February 21 that the absence of sabotage was proof of Japanese American cunning: "I believe that we are just being lulled into a false sense of security and the only reason we haven't had a disaster in California is because it has been timed for a different date. . . . Our day of reckoning is bound to come . . . ."[26] A few days later, the *Los Angeles Times* and other local newspapers carried huge headlines about the alleged "L.A. Air Raid." Shortly after midnight on February 25, air raid sirens caused panic-stricken anti-aircraft gunners to fire more than 1,400 shells into the early morning sky. Buried in small print was an admission that no enemy planes had flown over the city.

By Spring 1942 the mass evacuation was well underway, supervised by U.S. Army troops in full combat gear, replete with fixed bayonets. Their commander, General John L. DeWitt, declared: "A Jap's a Jap. They are a dangerous element . . . there is no difference whether he is an American citizen . . . he is still a Japanese, and you can't change him . . . ."[27] Evacuees were forced into local racetracks, livestock exposition facilities, and fairgrounds. Between May 7 and October 27, 1942, Santa Anita Racetrack housed 18,719 Japanese Americans in horse stalls and flimsy tarpaper barracks.[28] By early August 1942, the U.S. Army announced that 110,723 persons of Japanese ancestry had been removed from their homes throughout the West Coast and placed in temporary regional "assembly centers."

Further incarceration was unnecessary and could have been avoided. By mid-June 1942 the White House and the Pentagon knew that the U.S. victory in the Battle of Midway had removed any Imperial Japanese invasion threat to Hawaii, let alone the West Coast. Postwar research by scholars and a congressional commission confirm that federal officials withheld information and lied about the "military necessity" of the evacuation.[29] However, Autumn 1942 saw the further movement of over 110,000 adults and children from local assembly centers to concentration camps for the remainder of the war. With the exception of two sites in remote rural areas of California, Tule Lake near the Oregon border and Manzanar in the Owens Valley, the camps were far removed from the West Coast: Poston and Gila River in Arizona; Rohwer and Jerome in Arkansas; Minidoka, Idaho; Heart Mountain, Wyoming; Granada (Amache), Colorado; and Topaz, Utah. Los Angeles' Japanese Americans were dispersed among all of the ten major War Relocation Authority camps. Many community leaders and Latin American Japanese were imprisoned at other isolated sites such as Death Valley, Crystal City (Texas), and Moab (Utah).

Over 33,000 Japanese Americans, including women, served in the U.S. armed forces in World War II. Hundreds played critical roles as translators and agents of the Military Intelligence Service in the Pacific and Asia. The most publicized combat unit was the racially segregated 442nd ("Go For Broke") Regimental Combat Team that fought in Italy and France, and helped liberate Jewish survivors of Nazi death camps. The 442nd became the most heavily decorated unit of its kind in the history of the U.S. Army, and its highly publicized exploits dispelled prewar doubts about the loyalty of Japanese Americans.[30]

The evacuation orders were finally rescinded on January 2, 1945. There was opposition to the return of Japanese Americans to the West Coast. Returnees found that household possessions had been stolen, and shops and farms were looted and stripped bare. They were turned away at markets and real estate offices, local bureaucrats denied and delayed applications for business licenses, insurance companies demanded that evacuees forfeit their original policies and begin paying premiums anew at higher rates, and both public and private employers refused to count the incarceration years toward retirement benefits. Verbal abuse and violence were a daily fact of life. One exception was the Pacific Coast Committee on American Principles and Fair Play, an umbrella organization for private, federal, state and local groups and agencies as well as Black, Filipino, and Korean community representatives. The committee agreed that "any attempt to make capital for their racial groups at the expense of the Japanese would be sawing off the limbs on which they themselves sat."[31]

Public and private assistance was minimal. Destitute families formed communal residences in the crowded inner city, where they lived amidst poor Blacks and Latinos before moving into areas vacated by the postwar "White flight" to the suburbs. Returnees lost more land and money through escheat actions between 1944-1952 when the State of California offered one-half of the price to county officials when escheated lands were sold. In 1948 Congress passed the Japanese American Evacuation Claims Act, a token effort that processed relatively few claims. Forty years would pass until a nationwide movement for "redress" resulted in an official presidential apology and cash payments to survivors.[32]

WORLD WAR II:
A TURNING POINT FOR ASIAN PACIFIC AMERICANS

For Japanese Americans, the war was a time of fear and anxiety. Other Asian Pacific Angelenos, however, rejoiced in seeing the

United States finally involved in the war against the Japanese Empire. A Filipino American boxer made newspaper headlines by beating up Japanese Americans on the street. Asians feared being mistaken for Japanese, and wore lapel tags that identified them as Filipinos, Chinese or Koreans. Vernacular newspapers and periodicals highlighted contributions to U.S. War Bond drives and the Red Cross. The war provided an opportunity for the formerly suspected and scorned to tout their 200 percent Americanism.

Filipinos saw a chance for acceptance as equals as news stories made martyrs of Filipinos who fought and surrendered alongside U.S. units in the Philippines. The brutality of Japanese Imperial Army troops toward American and Filipino prisoners quieted intense anti-Filipino sentiment throughout California as U.S. propaganda depicted formerly despised peoples of color as important allies against Imperial Japan and her Axis partners in Europe. On February 19, 1942, the day President Roosevelt signed EO 9066 for the mass removal of Japanese Americans, news stories reflected the war's starkly contrasting effect on other Asian Americans. Filipinos celebrated President Roosevelt's authorization of the First Filipino Infantry Regiment "in recognition of the intense loyalty and patriotism of those Filipinos now residing in the United States."[33] Draft laws were changed to include Filipinos, and some 7,000 served in two segregated regiments. Deployed to the Pacific, Filipino troops were praised for unique and dangerous assignments behind enemy lines, where they gathered intelligence and sabotaged logistics and communications. At home, Filipino soldiers learned that their patriotism was not respected by fellow Americans. Filipinos stationed at Camp Beale were refused service at shops in Marysville, or restricted to segregated sections of theaters; visiting wives were denied rooms at local hotels. But the war provided opportunities for Filipinos. Citizenship was granted to those who served in the U.S. armed services. The state's alien land laws were interpreted to permit Filipinos to take over lands formerly farmed by Japanese Americans. Defense industry jobs were officially color-blind and paid well. Filipinos bought homes and settled throughout Los Angeles County, from the San Fernando Valley to Long Beach, Carson, Torrance, and Gardena. In 1946, Filipinos who had immigrated to the U.S. were granted citizenship and an annual quota of 100. Unfortunately, in spite of President Roosevelt's promise of citizenship to any Filipino who fought against Imperial Japan, some 10,000 surviving Southern California Filipino veterans (average age 75) had to wait until November 1990 for the U.S. government to finally respond to their demands that the president's wartime pledge be fulfilled.[34] President Bill Clinton proclaimed October 20, 1996 as a day honoring Filipino veterans of World War II.

Korean American nationalists saw America's entry into the war as a long awaited opportunity to liberate their homeland. They saw little difference between Japanese Americans and Imperial Japan and supported the removal of all Japanese from the Pacific Coast. The Manghokun or Tiger Brigade, a special 109 member Korean volunteer unit of the California National Guard, trained in Exposition Park on weekend afternoons.[35] The war created problems for Korean immigrants who were identified by the federal government as "enemy aliens" because they were officially classified as subjects of the Japanese Empire. One Korean American, Young Oak Kim, joined the segregated 442nd Regimental Combat Team, comprised of Japanese Americans, and earned promotions and several decorations for combat heroism in Europe.[36] While some Korean Americans sympathized with Japanese Americans, others moved to Southern California where they could buy property left by evacuees.

Chinese Americans also benefitted from U.S. involvement in the war against Imperial Japan. In 1943, in a cosmetic show of support for a wartime ally, Congress relaxed the total ban on Chinese immigration that had been in place since 1882, with a token quota of 105 per year. In 1946 wives of Chinese Americans were allowed to enter as non-quota immigrants, and nearly 10,000 arrived by 1952. Some 16,000 Chinese Americans served in the U.S. armed forces. Unlike Japanese Americans, they were fully integrated and even accepted as officers by the U.S. Navy. After 1949, when the Communists conquered mainland China and subsequently entered the Korean War on the side of North Korea, Chinese Americans became targets of Cold War and McCarthy-era paranoia. Surveillance and harassment of Chinese Americans by federal agencies such as the FBI, CIA, and INS did not diminish until the early 1970s, when President Richard M. Nixon's surprise visit to mainland China began a gradual rapprochement between the two nations.

Asian Indians lobbied Congress for relaxation of immigration and naturalization policies, arguing that such action would be evidence of American rejection of Nazi claims of Nordic racial superiority. Imperial Japanese Army and Navy advances into British India and the Indian Ocean alarmed strategic planners who feared Indian nationalists' support for Japan against the Allies, and in 1946 Congress supported a small immigration quota and naturalization rights for Asian Indians. Between 1947 and 1965, 1,772 Asian Indians became naturalized U.S. citizens, including Dalip Singh Saund, a successful Punjabi Sikh farmer in the Imperial Valley who had arrived in California in 1919. Saund won election to the House of Representatives in 1956.[37]

The end of World War II was a turning point for Asian Pacific Americans for a variety of reasons. Their wartime heroism in the U.S. armed forces was highly publicized and reduced prewar paranoia about their loyalty. Imperial Japan was unconditionally defeated and occupied, and transformed from wartime enemy to a key Cold War U.S. ally in Asia. North Korean and Chinese Communist troops fought U.S. forces to a bloody standstill in Korea (1950-1953), but widespread media coverage created sympathy for refugees from the war zone. Large numbers of U.S. military personnel served in Occupied Japan (1945-1952) and saw combat in Korea and more recently in Vietnam and Southeast Asia. Many returned with positive impressions of Asian culture and Asian wives. The civil rights movement of the 1950s and social and cultural revolutions in the 1960s and 1970s also saw a dramatic increase in multiracial outmarriages, particularly between Asian American women and non-Asian males. Popular stereotypes of Asians and Pacific Islanders began to shift from negative prewar "Yellow Peril" images to well-intentioned but patronizing postwar labels like "Model Minority"[38] and "200 percent Americans."[39]

NOTES

[1] William Lytle Schurz, *The Manila Galleon* (New York: E.P. Dutton and Co., Inc., 1939). Official Japanese delegations visited Mexico City in the early 1600s; see Zelia Nuttal, *The Earliest Historical Relations Between Mexico and Japan from Original Documents in Spain and Japan* (Berkeley: University of California Press, American Archaeology and Ethnology Series, 1906).

[2] William Mason and Roberta Kirkhart Mason, "The Founding Forty-Four," *Westways* (July 1976): 23.

[3] See "Los Angeles Massacre Site" in California State Office of Historic Preservation, *Five Views: An Ethnic Sites Survey for California* (Sacramento: California Office of Historic Preservation, State of California Resources Agency, Department of Parks & Recreation, 1990), 145-46.

[4] Sucheng Chan, *This Bittersweet Soil: The Chinese in California Agriculture, 1860-1910* (Berkeley: University of California Press, 1986), 46-50, 115-159.

[5] Alexander Saxton, *The Indispensable Enemy: Labor and the Anti-Chinese Movement in California* (Berkeley: University of California Press, 1971).

[6] Paul M. DeFalla, "Lantern in the Sky," *Southern California Quarterly* 42 (March 1960): 57-88.

[7] Sucheng Chan, *This Bittersweet Soil*, 42-33. Also see Roger Daniels, *Asian America: Chinese and Japanese in the United States Since 1850* (Seattle: University of Washington Press, 1988).

[8] Yuji Ichioka, *The Issei: The World of the First Generation Japanese Immigrants, 1885-1924* (New York: The Free Press, 1988).

[9] William M. Mason and John H. McKinstry, *The Japanese of Los Angeles, 1869-1900*, Contribution in History No. 1 (Los Angeles County Museum of Natural History, 1969).

[10] Lane Ryo Hirabayashi, Akemi Kikumura-Yano, and James A. Hirabayashi, eds., *New World, New Lives: Globalization and People of Japanese Descent in the Americas and from Latin America in Japan* (Palo Alto, CA: Stanford University Press, 2002). Also see Akemi Kikumura-Yano, ed., *Encyclopedia of the Japanese Descendants in the Americas: An Illustrated History of the Nikkei* (Walnut Creek, CA: Altamira Press, 2002).

[11] Tomas Almaguer, "Racial Domination and Class Conflict in Capitalist Agriculture: The Oxnard Sugar Beet Workers' Strike of 1903," *Labor History* 25 (Summer 1984): 325-50.

[12] John Modell, *The Economics and Politics of Racial Accommodation: The Japanese of Los Angeles, 1900-1942* (Urbana: University of Illinois Press, 1977), 69-70, 94.

[13] Karen Leonard, *Ethnic Choices: California's Punjabi-Mexican Americans* (Philadelphia: Temple University Press, 1991).

[14] Joan Jensen, "The Hindu Conspiracy: A Reassessment," *Pacific Historical Review* 48 (1979): 65-83.

[15] See the biography of Mary Paik Lee, a Korean woman who settled in Riverside, CA, in Sucheng Chan, ed., *Quiet Odyssey: A Pioneer Korean Woman in America* (Seattle: University of Washington Press, 1990); Akemi Kikumura, *Through Harsh Winters: The Life of a Japanese Immigrant Woman* (Novato, CA: Chandler and Sharp, 1981); Evelyn Nakano Glenn, *Issei, Nisei, War Bride: Three Generations of Japanese American Women in Domestic Service* (Philadelphia: Temple University Press, 1986); Yuji Ichioka, "Ameyuki-san: Japanese Prostitutes in Nineteenth Century America," *Amerasia Journal* 4:1 (1977): 1-22.

[16] Ivan Light, "From Vice District to Tourist Attraction: The Moral Career of American Chinatowns, 1880-1940," *Pacific Historical Review* 43 (August 1974): 67-94.

[17] Christopher Salter, "The Chinese of Los Angeles," *Urban Resources* (Spring 1984):15-20, 28.

[18] See Lon Kurashige, "The Problem of Biculturalism: Japanese American Identity and Festival before World War II," *Journal of American History* 86 (March 2000): 1632-1654; and *Japanese American Celebration and Conflict: A History of Ethnic Identity and Festival in Los Angeles, 1934-1990* (Berkeley: University of California Press, 2002).

[19] Linda Shin, "Koreans in America, 1903-1945," *Amerasia Journal* 1 (November 1971): 33-34.

[20] Wayne Patterson and Hyung-chan Kim, *The Koreans in America* (Minneapolis: Lerner Publications, 1977), 34.

[21] Carlos Bulosan, *America Is in the Heart: A Personal History* (1946. Reprint. Seattle: University of Washington Press, 1973), 143.

[22] See Carey McWilliams, *Brothers Under the Skin*, rev. ed. (Boston: Little Brown, 1964), 242.

[23] Eui-Young Yu, Earl H. Phillips, and Eun Sik, eds., *Koreans in Los Angeles: Prospects and Promises* (California State University, Los Angeles: Koryo Research Institute, Center for Korean-American and Korean Studies, 1982), 17.

[24] "Pearl Harbor" was unrivaled as the American synonym for "surprise attack" until "9/11," referring to the terrorist attacks on the World Trade Towers in New York City and the Pentagon on September 11, 2001.

[25] Morton Grodzins, *Americans Betrayed: Politics and the Japanese American Evacuation* (Chicago: University of Chicago Press, 1949), 103.

[26] Roger Daniels, *Concentration Campus USA: Japanese Americans and World War II* (New York: Holt, Rinehart & Winston, 1971), 76.

[27] Bill Hosokawa, *Nisei: The Quiet Americans* (New York: William Morrow, 1969), 260.

[28] Anthony L. Lehman, *Birthright of Barbed Wire: The Santa Anita Assembly Center for the Japanese* (Los Angeles: Westernlore Press, 1970).

[29] Peter Irons, *Justice At War: The Story of the Japanese American Internment Cases* (New York: Oxford University Press, 1983); Commission on Wartime Relocation and Internment of Civilians, *Personal Justice Denied:*

Report of the Commission on Wartime Relocation and Internment of Civilians (1982 and 1983. Reprint. Seattle: University of Washington Press, 1997); Roger Daniels, *Prisoners Without Trial: Japanese Americans In World War II* (New York: Hill and Wang, 1993); and Michi Weglyn, *Years of Infamy: The Untold Story of America's Concentration Camps* (New York: Morrow, 1976).

[30] Lyn Crost, *Honor By Fire: Japanese Americans at War in Europe and the Pacific* (Novato, CA: Presidio Press, 1994); and Orville C. Shirey, *Americans: The Story of the 442nd Combat Team* (Washington, D.C.: Infantry Journal Press, 1946).

[31] Daniels, *Concentration Camps USA*, 158.

[32] Donald Teruo Hata, Jr. and Nadine Ishitani Hata, "Justice Delayed But Not Denied?" in Kay Saunders and Roger Daniels, eds., *Alien Justice: Wartime Internment in Australia and North America* (Queensland, Australia: University of Queensland Press, 2000), 221-233.

[33] Bienvenido Santos, "Filipinos in War," *Far Eastern Survey*, 11 (30 November 1942): 249.

[34] "At Long Last, Justice for Filipino Vets," *Los Angeles Times*, 1 December 1990, sec. M, p. 6; George Ramos, "Long Fight Over for Filipino Vets," *Ibid.*, 18 December 1990, sec. A, pp. 3, 39.

[35] Bong-Youn Choy, *Koreans in America* (Chicago: Nelson Hall, 1979), 326.

[36] Masayo Umezawa Duus, *Unlikely Liberators: The Men of the 100th and 442nd* (Honolulu: University of Hawaii Press, 1987).

[37] D. S. Saund, *Congressman from India* (New York: Dutton, 1960).

[38] William Petersen, "Success Story, Japanese-American Style," *New York Times Magazine*, 9 January 1966, 20.

[39] "Success Story: Outwhiting the Whites," *Newsweek*, 12 June 1971, 24-25.

Chapter 3

"ALL MEN UP AND NO MAN DOWN"
Black Angelenos Confront
Refracted Racism, 1900-1940

Delores Nason McBroome

Los Angeles's African American population in 1900 totaled 2131 residents, making it the second largest black community in the West. This small group created a carefully wrought network of community organizations promoted by a local African American press that served as a springboard for political activism and identity in Los Angeles until World War II. Some community members, such as Dr. J. Alexander Somerville in 1903, admired the "openness of the city" and its lack of segregated Negro districts. Despite the apparent openness of the city, black residents formed the Afro-American Council in 1900 to offset any threat of discrimination that increasing migration to Los Angeles might present.[1] This council held annual statewide congresses in the early 1900s to advocate the advancement of African Americans in California. Vigilance among black Angelenos against southern-style Jim Crow segregation united the African American community and defined its hopes for a color-blind society proffering economic and political opportunities for their advancement.

The confluence of the local African American press in Los Angeles with the socio-political associations of the Afro-American Council, the Los Angeles Forum, the National Association for the Advancement of Colored People [NAACP], and the All-American

League successfully maintained the "openness" of Los Angeles from 1900 through the First World War era. Yet the practices of Jim Crow segregation began to overtake the city by the 1920s. When Black Angelenos turned to their local branches of political associations such as the NAACP, the National Urban League, and the United Negro Improvement Association [UNIA] to confront and combat a refracted form of racism in their western community, they discovered that the "openness" of the city had evaporated as Los Angeles's population and economic institutions rapidly expanded.

Community vigilance against southern-style Jim Crow segregation not only united the small African American community in Los Angeles but also promoted a shared sense of political and economic activism that historian Douglas Flamming portrays as "middle class in spirit and outlook."[2] One of Los Angeles's leading African American news publications, the *Liberator*, advanced the idea that southern California could become "a place where Negroes could enjoy all the rights of citizenship."[3] The *Liberator's* publisher, Jefferson L. Edmonds, applied many of the tactics of Progressive reform to the issue of racial advancement in California. Edmonds and other African American publicists, such as Frederick Roberts, John Neimore, Charlotta and Joe Bass, created a clear and "optimistic, middle-class vision of what black life could become in Los Angeles."[4]

Jefferson L. Edmonds's background helped to shape his vision for political activism in California. Born a slave in Virginia in 1845, Edmonds gained his freedom after the Civil War and migrated to Crawfordsville, Mississippi where he attended freedman schools to gain an education. He taught in black schools and then purchased his own farm in Mississippi. Edmonds developed a strong interest in political activism and served as a Mississippi State Assemblyman during the Reconstruction era. He witnessed first-hand the introduction of Jim Crow practices that subverted Southern Reconstruction in the 1870s and renounced the growing racial violence and lynching that swept the South. Leaving Mississippi after 1886, Edmonds claimed that "the only thing that we are proud of in connection with the fact that we were born in the South, is that we left it."[5] When he arrived in Los Angeles,

Edmonds joined an active African American community of men and women dedicated to promoting a better life for themselves and their families in California. By 1900 he started the *Liberator*, a monthly news magazine, that he hoped would serve as an educational forum providing black Angelenos with political and economic tactics that could advance their civil rights.

The African American population of Los Angeles received a boost in 1903 when the Southern Pacific Railroad imported almost two thousand African Americans to break a strike led by Mexican construction workers. Many of these newcomers found homes in Los Angeles; and a large number settled in the area around the Southern Pacific Station at Fifth and Central Avenue in Los Angeles.[6] These newcomers found that they could purchase homes in Los Angeles for moderate rates, and they quickly began to share the community vision for black Angelenos that Edmonds and others promoted.

Black Angelenos found the local African American press to be fiercely opposed to the spread of race prejudice. Even Harrison Gray Otis, the Anglo publisher of the *Los Angeles Times*, Jefferson L. Edmonds, publisher of the *Liberator*, and John Neimore, editor of the African American *Eagle*, consistently opposed extensions of Jim Crow racial practices to California. A member of the 1860 Republican national convention that nominated Abraham Lincoln for the Presidency and then a lieutenant colonel in the Union Army, Harrison Gray Otis remained a staunch radical Republican well into the 20th century. John Neimore, black Angeleno and editor of the *California Eagle*, editorialized that Otis "has treated the Brother in Black with considerate judgment, moderation and even handed justice, his contention being that all men are created equal and that no man should be discriminated against because of his color or previous condition."[7] The lack of hostility that African Americans observed in the *Los Angeles Times* during the first decade of the 20th century encouraged many to see the city as a haven for the industrious black man. Robert C. Owens, an African American entrepreneur and community booster, stated in the *Colored American Magazine* that "It is truly hoped that Colored men . . . who want to better their condition and enjoy every political right as American citizens should come to the golden West."[8] For Owens and many other black Angelenos, it appeared that Los Angeles and Southern California offered a safe haven from racism and opportunities for a better life.

Determined to stay in Los Angeles, many African Americans purchased homes in the city at moderate prices during the early 1900s. By 1910 home ownership among black Angelenos remained extremely high in contrast to other urban cities throughout the nation. The 1910 census showed that only 2.4 percent of African Americans in New York City purchased homes and only 11 percent in New Orleans; whereas over one third of black Angelenos (36.1 percent) owned homes.[9] The tendency that existed in most urban communities to consolidate African American neighborhoods did not flourish in Los Angeles until the post World War I era. From 1900 to 1920, African Americans could find residency in six areas of the city: 1) West Temple Street to Occidental Boulevard; 2) First to Third Streets and San Pedro to Santa Fe Streets; 3) Seventh to Ninth Streets and Mateo to Santa Fe Streets; 4) Boyle Heights (First to Broadway and Evergreen to Savannah); 5) Thirty-fifth Street and Normandie Avenue; and 6) the Pico Heights.[10] This variety of African American neighborhoods contributed to the sense of "openness" upon which many black residents commented.

While black Angelenos participated in the early "bugalow boom" of Los Angeles and purchased "California cottages" for their families, de facto residential segregation and discrimination in employment did exist in Los Angeles and gained ground after World War I.[11] The hardships of southern agriculturalists—a stifling system of share-cropping, tenant farming, and a post-war glut of cotton—exacerbated by boll weevil infestations and numerous periods of flood and drought brought new migrants to Los Angeles during the 1920s.[12] Black Angelenos also confronted larger numbers of white southerners coming to Los Angeles who arrived with a strongly rooted sense of racial prejudice against African Americans. These white southerners introduced to Los Angeles the Jim Crow practices they had experienced in the American South.[13] This new threat of southern segregation practices extending to Los Angeles found strong opposition among the socio-political organizations of black Angelenos during the 1920s. These African American associations, shaped and promoted by the visions of the local black press, served as a support network and staging arena for political and civil rights activism.

The Los Angeles Forum served as one of the most important early socio-political associations for black Angelenos. Organized in 1903 by the efforts of three men—the Reverend J. E. Edwards, pastor of the First AME Church, Jefferson L. Edmonds, editor of the *Liberator*, and lawyer Frederick Roberts—the Forum encouraged "united effort on the part of Negroes for their advance and [strengthened] them along lines of moral, social, intellectual, financial and Christian ethics."[14] Moving from the First AME Church to the Odd Fellows' Hall, it met every Sunday at four p.m. for lectures, public debate and political discussions. Through its subcommittees the Forum maintained its status as the premier social institution for black Angelenos for over three decades. Its "Committee on Strangers" introduced newcomers to the city and made them aware of the existing community of black residents and the civic issues facing it. As part of a campaign to eradicate vice among the African American community, this committee introduced newcomers to the "right" sort of people.[15] As the influx of migrants to Los Angeles increased during the 1920s and '30s, the Forum's Committee on Strangers found it more difficult to canvass the black neighborhoods of Los Angeles and integrate newcomers into the established leadership groups.

The Forum introduced popular socio-political ideas of the age and often influenced its members to participate in entrepreneurial ventures. In 1911, the Forum promoted the all-black colony of agriculturalists and independent laborers at Allensworth in Tulare County. Later it would offer vigorous support for a plan to colonize African Americans from southern California to a new settlement of agriculturalists in Baja, California. Led by Theodore Troy and enjoying the enthusiastic support of one of Los Angeles's most prominent African American lawyers, Hugh Macbeth, Baja's Little Liberia typified the "back-to-the-soil movement" so popular in the early 20th century among African Americans. Black boosters in southern California adapted the opposing policies of Booker T. Washington and W. E. B. DuBois to a meld of economic and political activism on several fronts. According to Douglas Flamming:

... Race men and women always held one thing in common: hope. They
believed that things could get better if people would join together and
try to remake society. They saw Los Angeles as an unfinished project,
or, better yet, as an ongoing one. They remained consistently involved
in city affairs. Charlotta Bass [African American publisher of the Los
Angeles newspaper, *The California* Eagle] over the course of her long
life, probably had more harsh words to say about Los Angeles than
any other Angeleno, but it was equally true—and an absolutely vital
point—that she loved the city and believed in its possibilities. For
Charlotta Bass and thousands of other local blacks, Los Angeles was
worth fighting for.[16]

As a result of black Angelenos' determination to preserve the
openness of all avenues of economic and social activities for their
welfare, civic engagement took on a myriad number of tasks.

The Los Angeles Forum advertised its discussions to be unfettered
by any one controlling ideology or viewpoint. Some black Angelenos
viewed the Forum as their "all-American town meeting" where
people could hear differing viewpoints from participants whose
membership in various other organizations varied. All groups found
sanctuary in the Los Angeles Forum.[17] It became a common practice
to select articles from contemporary periodicals as discussion topics
for the Forum meetings. In this way, participants remained current
with ideas and movements that spanned the nation during the early
twentieth century.

The articulation of the Shenk Rule in 1912 caused participants at
the Forum as well as many other black Angelenos much concern
about the encroachment of Jim Crow practices in Los Angeles.
By invitation, C.W. Holden, an African American entrepreneur,
joined a white acquaintance for a beer at a public saloon. The
bartender then charged Holden a dollar for his beer while the
white customer paid a nickel. When Holden's white friend asked
that the mayor revoke the saloon's license, Los Angeles's City
Attorney, John Shenk, maintained that "it was neither extortion
or a violation of the Civil Rights Act to charge a Negro more for
an article than a white man." His decision became known as the
Shenk Rule and soon became a prevalent practice among many of
the city's establishments. Jefferson L. Edmonds editorialized in *The
Liberator* about ice cream parlors and lunch counters that charged
five dollars for a dish of ice cream served to African American

customers. Edmonds's editorials advocating that black Angelenos should vote against Shenk in the mayoral race of 1913 resulted in Shenk's defeat by only a small margin.[18] The political tactic that Edmonds advocated found resonance with black Angelenos seeking to confront racism in their city.

Another ominous sign of the city's altering policies towards African Americans surfaced a year later when a group of white lawyers protested leasing office space to black tenants in the Copp Building thereby forcing the blacks to leave the building.[19] While some black Angelenos confronted incipient Jim Crow practices in the pre-war years, others enjoyed acceptance and association within the white community. Hugh Macbeth, an African American attorney and perhaps the first man to urge admission of black attorneys to the Los Angeles Bar Association, not only had his office in the integrated Lissner Building on South Spring Street but also became one of the founding members of the Lawyers Club of Los Angeles. This group of predominantly white attorneys and leading members of the city organized in 1931 to foster liberal discussion of economics and law so as to "make an effort to bring the legal profession closer to the general public."[20]

Macbeth exemplified the tendency of many black Angelenos to meld different views and ideologies within a guiding creed of entrepreneurial enterprise and boosterism for the black community. As general counsel for the International Community Welfare League, Macbeth promoted the United States' recognition of revolutionary Mexico in order to regularize relations between the Mexican government and the United States. Seeking to stabilize the agricultural colony of Little Liberia in Baja, California, Macbeth stated in the *Los Angeles Times* that "If Los Angeles continues to grow it will soon be the Chicago of the West, and Lower California will eventually be the bread basket of Los Angeles. That's why I am giving my best efforts to this colonization plan. It appeals to me as being a wonderful opportunity for colored people."[21] Macbeth carefully couched the plans for Little Liberia in an inclusive fashion that promised opportunities for white investors in Mexico when he said that "the Negro colony of Lower California will serve as an entering wedge for the white man in Mexico. . . . as the Negro gains a foothold there [Mexico] and proves his value as a citizen, the Mexican will be more friendly to American capital."[22]

Macbeth's bid for U.S. recognition of the Mexican government came at the end of the first revolutionary decade in Mexico and spoke directly to the ambitions of many white businessmen in Los Angeles and southern California. Recognizing that President Woodrow Wilson's military ventures in Mexico, beginning in 1914 at Vera Cruz and ending with General Pershing's punitive expedition against Pancho Villa in northern Mexico between 1916 and 1917, helped to strain U.S.-Mexican relations, Macbeth appealed to diplomacy rather than military action to resolve the differences and open channels for businessmen such as Harrison Grey Otis and his son-in-law, Harry Chandler of the California & Mexican Ranch in the Mexicali Valley. Numerous Los Angeles investors in the Colorado River Land Company sought to protect their title to over 835,000 acres in northern Mexico stretching from the Cocopas Range to the gulf and north to the border west of Calexico.[23] Macbeth's entreaties to improve diplomacy for African American ventures in Mexico echoed the concerns of many white businessmen in Los Angeles who helped to organize the National Association for the Protection of American Rights in Mexico. This group, created in New York City in 1918, included Thomas E. Gibbon, Los Angeles attorney and investor in the Colorado River Land Company and sought diplomatic assurances for the protection of American investments in Mexico .[24] The discovery of oil in large quantities by Edward Doheny and his associates also attracted the attention of other large oil interests including Standard Oil Company, the Waters-Pierce Company and the British interests of Lord Cowdray during the early years of the Carranza administration in Mexico.[25] Fearing the nationalization of their interests, many of the oil companies' investors joined the National Association for the Protection of American Rights in Mexico. While the scale of their holdings eclipsed the small African American colony of Little Liberia, their entrepreneurial activities demanded similar access to Mexican lands.

Ironically, other black Angelenos found themselves the beneficiaries of the deterioration of U.S.-Mexican diplomacy as it offered cinematic subjects for the creation of African American films featuring black soldiers in the Pershing Expedition. An all-black corporation, the Lincoln Motion Picture Company, organized in May 1916 with Noble M. Johnson as its president and Clarence A. Brooks as Secretary. Noble Johnson, the first African American employed as an actor by Universal Film Company of Los Angeles, achieved star status in "The Trooper of Troop K." This three-part photoplay commemorated the lives of "brave Negro soldiers" at the battle of Carrizal, Mexico on June 21, 1916. In another of the popular Lincoln Motion Pictures, Clarence Brooks plays a Race lawyer in *By Right of Birth*, scripted by Noble Johnson's brother, George.[26] The films of the Lincoln Motion Picture Company and the more limited opportunities offered by Universal Film Company afforded black Angelenos a cinematic identity that portrayed bravery and political activism. *The Realization of a Negro's Ambition* became the first production of the Lincoln Motion Picture Company and fittingly portrayed a Tuskegee graduate "who goes to California and, through heroism and strong middle-class virtues, acquires wealth and gets the girl.[27] These images found an eager audience among black Angelenos during the second decade of the century.

The efforts of the Lincoln Motion Picture Company are all the more significant when contrasted to the depiction of African Americans in the daily newspapers. Although the *Los Angeles Morning Tribune* and the *Los Angeles Evening Express* took the time to eulogize Booker T. Washington upon his death in 1915, the more frequent news accounts concerning African Americans were not as complimentary. *The California Eagle* complained in April, 1916 that "only the darkest side of [Negro] life is pictured in the white dailies."[28] The *Eagle* cited an example of hasty judgment exercised by the press in the case of an African American woman, Edna Barnes. Mrs. Barnes, employed as a housekeeper for a white family living in Los Angeles, faced criminal charges for poisoning an infant. The *Eagle* resented white reports portraying Mrs. Barnes as "either insane or infuriated because she was about to be dismissed from service, and poisoned the baby to get even."[29] Hugh Macbeth served as counsel for Edna Barnes and presented evidence from eye witnesses that the infant ingested the poison after Mrs. Barnes had left the house. News reports such as this left an impression that black Angelenos were prejudged as guilty because of race rather than apparent evidence.

As a result many black Angelenos promoted the objectives of the All-American League during this time to assure political democracy be extended to all people. Hugh Macbeth became the chief proponent of the Los Angeles chapter of the League. Its founding principles succinctly stated:

> And while the founders of the All-American League are prompted primarily by a desire to secure for the American Negroes a "place in the American sun"—above and beyond all other things these founders are prompted by the firm knowledge that the ultimate security of our entire scheme of civilization depends upon the opportunity for every class of American citizens to secure on equal terms a "place in the American sun." The founders of the All-American League are insisting for the Negro Americans and all other classes of American citizens the same measure of opportunity and the same degree of responsibility as is demanded of the very highest element of American citizenship.[30]

The All-American League sought to bring about a "national revival" to promote patriotism and toleration on the eve of World War I. Claiming that its "highest aim will be to strike away the bars and blocks which permit the toleration or permissive recognition of departure from or infringement" of just government, the All-American League held meetings to discuss the need to check racism at home before confronting the horrors of European animosities abroad.[31] The League desired "that America will spare itself the terror of the present European internecine strife by a proper and amicable adjustment of the present racial animosities and friction, that representatives of the largest class of American undesirables— the American Negroes—have in the largest spirit of humanity and patriotism founded this All American League. It is because we are confident that America, to stand and endure as a nation or as a civilized entity, must be in truth dedicated to the principle of absolute equality of all men in point of opportunity—that America will pass from the stage of action in bloody strife unless such is done, that this League has founded."[32] Still believing that California offered economic and social opportunities, black Angelenos showed keen awareness of Jim Crow intolerance throughout the nation.

Black Angelenos feared increasing "makeshifts, curbed opportunities, restrictions, and disfranchisement" that represented a refracted racial policy extending even to Los Angeles. This motivated black Angelenos to take part in the All-American League throughout the period of World War I. Styling the annual conventions of the League as "conclaves," black Angelenos met at Los Angeles's Exposition Hall on State Street for a "stock taking day." Exposition Hall with its surrounding rose gardens opened to the public in 1913 and offered the All-American League enough space for the conclave's barbecues and addresses. League branches included members from San Francisco, Oakland, Sacramento, San Diego, Calexico, Fresno, and Bakersfield. The League soon took on many of the functions of the Los Angeles Forum in that it promoted on a statewide basis an arena for political discussion for confronting racism. While the Forum more obliquely addressed the competing philosophies of Booker T. Washington and W. E. B. DuBois, the League positioned itself to be "the connecting link between two great schools, viz. Industrialism and Philosophical Education."[33] Tailored to statewide concerns, the League held numerous addresses on the "Back to the Soil" movement advocated by men such as C. E. Orr from Fresno county. Orr urged his fellow members at the League's 1916 conclave to become agriculturalists and producers.[34]

Although the *Los Angeles Post* reported the All-American League's objectives to be political in nature, the League considered its civic functions more broadly concerned with promoting racial justice. Its motto became "All men up and no man down."[35] League meetings often took up issues of discrimination against black Angelenos as in the case of James Lee, a civil service employee dismissed without charges by the County Superintendent of Machinery.[36] It also printed its constitution and sold it for ten cents at the office of League President Hugh Macbeth.

The programs of the All-American League took on the long-held interests of its president when it promoted inter-racial progress as well as the achievements of African Americans. Macbeth made certain to have speeches address the need to obliterate the color line in America and promote inter-racial cooperation. The 1917 annual conclave program listed addressed by the "leading colored, white, and Japanese American citizens of the State."[37] Often using the industriousness and business success of Japanese Americans living in California as an example to be emulated, Macbeth encouraged black Angelenos to follow the Japanese Americans' example of becoming entrepreneurs and looking to the soil. "Become producers, and—when we do that—all things will be added unto us."[38] Throughout the next two decades, Macbeth encouraged inter-racial cooperation and unity by his membership and participation as Executive Secretary of the California Race Relations Commission in the 1930s, as author of the California Race Relations Bill of 1937, and author of *Better Race Relations, America's First Line of Defense.*[39]

In his annual address of 1917, Macbeth outlined the growing resentment of African Americans to "the inadequacy and inequality of opportunity in the Southern States, [where] thousands of Colored American laborers have abandoned their Southern homes and have sought the labor market of the North and East, where the spirit of true Americanism finds truer expression."[40] Although he did not mention the West as a region where discrimination existed, Macbeth engaged in numerous associations throughout his life that served as watch guards against racial intolerance.

During the first World War Macbeth stood firmly behind American efforts to end the war abroad and served as a Four Minute Man for several of the motion picture companies of Los Angeles.[41] His four-minute patriotic speeches played in theaters throughout the city and indicated his acceptance by the city's white leaders as well. Macbeth seemed focused upon efforts of German saboteurs and espionage agents throughout the war. As early as April 7, 1917, Macbeth warned in his annual All-American League address about the dangers of foreign espionage: "And in the meantime America pays the price of permitting in her borders organizations whose reference is to foreign allegiance in that while on the verge of war with a European power, our nation finds itself in the grip of a system of foreign espionage whose agents exist in numbers to the extent of over a hundred thousand."[42] Macbeth's trips to Baja, Mexico convinced him that German agents sought to subvert the loyalty of African Americans to the United States.

In May 1918, Macbeth sent a letter to the Director of Negro Economics in the U.S. Department of Labor reporting an encounter he had with a German man in Ensenada during the summer of

1917. Macbeth wrote that the German told him: "I notice that you report to the American Colonel. You don't have to do that. The American people have some of you Negroes fooled, but within the next six months Germany is going to show them that more than half of the American Negroes are on Germany's side and don't care a snap of their finger for the American Government offices who have oppressed them."[43] Other surveillance entries indicated that Bureau of Investigation agents tracked Macbeth's activities on behalf of the Little Liberia colony and his travels in Baja. Unfortunately the Bureau's agent, Fred C. Boden, characterized Macbeth as encouraging "young colored men to leave the United States and go to Mexico so as to evade the draft."[44]

Boden's spin on Macbeth's activities mirrored the desire of the Anti-Radical Division of the Bureau of Justice to suppress African American radicalism whether it be real or imagined. Since the Bureau enforced the Conscription Act during the First World War, it zealously conducted numerous "slacker raids," jailing thousands of men until they could prove their compliance with the Conscription Act. Surveillance records of African Americans suspected of shirking the draft number over a thousand case files; and failure to register with draft boards in California is the subject of much conjecture in the federal surveillance records.[45]

A review of the Bureau of Investigation's case files indicates that the agency believed the growth of African American radicalism to be a major target of investigation during the Red Scare of 1919 and 1920. The end of the First World War created two new foci for intelligence agencies: 1) concern about the growth of Bolshevik radicalism at home and abroad and 2) a belief that Japan sought to cultivate African American sympathies. Attorney General A. Mitchell Parlmer labeled A. Philip Randolph, the editor of the African American magazine *The Messenger*, the "most dangerous Negro" in the county and the Justice Department directed U.S. attorneys to stifle *The Messenger* as well as the more moderate *Crisis*, the official publication of the National Association for the Advancement of Colored People.[46] Black Angelenos read and discussed both publications through their Forum, League, and NAACP associations. The concomitant fear of Japanese intrigue among African American communities found resonance among those bureau agents who followed the gatherings of Marcus Garvey as he often characterized Japan as an oppressed colored nation suffering from imperialist objectives. Tom Brady, a black Angeleno and bootblack, informed one Bureau agent that Mexico and Japan plan trouble against the U.S. and "are planning war in California." This remark engendered its own case file opened by Agent George T. Holman who forwarded it to Washington, D.C.[47]

Despite the earnest entreaties of Hugh Macbeth while President of the All-American League, most black Angelenos did not consider the feasibility of strategically allying with other minority groups in California. African Americans and Asian Americans acted independently from one another despite their similar struggles against racial restrictions and economic limitations. By 1919 the California State Board of Control reported that Japanese leased over 33,000 acres of land in the Imperial Valley.[48] These Japanese agriculturalists too often appeared as competitors, not as labor allies, to the African American farmers of the region. The *Chicago Defender* in 1924 ran a cartoon depicting a California white farmer throwing a brick with a message "Land Shall be Sold to Caucasians Only" that bounced off a Japanese and struck an African American. The cartoon's caption read: "Perhaps It Wasn't Intended for Us, But . . . ."[49] Although the *Defender* cartoon aimed against racial discrimination, the paper advocated restrictions upon Japanese and other immigrants.

Labor concerns after World War I included numerous ideas about adverse effects from rapid demobilization of the armed forces. Secretary of the Interior, Franklin K. Lane from California, publicized his idea for veterans colonizing agricultural communities with federal-state cooperation. States would provide land for veterans' colonies while the federal government would provide money for land reclamation.[50] Although the Lane-Mondell Bill suffered defeat, the arguments of its opponents highlighted the opposition to "back-to-the-soil" programs from white agricultural leaders and organizations, including the United States Department of Agriculture and the National Grange which helped to defeat the bill.[51] With little support for agricultural colonization from the state and federal governments, the claims for "back-to-the-soil" movements, such as those established at Allensworth, California and Little Liberia in Baja, began to dwindle during the 1920s.

The focus of many black Angelenos during the decade following the war shifted from the expectations of agricultural and entrepreneurial opportunities to urban confrontations against creeping Jim Crow practices. The major difference in the efficacy of the socio-political associations of black Angelenos in the 1920s and '30s from earlier decades hinged upon the ability of black leaders to integrate newcomers to the community and into the work force. As population boomed, this became more and more difficult for the Los Angeles Forum and local chapters of the NAACP, the UNIA and National Urban League. These associations waged most of the struggles against racial practices in Los Angeles that seemed refracted from southern Jim Crow practices. The increasing occurrences of this refracted racism alarmed many black Angelenos and provided them with common bonds to other African American communities throughout the nation. Just as the Red Summer of 1919 created tensions in many northern cities when black residents sought to cool off from the summer heat by frequenting beach areas claimed for whites only, Los Angeles experienced new problems with segregation of public swimming pools, continued diminished economic opportunities, and the growth of the Ku Klux Klan in southern California. The political activist associations that black Angelenos created—the Los Angeles Forum, the wartime All-American League, and membership in the NAACP and UNIA—now served as the springboards for confronting racism during the 1920s and '30s. Douglas Flamming suggests that this "civil rights activism was not a 'movement.' . . . It was instead a way of life, an act of faith, a lifelong mission. . . . When the dueling forces of decadence and intolerance swept across Los Angeles, the city's Race leaders saw their faith and determination sorely tested."[52]

As Los Angeles's population boomed during the 1920s, the African American community more than doubled from 15,579 in 1920 to 38,894 in 1930, making it "the third-fastest-growing Race community in urban America."[53] Migrants came predominantly from southern states where Jim Crow practices seemed to intensify after the war. The *California Eagle* voiced Hugh Macbeth's concerns about the organization of a Ku Klux Klan local in Los Angeles in 1921 just weeks after the devastating riot of Tulsa, Oklahoma's Greenwood community known as the "black Wall Street."[54] The existence of the Klan surfaced after Los Angeles Mayor Meredith Snyder and Edwin W. Widney, City Prosecutor, negotiated with the Garrick Theater and the Moving Picture Producers Association to have D. W. Griffiths's *The Clansman* removed in June 1921. Widney soon received a visit from the Grand Goblin of the Klan's Pacific States Division, William S. Coburn, who had recently moved to Los Angeles.[55] Although Coburn maintained that he thought it essential that *The Clansman* be shown to support white supremacy, Edwin Widney reported the visit and Coburn's demands to the *Los Angeles Times* which began to publish a series of articles opposing the Klan's growth in the city. Fred Roberts, editor of the *New Age* newspaper and black Assemblyman from the 74th District of Central Avenue since 1918, stated that neither "Los Angeles nor California will grant any lasting place to this 'Klan.' It is too un-American and too much out of step with the spirit of the West."[56]

Klan efforts to gain a foothold in Los Angeles continued throughout much of the 1920s and included efforts to elect pro-Klansmen to office in Watts. In 1925 the *California Eagle* published a letter written by Klan leader G. W. Price, intercepted by the Watts Police Department and forwarded to the *Eagle's* publisher and editor, Charlotta and Joe Bass. Price argued that the *Eagle* fabricated the letter. The case went to court as *The People of the State of Calif.*, v. *J. B. Bass, C. A. Spear Bass and Robt. T. Anderson*. Hugh Macbeth and Lewis K. Beeks won the case for the defendants and helped to hasten the Klan's decline in Los Angeles.[57]

Concurrent with the rise of Klan racism appearing in Los Angeles after the wartime migration from southern states to California, other African American migrants came prepared to confront Jim Crow practices wherever they existed. Dr. H. Claude Hudson, an African American dentist who came to Los Angeles after World War I, exemplified the newcomers who brought considerable experience in political activism. Before settling in Los Angeles, Hudson had served as president of the local NAACP in Shreveport, Louisiana. Characterized as "fearless and outspoken almost to a fault," Hudson soon found popularity among black Angelenos who wanted new and more active leadership within the Los Angeles branch of the NAACP.[58] Elected as President of the Los Angeles NAACP in 1924, Hudson confronted race segregation in

Toddler on the lawn of a bungalow on West 37th Street, circa 1930

the city's new swimming pool policy adopted by the Los Angeles Playground Commission in July 1925. The Commission introduced the International Day formula which meant that Exposition Park, heavily used by African Americans would be open to them only on Monday afternoons; Arroyo Pool would be open to black Angelenos on Wednesday afternoons and North Broadway pool would be open on Friday afternoons. The recently opened Vignes Pool that attracted few African Americans would be open to them every day of the week. Known as the "Bath House Battle," the Hudson and the local NAACP brought the case to court in *George Cushnie* v. *City of Los Angeles* in late 1925.[59]

A nationwide press release from the NAACP officials in New York raised awareness and expectations for the prosecution of the Cushnie case. Los Angeles's city attorney requested that a judge dismiss the case because swimming pool segregation, which violated California's civil rights statutes, did not apply to Los Angeles because it had adopted a new city charter in 1923 stating that it had the power "to make and enforce all laws and regulations in respect to municipal affairs."[60] The case went to trial in December 1926 only to decide the question as to whether Los Angeles provided equal accommodation for both races in accord with the *Plessy* v. *Ferguson* Supreme Court decision of 1896 and the Fourteenth Amendment to the Constitution. The trial court decided that the city had made "substantial accommodations for colored groups" and the International Day formula could stand.[61] California's Superior Court ruled in 1932 that Los Angeles could no longer segregate its pools; however, the practice continued to be locally enforced well into the 1940s. African Americans could come to the Santa Monica Pier Amusement Park, but they found themselves segregated to a small area of beach and forced by police officers to leave the beach by dusk while whites could remain there after dark.[62]

The vision for a color-blind society in California significantly began to wane after the NAACP's defeat in the Bath House Battle and in its struggle against restrictive housing covenants during the 1920s. Although home ownership among black Angelenos remained high during the first half of the 1920s, more racially restrictive covenants began to exclude African Americans from areas away from Central Avenue.

The court case, *George H. Letteau et al. v. William A. Long, et al* [commonly referred to as the Long Case], protested racial housing restrictions. Threatened with eviction from their newly purchased home that had been owned by previous African Americans, the Longs learned that the original Entwistle tract of land owned by the Letteau family had occupancy restrictions against blacks that, if violated, meant the home would revert to the Letteau family.[63] With the unexpected death of the Longs' attorney, E. Burton Ceruti, legal proceedings fell apart. Although the local NAACP contacted new lawyers on Eunice Long's behalf, they failed to meet the deadline for appealing the case and Eunice Long, whose husband died during the court proceedings, suffered eviction.

The mid-1920s served as a watershed for race relations in Los Angeles as Jim Crow practices, so long kept at arm's length, now surfaced with vigor as the city expanded its population and allowed greater segregation through city policies and restrictive housing covenants. The 1926 case, *Corrigan v. Buckley*, brought before the U.S. Supreme Court upheld racially restrictive housing covenants and would not be challenged again until 1948.[64] Hope confronting despair became a new metaphor for the experience of black Angelenos as the hardships of the Great Depression began. The Harlem Renaissance writers, Wallace Thurman and Arna Bontemps, met while in school at the University of Southern California and provided a literary setting for black Angelenos in this period. In 1931 Arna Bontemps wrote *God Sends Sunday*, a novel describing 'the hope and despair southern migrants found on Central Avenue, the 'Beale Street of the West.'"[65]

Even before the depression era's chill, black Angelenos found their employment opportunities limited. The 1926 survey conducted by Charles S. Johnson, sociologist and Director of the National Urban League's Department of Research and Investigation, reported that many Los Angeles manufacturers refused to hire African Americans because they had never done so before. The 1930 census showed that eighty-seven percent of black females and forty percent of black men employed in Los Angeles served as household servants. Twenty-two percent of employed black males found jobs as janitors and laborers, while seventeen percent of employed black males served as porters or waiters in the transportation sector.[66] Even the formation of the Congress of Industrial Organizations (CIO) in 1936 failed to help black Angelenos as they were excluded or severely restricted from industrial employment.

The anti-poverty programs of Franklin Roosevelt's New Deal offered black Angelenos some respite from the Depression. Yet the New Deal programs frequently institutionalized racial segregation. In contrast to the National Youth Administration's [NYA] programs in Oakland where C. L. Dellums and the NAACP fought segregation, Los Angeles acquiesced to discriminatory policies in the NYA as well as the Civilian Conservation Corps [CCC] which maintained separate work camps. C. L. Dellums, President of the Alameda Branch NAACP, served on a State Advisory Committee for the reorganization of the California NYA, and said that it took two years to abolish the segregated centers. He recalled one meeting of the committee at Asilomar attended by Helen Gahagan Douglas, the white congressional representative for the predominantly African American Central Avenue district of Los Angeles. "She was on the committee. She was really something. That beautiful girl did a job on there. She led the fight with us to get rid of segregation and discrimination."[67] The promise of the New Deal programs effected a political change among the voting patterns of many black Angelenos during the 1930s. Democrat Augustus F. Hawkins campaigned vigorously against the long-term African American Assemblyman from Los Angeles, Frederick Roberts, in 1934. The election of Assemblyman Hawkins gave strong indication that black voters supported President Roosevelt's New Deal programs that Hawkins promoted.

One of the most interesting effects of the New Deal upon black Angelenos occurred as younger members of the community began to view the "black middle-class leadership in the city" as a "great army of stuffed shirts."[68] When the Los Angeles NAACP failed to support the nine Scottsboro Boys convicted of gang-raping two white women in Alabama in 1931, a young African American attorney, Loren Miller, attacked the "accommodationism" of Los Angeles's black middle class leaders and stated that "No city is more in need of intelligent leadership than this one where mountebanks flourish at every street corner."[69] Seeking to support the Scottsboro

Leon Washington, editor and publisher of the Los Angeles Sentinel, ca. late 1930s

Boys, some Black Angelenos gravitated toward the Los Angeles Communist Party. The rhetoric of shared class exploitation failed to recruit most African Americans to the Communist Party because class exploitation shared by minorities did not describe the economic reality of black Angelenos. Excluded from manufacturing and therefore not actively recruited by the CIO for membership as were Mexican workers, blacks perceived their economic plight as singular and constricted.

Black Angelenos on the eve of World War II continued to experience a refracted form of racism in Los Angeles. Confronting segregation policies whenever possible in the 1920s and '30s, African American leaders found that their socio-political organizations still offered the best hope for political redress. It should be noted that the vibrant African American press helped sustain and publicize these associations throughout the first four decades of the twentieth century. In 1932 Charlotta Bass hired Leon Washington as a reporter for the *California Eagle.* Not content with reporting the news, Washington started a new paper for black Angelenos called the *Los Angeles Sentinel.* Ratcheting up the tactics of political activism, Washington published a series of reports on discrimination along Central Avenue and accompanied them with photographs. He also advocated a "Don't Spend Where You Can't Work" campaign and targeted those businesses that he knew to have discriminatory hiring policies.[70]

The rising leadership of Augustus Hawkins, Loren Miller, and Leon Washington presaged a new generation of civil rights activism in Los Angeles; yet, they could not have succeeded in mobilizing support without the socio-political network of associations that an older generation of black Angelenos carefully nurtured from 1900 to 1940. The failure of black Angelenos to advance their civil rights in the period from the 1920s to the eve of World War II resulted from the community's inability to maintain a cohesiveness among its expanding black population and its isolation from the industrial and manufacturing sectors of the city's economy. Unable to participate in the union efforts led by the CIO during the 1930s because manufacturers did not hire African Americans, black Angelenos lost their sense of "openness" to economic ventures that had recommended Los Angeles to them in earlier decades.

NOTES

[1] Patricia Adler, "Paradise West: A Study of Negro Attitudes Toward the City of Los Angeles." TMs (photocopy), Paper for History 680, UCLA (May 22, 1969), p. 7, 10-11, Elizabeth and James Abajian Collection of Afro-Americana, Bancroft Library, Berkeley, California; Lawrence B. de Graaf, "The City of Black Angels: Emergence of the Los Angeles Ghetto, 1890-1930," *Pacific Historical* Review 39 (August 1970): 323-324; Lawrence B. De Graaf and Quintard Taylor, "Introduction," *Seeking El Dorado: African Americans in California,* eds. Lawrence B. De Graaf, Kevin Mulroy, & Quintard Taylor (Los Angeles, Seattle and London: Autry Museum of Western Heritage in association with the University of Washington Press, 2001), 15; Census records for Los Angeles County total 2,841 residents and are taken from the Geospatial & Statistical Data Center, "Historical Census Browser—County Level Results for 1900." http://fisher.lib.virginia.edu/ collections/stats/histcensus/php/start. php?year=V1900 (21 July 2005).

[2] I am deeply indebted to the remarkable work and scholarly generosity of Douglas Flamming whose history of African Americans in Los Angeles is the most complete work to date on the subject of the extension of Jim Crow attitudes to Los Angeles. Douglas Flamming, *Bound for Freedom: Black Los Angeles in Jim Crow America* (Berkeley and Los Angeles: University of California Press, 2005): 55. 40.

[3] Lonnie G. Bunch, III, "'The Greatest State for the Negro': Jefferson L. Edmonds, Black Propagandist of the California Dream" in *Seeking El Dorado: African Americans in California,* eds. Lawrence B. De Graaf, Kevin Mulroy, & Quintard Taylor (Los Angeles, Seattle and London: Autry Museum of Western Heritage in association with the University of Washington Press, 2001), 131.

[4] Bunch, "The Greatest State for the Negro," 131.

[5] *Ibid.,* 132.

[6] de Graaf, "The City of Black Angels," p. 330; Works Progress Administration, "Historical Background of Negro Survey for Los Angeles." *Index of American Design.* Federal Art Project, Box 2, Items B 2-6. Los Angeles: WPA, 1935, The Huntington Library, San Marino, California.

[7] *California Eagle,* 5 September 1903.

[8] Flamming, *Bound for Freedom,* p. 56.

[9] Lonnie G. Bunch, "A Past Not Necessarily Prologue: The Afro-American in Los Angeles," in *20th Century Los Angeles: Power, Promotion, and Social Conflict,* ed. by Norman M. Klein and Martin J. Schiesl (Claremont, CA: Regina Books, 1990): 103-104.

[10] Bunch, "A Past Not Necessarily Prologue," 104.

[11] In his history on the emergence of the Los Angeles ghetto, Lawrence de Graaf describes these homes as consisting of four to five rooms at a cost between $900 and $2500; de Graaf, "City of Black Angels," 343.

[12] Adler, "Paradise West," 17.

[13] Adler, "Paradise West," 17.

[14] de Graaf and Taylor, "Introduction," 19-20; Bunch, "A Past Not Necessarily a Prologue," 107.

[15] It has been suggested that breaking the prevalent church-dominated pattern of black community might have been one of the primary objectives of the Los Angeles Forum. Bunch, "A Past Not Necessarily a Prologue," 107; Hugh Harlan, *The Story of the Negro in Los Angles County* (San Francisco: R. & E. Research Associates, 1970 [reprint], 15.

[16] Flamming, *Bound for Freedom*, 127.

[17] E. Frederick Anderson. *The Development of Leadership and Organization Building in the Black Community of Los Angeles from 1900 through World War II,* (Saratoga, CA: Century Twenty One Publishing, 1980), 53.

[18] Bunch, "The Greatest State for the Negro," 142.

[19] Bunch, "A Past Not Necessarily Prologue," 105-106.

[20] W. W. Robinson, *Lawyers of Los Angeles: A History of the Los Angeles Bar Association and of the Bar of Los Angeles County* (Los Angeles Bar Association, 1959), 290-291.

[21] *Los Angeles Times* 40 (16 October 1921), Part II: p. 10.

[22] *Ibid.*

[23] U.S. Bureau of Foreign and Domestic Commerce. *Mexican West Coast and Lower California* in Special Agents Series—No. 220 (Washington, D.C.: Government Printing Office, 1923), 283, 306.

[24] T. E. Gibbon, Los Angeles, to Mr. James D. Sherhan, V.P, International Land & Livestock Co., Chicago, 8 May 1919. Bergman Collection. Papers of T. E. Gibbon, Box 31, The Huntington Library, San Marino, CA.

[25] Thomas Edward Gibbon. *Mexico Under Carranza: A Lawyer's Indictment of the Crowning Infamy of Four Hundred Years of Misrule* (New York: Doubleday, Page & Company, 1919), 103. In 1921, the American journalist John Kenneth Turner wrote a series of articles in a Mexico City newspaper claiming an "interventionist campaign long conducted in the U.S. and charging the oil interests headed by E. L. Doheny with responsibility therefore." "Doheny's Disclaimer Refuted," *The Mexican Review* (January 1921), 36.

[26] George P. Johnson Negro Film Collection. University of California, Los Angeles. Caballero Addition, dm 4/93, Box 52, f.13, 35.

[27] Flamming, *Bound for Freedom*, 89.

[28] *California Eagle*, 25 April 1916.

[29] *Ibid.*, 29 April 1916.

30 *Ibid.*, 8 January 1916.
31 *Ibid.*
32 *Ibid.*
33 *Ibid.*, 8 July 1916.
34 *Ibid.*, 26 February 1916.
35 *Ibid.*, 25 March 1916.
36 *Ibid.*, 12 February 1916: 4.
37 *Ibid.*, 6 January 1917: 4.
38 *Ibid.*, 2 March 1918.
39 *Who's Who in California*, I, (1942-1943), 568.
40 *California Eagle*, 7 April 1917: 8.
41 *Ibid.*, 26 January 1918.
42 *Ibid.*, 7 April 1917: 8.
43 U.S. Department of Justice—Bureau of Investigation, *Surveillance of Black Americans, 1916-1925*. National Archives and Records Administration,RG65, F.B.I., Reel 10: 0140.
44 U.S. Department of Justice—Bureau of Investigation, *Surveillance of Black Americans*, Reel 10: 0135, Casefile OG132476.
45 U.S. Department of Justice—Bureau of Investigation, *Surveillance of Black Americans. 1916-1925*, Reel 9: 0420, Casefile 0G30791: Failure to Register, California. 1917.
46 U.S. Department of Justice—Bureau of Investigation, *Surveillance of Black Americans. 1916-1925*, n. 4.
47 U.S. Department of Justice—Bureau of Investigation, *Surveillance of Black Americans, 1916-1925*. RG65, Reel 13, Casefile 0G375308: Japanese/Mexican Collaboration, California, 1919.
48 California State Board of Control, *California and the Oriental: Japanese, Chinese, and Hindus* (Sacramento: California State Printing Office, 1920; reprint, New York: Arno Press, 1978), 48.
49 David J. Hellwig, "Afro-American Reactions to the Japanese and the Anti-Japanese Movement, 1906-1924," *Phylon* 38 (1st Qtr., 1977), 93.
50 Bill G. Reid, "Franklin K. Lane's Idea for Veterans' Colonization 1918-1921," *Pacific Historical Review* 33 (November 1964): 455-456.
51 Reid, "Franklin K. Lane's Idea," 459.
52 Flamming, *Bound for Freedom*, 195-196.
53 de Graaf and Taylor, "Introduction," 22; Flamming, *Bound for Freedom*, 197.
54 Flamming, *Bound for Freedom*, 199.
55 *Ibid.*, 200.
56 *Ibid.*
57 *Ibid.*, 209-210.
58 Adler, "Paradise West," 14; Flamming, *Bound for Freedom*, 213.
59 Flamming, *Bound for Freedom*, 216-217.
60 *Ibid.*, 217.

[61] *Ibid.*

[62] Josh Sides, *L.A. City Limits: African American Los Angeles from the Great Depression to the Present* (Berkeley, Los Angeles and London: University of California Press, 2003), 21.

[63] Flamming, *Bound for Freedom*, 218-220.

[64] Sides, *L.A. City Limits*, 18.

[65] Quintard Taylor, *In Search of the Racial Frontier: African Americans in the American West, 1528-1990* (New York and London: W.W. Norton & Company, 1998), 245.

[66] Sides, *L.A. City Limits*, 24, 26.

[67] Joyce Henderson, *C. L. Dellums: International President of the Brotherhood of Sleeping Car Porters and Civil Rights Leader.* (Berkeley: Regional Oral History Office, Bancroft Library, 1973), 82.

[68] Sides, *L.A. City Limits*, 30.

[69] *Ibid.*

[70] *Ibid.*

PART TWO

AFTER 1945

Chapter 4

INTO THE MAINSTREAM
Asians & Pacific Islanders
in Post-1945 Los Angeles

Nadine and Donald Hata

The place of Asians and Pacific Islanders in post-World War II
America was transformed by U.S. involvement in Asia during
the Cold War and by dramatic reforms in immigration and civil
rights policies at home. In 1952, the U.S. Supreme Court ruled
that California's alien land laws, which prohibited the lease or
purchase of land by Asian aliens, were unconstitutional and in
violation of the due process and equal protection clauses of the
Fourteenth Amendment (*Fujii* v. *State*). The 1952 Walter-McCarran
Act (Immigration and Nationality Act) weakened the rigid quota
restrictions of the 1924 federal immigration law and provided that
all races were eligible for naturalization and citizenship, but the
remaining quota system still discriminated against immigrants
from Asia and the Pacific. Racial quotas were finally abandoned by
the Immigration and Nationality Act of 1965. It dramatically altered
the faces of Asian Pacific America by abolishing the racist policy
that had given special preference to immigrants from Europe.

Prewar terms like "Orient" and "Oriental American" were laden
with condescending colonial overtones, and were replaced with
"Asians" and "Asian Pacific Americans." The heterogeneity of the
Asian Pacific American population was reflected in the U.S. Census
Bureau's definition of "Asian" as referring to "people having origins

in any of the original peoples of the Far East, Southeast Asia, or the Indian subcontinent (for example, Cambodia, China, India, Japan, Korea, Malaysia, Pakistan, the Philippine Islands, Thailand, and Vietnam)." Since 1980 the U.S. Census has categorized Asians as: Asian Indian, Chinese, Filipino, Japanese, Korean, and Vietnamese. Pacific Islanders are defined as Native Hawaiian, Guamanian or Chamorro, and Samoan.[1]

The absolute numbers of Asian Pacific Americans have soared since 1965. Their total U.S. population grew from 0.7 percent in 1970 to 3.6 percent in 2000. At the end of the 20th century, two out of every five immigrants came from across the Pacific, and Los Angeles replaced Angel Island in San Francisco Bay as the Ellis Island of the West Coast. Today 12 percent of Los Angeles County's population is comprised of Asian and Pacific Islanders.[2]

INTO THE SUBURBS AND THE MIDDLE CLASS

After World War II Asians and Pacific Islanders were dispersed throughout the greater Los Angeles basin, far beyond inner city enclaves like Chinatown, Little Tokyo, and Koreatown. With few exceptions, they were welcomed into suburban bedroom communities throughout Southern California. By the late 1990s, whether they were cutting-edge computer corporations or mom and pop shops, many Asian Pacific Americans had moved from the margins into the middle class mainstream.

Immigration from the Philippines increased sharply after 1965, and by the 1980s over three-fourths of the Filipinos in the United States were immigrants. By 1984, most of the 664,938 immigrants were urban, educated, middle-class professionals and women who achieved the highest household incomes of all immigrants during their first ten years in the country. Concentrations of Filipino residences in areas adjacent to hospitals reflect their involvement in healthcare-related occupations.[3] More recently, the shortage of credentialed teachers has encouraged private recruiters to seek experienced foreign teachers from English-speaking countries such as the Philippines, 58 of whom arrived in 2002 to teach in the Compton School District.[4]

The Korean War (1950-53) brought thousands of students and war brides to the United States. Los Angeles County's pre-1965 total of 5,000 Koreans swelled to 145,431 in 1990. The strongest community organization was the network of 430 churches, most of them Protestant. A 1983 study of Korean businesses in Los Angeles County found that "Koreans account for less than 1% of the county population but own 2.6% of the businesses."[5] According to 1997 and 2000 census reports, "a majority of Koreans either operate their own business or work for a business owned by other Koreans" in inner city ghettoes or middle-class suburbs. Nearly 44 percent of Koreans twenty-five years or older were college graduates but were unable to find suitable employment because of "language difficulties and unfamiliarity with American culture." The 2000 Census found that the 257,975 Koreans living in Los Angeles, Riverside, Orange, San Bernardino, and Ventura counties comprised nearly one-fourth of all Koreans living in the United States.[6]

Asian Indians are dispersed throughout the Los Angeles basin, but a substantial suburban community emerged in Artesia and neighboring Norwalk by 1980. In the 1960s and 1970s Indian immigrants were largely graduate students and professionals such as doctors, engineers and technicians. A second wave of arrivals in 1970-1980 were entrepreneurs who invested in Artesia's depressed business district on Pioneer Boulevard. The area was easily accessible to the 12,000 Asian Indians in the surrounding communities, and by 1988 some two dozen businesses were owned or managed by immigrants from the Bombay area. But their success also created resentment. A controversy arose in 1991 when Caltrans was asked to put up a "Little India— Next Exit" freeway sign. The mayor of Artesia opposed the request and said: "This is Artesia and not India. If you don't like our decision, please pack up and leave this city and move to some other place or go back to India . . . ." The brouhaha arose again in 2004 when the request for a sign was opposed by citizens of Portuguese descent whose "dairy-farming ancestors helped found the city."[7]

Refugees from the war in Southeast Asia streamed into California during the 1970s and 1980s. Prior to 1975 Vietnamese immigrants were largely educated, urban and professional. This changed when the abrupt U.S. military withdrawal from Southeast Asia led to an exodus of refugees. A massive influx of destitute Vietnamese, Laotians, Cambodians, Hmong and Mien caused extraordinary demographic changes in Southern California. Between 1980-1990, the Vietnamese population rose 217 percent in Orange County and 118 percent in Los Angeles County. In 1982 residents of Westminster who resented their presence held "emotional and ugly" meetings that the city's mayor described as "like being with the Ku Klux Klan." [8] Overt racism eventually gave way to grudging respect, however, and Bolsa Avenue continues to thrive. In 1988, the Westminster City Council officially designated it "Little Saigon," and Governor George Deukmejian unveiled a freeway sign in June as part of a Republican Party effort to draw support from Vietnamese Americans. The 89,000 Vietnamese living in Los Angeles County in 2000 have settled in parts of the San Fernando Valley, Long Beach, and the South Bay.

The 30,000 Cambodians who live in Los Angeles County comprise California's second largest Southeast Asian community. War refugees who survived atrocities committed by the Pol Pot regime found life in America particularly difficult, with high rates of depression, and single-parent families headed by widows of the genocide. During the 1980s, California's doughnut shops were dominated by Cambodian entrepreneurs led by pioneer Ted Ngoy. Of the 1,500 businesses listed in the Cambodian Yellow Pages, some 80 percent were doughnut shops, attractive because they could be started with very little capital and provided jobs for the entire family.[9] By 1990, Cambodians had created Little Phnom Penh in the heart of downtown Long Beach. They pooled resources, raised funds and secured low-interest government loans to open grocery stores, restaurants, Buddhist temples, newspapers and social service agencies.[10] Other South and Southeast Asians in Los Angeles County include small and widely dispersed communities of Sri Lankans (3,225), Laotians (4,105), Pakistanis (6,548), Indonesians (9,554), and Thais (24,048).[11]

In 2000, of the 2.3 million Chinese in the United States, 329,352 were in Los Angeles County. Chinese Americans constitute only 3.5 percent of the population of the county, but their impact on the region's economy has been enormous. The influx from Taiwan and Hong Kong made Monterey Park the "nation's first suburban Chinatown." The increase of Chinese from 14 to 40 percent of the city's 60,000 residents caused a backlash, but their numbers continued to grow, and by 1990 Monterey Park became the first U.S. mainland city whose majority population was Asian American.[12] Chinese entrepreneurs, often borrowing from one of California's twenty-eight Chinese community-owned banks, provided jobs in areas beyond the ubiquitous restaurants and small shops in Los Angeles' Chinatown. In the San Gabriel Valley 100 Asian restaurants and shops line a one-mile stretch of Valley Boulevard. The new San Gabriel Square mall, which is bigger than the Rose Bowl, became the center of the valley's new Chinatown.[13] Taiwanese immigrant Roger Chen's sixteen 99 Price and 99 Ranch markets generated $150 million in sales in the United States and Canada. Based in Southern California, Chen's upscale supermarket chain and other Asian ethnic food firms such as Hong Kong Markets capitalized on the surge of Asian immigration in the 1980s. William Mow established the Southern California apparel company that became Bugle Boy, "the largest privately held apparel company in the United States" with annual sales as high as $500 million.[14] A positive image of Chinese as benevolent bosses made headlines when John Tu and David Sun, co-founders of Kingston Technology Corporation, a computer memory company, shared a $100-million bonus package with their non-Chinese employees who said they were treated "like family."[15]

During the 1950s and into the late 1960s, Japanese Americans began a steady migration from the inner city to new residential concentrations in Monterey Park, Crenshaw and Gardena. Landscape gardening employed 70 percent of all Japanese American males. Many subsequently moved on to retail shops and civil service jobs, but 20 percent were still working as gardeners in 1970.[16] During the 1970s and 1980s some moved to more affluent suburbs on the Palos Verdes peninsula and Irvine in Orange County. The old concentration of Japanese Americans in the Torrance-Gardena area has been augmented by the arrival of Koreans and other Asians and Pacific Islanders, as well as Japanese nationals who work for Japan-based corporations such as Toyota, Nissan, and Honda. The result has been a thriving community of temples and churches, restaurants, markets and specialty stores, and cultural and athletic organizations. More than half of all Japanese Americans now marry into other racial and ethnic groups.

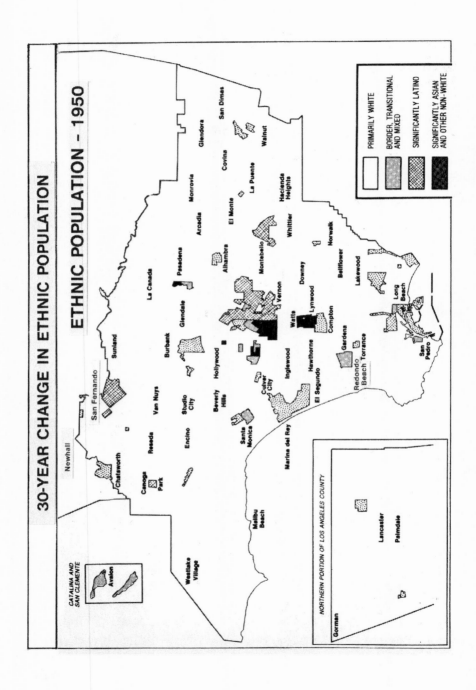

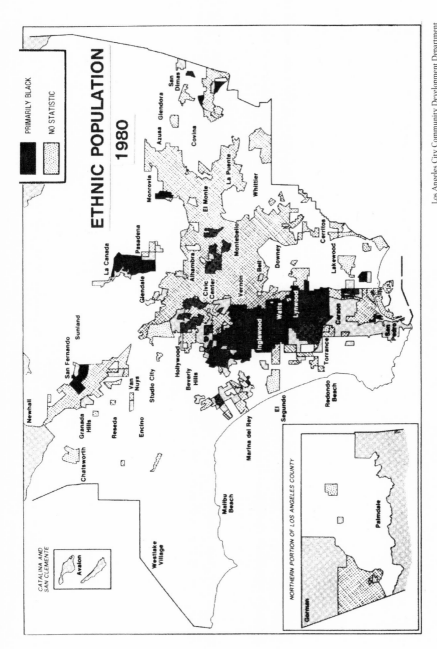

Los Angeles City Community Development Department

In 1950 the majority of Angelenos were white, with Latinos and Blacks the only sizable minorities; by 1980, the minorities were approaching the majority

Of the various Pacific Islander communities in Los Angeles County in 2000, the majority of Samoans (12,800) lived in the Carson, Long Beach, and Wilmington nexus. Native Hawaiians (4,300) and Guamanians or Chamorros (3,200) were concentrated in the South Bay. Many shared ties to the U.S. Navy and jobs associated with maritime trade.[17]

MYTH OF THE "MODEL MINORITY"

As the civil rights movement turned increasingly violent during the 1960s and 1970s, Japanese Americans were hailed by liberals and conservatives alike as "a model minority" whose posture of self-help and self-effacing accommodation in the face of adversity should be emulated by more outspoken and militant minorities.[18] As a group, Asian Pacific Americans were perceived as having no problems and needing no public social services because they "pull themselves up by their own bootstraps" and "take care of their own." Numerous studies refuted these misleading images. A 1985 Los Angeles United Way report on Koreans found that social service agencies were unable to quickly provide jobs and medical care to the rapidly increasing newcomers. Los Angeles' first subsidized housing project for Korean Americans was completed in 1990, but the 60 units did not meet the needs of the county's more than 40,000 Korean senior citizens. The 1990 Census found as many as 15 percent of Southern California's Chinese at or below the poverty level. Many Samoans were unemployed or trapped in poorly paid jobs, while Filipino health professionals were unable to practice because of California's rigid licensing restrictions. A December 1993 UCLA Urban Planning Program study reported: "there are more than 124,000 Asian poor in Los Angeles County. In central urban areas, one in five Asians is poor."[19]

Many Asian Pacific Americans still remain far removed from the American Dream. Some are dependent on exploitative employers who themselves are sometimes former refugees. In August 1995, 72 Thai garment workers were discovered in an El Monte sweatshop where they had worked under abusive conditions and had been confined behind barbed wire, some for as long as three years.[20] Amerasian children were an often-ignored legacy of U.S. military deployments in Asia. The 1987 Amerasian Homecoming

Act removed their immigration quotas, and by June 1991, more than 12,000 arrived. Many were taunted by Vietnamese Americans who called their mothers "traitors" and "prostitutes." Disillusioned and angry, some Amerasians joined gangs which offered a sense of family that they never had.[21] For many immigrant Asian women and children, life in America is a constant clash between traditional values that emphasize subservience and obedience, versus values in the larger society that encourage individuality and independence.

As in the past, public images of immigrants' homelands have a direct influence on their treatment here. By 1980, trade across the Pacific surpassed commerce across the Atlantic. With many Americans out of work, a severe trade imbalance, and America's humiliating descent to debtor-nation status, there was a need for scapegoats. Fears of the old "Yellow Peril" were fueled when Asian high technology products and autos were blamed for domestic unemployment and economic malaise. Articles about investments by Asian-based corporations headlined an "Asian takeover" theme. As early as September 1973, *Los Angeles Magazine*'s cover story was "Banzai! Meet the New Owners of Southern California." Violence, vandalism, and racist slurs directed against Asian Pacific Americans in Los Angeles mirrored events across the nation.[22] In 1986 the U.S. Commission on Civil Rights found bumper stickers in Los Angeles County that read "Toyota-Datsun-Honda-and Pearl Harbor" and "Unemployment Made in Japan." The U.S. Commission on Civil Rights observed that the "stereotype of Asians as foreigners make Asian Americans particularly vulnerable...."[23] One reason for the "foreigner" stereotype is that some Asian Pacific Americans continue to have strong ties with the nations from which they emigrated. Many Filipinos want to retire in the Philippines, and the Philippine government recognizes the importance of the remittance money sent back to relatives in the islands each year. In 1994 it was reported that Filipinos in the U.S. wired $1 billion dollars in cash annually to families in the Philippines.[24] The recent outcry against outsourcing American jobs to Asian countries such as India again raises the ugly specter of a backlash against Asian Pacific Americans.

In 1988 the California Attorney General's Asian and Pacific Islander Advisory Committee reported that "hate crimes and . . . violence

against Asian/Pacific Islander Americans are again on the increase."
In 1989 a Los Angeles County Human Relations Commission
report on hate crimes in the county's schools concluded that, while
Asian Pacific Americans comprised only 8.6 percent of the school
population, they represented no less than 14.5 percent of all victims
of racially-motivated hate crimes. Of 144 anti-Asian crimes, nearly
half "were attributed to anti-immigrant sentiments." Evidence
of anti-Asian sentiments included epithets, graffiti, vandalism,
and violence. The 1999 murder of Filipino postal worker Joseph
Ilieto in Chatsworth because he was "non-white and worked for
the government" shocked Filipinos in Los Angeles and across the
nation.[25] Violence and crime among Asian immigrants were also
on the rise. In 1984 the police chief of Monterey Park warned the
President's Commission on Organized Crime about Asian gangs
"struggling for control of the lucrative criminal enterprises in Los
Angeles and San Gabriel Valley."[26] By 1987 gang violence and
crime became a highly publicized political issue in other Asian
communities as well. Young Cambodians, many of whom had
lost parents and lacked role models, victimized other Cambodian
Americans. In October 1989, Long Beach's Cambodian and Latino
gangs began a war that by 1991 was one of the most violent in the
city's history.[27] Home invasion robberies by Asians have increased
in numbers, brutality, and audacity. Chinese and Southeast Asian
immigrants have been easy prey because of their reluctance to
cooperate with authorities and their fear of retaliation.

Inter-racial tensions involving Asian immigrants in the inner
city were highlighted in newspaper headlines such as: "Tale of 2
Cultures: Murders Refocus Spotlight On Tensions Between Koreans,
Blacks."[28] In the mid-1980s, Koreans and African American business
and religious groups attempted to improve communications and
sought community and political support. The efforts were largely
unsuccessful. In March 1991, hostility between Blacks and Koreans
intensified when a Black teenager was killed by a Korean merchant
over a bottle of orange juice in South-Central Los Angeles; outrage
ensued when Mrs. Soon Ja Du was found guilty of manslaughter
but not sentenced to spend time in jail. After a jury announced
not-guilty verdicts for the Los Angeles police officers accused
of beating Rodney King on April 29, 1992, Los Angeles became

a battleground between Blacks, Whites, Latinos, and Asians. Of 58 dead, two were Asian. During the three days of terror, Korean merchants were the hardest hit: 2,000 businesses were looted or burned and property damage was estimated at $359 million. In addition, 235 Chinese and two dozen Thai businesses were torched and pillaged.[29]

POLITICAL ACTIVISM AND EMPOWERMENT

Asian Pacific Angelinos have defended their hard won gains in moving from the margins into the mainstream after World War II. Japanese Americans were galvanized in 1969 when Thomas Noguchi, the flamboyant Los Angeles County Chief Coroner, was accused of incompetence and bizarre behavior, and summarily fired.[30] Noguchi was eventually reinstated, but only after an unprecedented coalition of Japanese American civic and cultural organizations drew public attention to the case through full page advertisements in the *Los Angeles Times*, with headlines such as "A Plea of Justice, If This Can Happen To One of Us, It Can Happen to You . . . . A nationally known doctor and scientist was humiliated, disgraced and fired from a civil service post without a hearing, amid charges . . . bizarre . . . degrading and odious . . . ."[31] Chinese Americans were shaken by a 1973 memorandum to all law enforcement agencies from the state attorney general about the alleged threat posed by Chinese benevolent associations. It bore a frightening resemblance to hate literature circulated by racists and nativists at the height of the anti-Chinese movement a century earlier: "Chinese benevolent associations. . . operate under the façade of a mutual aid society. . . the Tongs more closely resemble Mafia-like organizations . . . . The Chinese's primary interest in coming into the U.S. is to make money . . . an easy method is involvement in the drug market . . . Drugs are a way of life in the Orient."[32] Prewar racist epithets reappeared to haunt Japanese Americans during the U.S. Senate's Watergate hearings in 1973 when the attorney for President Richard Nixon's henchmen slurred Senator Daniel Inouye as "that little Jap."[33] Amidst the ensuing outrage, Asian Pacific American community leaders saw the need to create political alliances and other mechanisms in order to survive and prevail in future crises.

In the 1980s, activists among Los Angeles' various Asian Pacific American communities created a variety of civil rights and occupation-based groups and coalitions to publicly confront perceived injustices. The Asian American Bar Association lobbied for the appointment of more judges, and the Asian American Journalists Association sought more positions in both the print and electronic media. LEAP (Leadership Education for Asian Pacifics), a national, nonprofit, non-partisan, educational organization was founded in 1982 by a cross section of Asian and Pacific Americans, and based in Los Angeles' Little Tokyo. LEAP maintained close contacts with political parties and nurtured strong support from powerful corporate sponsors.

Community-based advocacy groups and protest movements became an accepted activity, and a diverse coalition emerged in support of "redress" for Japanese Americans incarcerated during World War II. [34] Bitter differences divided the community on issues such as monetary compensation versus an official apology, but overwhelming support for redress in Congress was secured through the combined clout of Japanese American senators Daniel Inouye and Spark Matsunaga—both decorated combat veterans of the 442nd Regimental Combat Team—and California congressmen Norman Mineta and Robert Matsui. Congress created the Commission on Wartime Relocation and Internment of Civilians in 1980. The commission held nationwide public hearings, including one in Los Angeles, and concluded that the wartime treatment of Japanese Americans was caused by "race prejudice, war hysteria and a failure of political leadership."[35] In the meantime, researchers in the U.S. National Archives discovered documents showing that government officials had lied to justify the mass removal of Japanese Americans into a gulag of concentration camps. A team of young Asian American attorneys, led by Dale Minami, a Sansei ("third generation") Japanese American from Gardena, pursued an obscure legal proceeding (a petition for a writ of error, *coram nobis*) to reopen and overturn U.S. Supreme Court decisions that had supported the wartime diaspora.[36] The redress campaign was an uphill battle, but victory eventually came when President Ronald Reagan signed the Civil Liberties Act of 1988 which provided for a presidential apology and a one-time, nontaxable $20,000 cash payment to each survivor. In 1990 President George Bush issued an official apology along with the first checks.[37] Redress arrived too late for at least half of the 120,000 incarcerees. Most of the immigrant pioneer Issei were dead, and only some 60,000 Nisei were still alive.

Asian and Pacific Islander college students and community activists demonstrated against the commercial development and gentrification of Little Tokyo, "glass ceiling" obstacles to top-management promotions, and alleged quotas restricting Asian Pacific American admissions at the Los Angeles and Berkeley campuses of the University of California. In the 1970s and 1980s both institutions were accused of discriminating against Asian applicants by establishing informal quotas like those used against Jews before World War II. UC officials denied the allegations but in 1989, against a backdrop of declining Asian Pacific American admissions and investigations by state and federal agencies, the UC Berkeley chancellor apologized for manipulating the admissions process. By 1995, Asians were more than half of all undergraduates and just under 50 percent of the total student body at UC Irvine; similar figures were given for UCLA and UC Riverside. Campus jokes sarcastically defined UCLA as the "University of Caucasians Lost Among Asians" and UCI (Irvine) as the "University of Chinese Immigrants."

There were few Asian teachers in Los Angeles' public schools before World War II, but by the late 1960s they were familiar faces in elementary, secondary, and college classrooms throughout the basin. By the late 1980s they also advanced to senior administrative positions. Two Japanese Americans from Gardena, Warren Furutani, elected in 1987 to the first of two terms, and George Kiriyama who replaced him in 1995, led the Board of Education of the Los Angeles City Unified School District, where each presided as board president. Confronting them as head of the powerful teachers' union, United Teachers of Los Angeles, was another Japanese American, Day Higuchi. In higher education, Bob Suzuki served as president of California State Polytechnic University, Pomona for nearly a decade. Jack Fujimoto was president of several campuses in the Los Angeles Community College District, and Neil Yoneji was appointed to an interim position as that district's first Asian Pacific American chancellor. Asian American women moved into senior community college posts as Evelyn Wong became president at West Los Angeles College and Nadine Ishitani Hata was appointed vice president for academic affairs at El Camino College in the South Bay.

A new postwar generation of Asian Pacific American lawyers emerged as advocates of civil rights, and many would later mete out justice from the bench. In the 1950s, Los Angeles attorney and fourth generation Californian Delbert Earl Wong became the first Chinese American judge in the continental United States. Nisei John Aiso was appointed to the Los Angeles Municipal Court in 1953 and later to the California Court of Appeals. Robert Takasugi, a Japanese American lawyer known for his fearless advocacy of underdogs in civil rights cases, was first appointed to the municipal court in East Los Angeles in 1973 and later promoted to the U.S. District Court. Katherine Doi Todd became the first Japanese American woman municipal court judge in Los Angeles in 1978 and was later elevated to the State Court of Appeals. Joyce Kennard, an immigrant from Indonesia who worked as a secretary to pay her way through Pasadena City College and law school at USC, was the first Asian American appointed to the California State Supreme Court in 1989. Two Japanese American judges, Lance Ito and Hiroshi Fujisaki, became household names when they presided over the highly publicized criminal and civil trials of O.J. Simpson in the mid-1990s. Wallace Tashima was confirmed in 1996 as the first Japanese American appointed to the U.S. 9th Circuit Court of Appeals. In 1997, Bill Lann Lee, the son of a Chinese immigrant laundryman and a lawyer for the NAACP Legal Defense Fund in Los Angeles, was appointed Assistant U.S. Attorney General for Civil Rights—the first Asian Pacific American to serve in that powerful federal post.

A rapidly expanding number of Asian Pacific candidates have been elected as city council members and mayors in suburban Los Angeles, Orange and Ventura counties, showing that they have moved into the political mainstream. With few exceptions, they ran as moderates and either lacked or did not cultivate an Asian ethnic voting bloc. Their success in local politics reflected their acceptance by broad cross sections of their suburban middle class constituencies. Women, such as Eunice Sato in Long Beach and Audrey Yamagata-Noji in Santa Ana, launched careers in electoral politics by gaining name recognition through service as school and community volunteers, and winning election to local school boards. Monterey Park voters elected several Asians beginning in 1960 when Al Song, a Korean, became the first Asian American on the city council. Song was followed by George Ige, a Japanese, who was elected to the city council in 1970 and later served as mayor. A Filipino, G. Monty Manibog, served on the city council from 1976 to 1978. In 1983 Monterey Park elected Lily Chen the nation's first Chinese woman mayor. Chen was swept out of office in the 1986 municipal election which some viewed as a neo-nativist and racist referendum against the highly visible influx of affluent Chinese immigrants.[38] She was followed by Judy Chu, who served three terms, twice as mayor, and survived by constructing a city-wide multiethnic coalition. In the late 1960s, Gardena began to elect at least one Japanese American to its city council in every election, starting with City Councilman and later Mayor Ken Nakaoka, a realtor.[39] George Nakano became the first Japanese American elected to the Torrance City Council in 1984. 1992 saw more victories in municipal elections across the basin: Peter D. Fajardo became the first Filipino elected to the Carson city council.[40] A year later Lorelie S. Olaes became Carson's first Filipina councilwoman. Westminster City Councilman Tony Lam's victory marked the first time a Vietnamese American was elected to public office. Several city council seats were won by Chinese Americans: Michael Gin in Redondo Beach, Carol J. Liu in La Canada-Flintridge and Benjamin Wong in West Covina. Michael Woo's election as the first Los Angeles City Council member of Chinese ancestry was summed up in these June 6, 1985 *Los Angeles Times* headlines: "Woo's Victory—Asians Come of Political Age" and "Woo: Asians Recognized as Growing Political Force." His 1993 bid to become Los Angeles' first Chinese American mayor failed, but Woo demonstrated the fund-raising potential of Asian candidates by soliciting contributions from across the nation and members of both major parties.

In the 1980s and 1990s an increasingly diverse cast of Asian Pacific Americans gained experience and public exposure, and exploited success in municipal politics to attract partisan endorsements and campaign funding to move up to the State Assembly, State Senate, and Congress. Monterey Park voters elected Al Song, a Democrat, to two terms as state assemblyman and state senator, and later sent Democrat Judy Chu to the State Assembly. Gardena realtor Paul Bannai, a Republican, moved from the Gardena City Council to the State Assembly. George Nakano completed two terms on the Torrance City Council and ran successfully as a moderate Democrat for two terms in the State Assembly. Carol Liu, a Democrat, was re-elected to the State Assembly in 2004. In that year, Garden Grove's Van Tran, a Republican, became the first Vietnamese American elected to the State Assembly. The first Asian Pacific American from the U.S. mainland in the U.S. Congress was Dalip Singh Saund, a naturalized Asian Indian from the Imperial Valley, who was elected as a Democrat to the House of Representatives in 1956. Other Asian Pacific Americans were elected to Congress from Hawaii and Northern California,[41] but it was not until the early 1990s that another from Southern California was elected—Republican Jay Kim of Diamond Bar. The first Korean American member of Congress, Kim was a naturalized citizen. A five-year investigation by the *Los Angeles Times* led to a conviction for campaign finance irregularities and the loss of his seat in 1998. Kim had clearly broken the law, and his plea for leniency—that he was an immigrant and unfamiliar with the rules—received no support from Asian Pacific Americans.

Equally important as their emergence as elected officials is the presence of Asian Pacific Americans at every level and in every dimension of the bureaucratic infrastructure. They implement and enforce policy as staff to elected officials, and they shape and make policy as members of official commissions, governing boards of major public and private organizations, and in powerful executive management positions. The first public hearings on Asian Pacific American civil rights problems were convened in 1973 by the California State Advisory Committee to the U.S. Commission on Civil Rights.[42] Richard Riordan's successful Los Angeles mayoral campaign was managed by a Chinese American woman, Jadine Nielsen, and he appointed William G. Ouchi, a Japanese American professor of management at UCLA, as his first chief of staff. Korean American Paul Kim and Japanese American Terry Hara became the first Asian Pacific American captains in the Los Angeles Police

Department, where Asian Pacific Americans comprise 4.5 percent of the total force. In Los Angeles County government, with a budget larger than many nations, powerful County Supervisor Kenneth Hahn appointed Gardena City Councilman Masani "Mas" Fukai as his senior deputy and chief of staff. Torrance attorney Angela Oh, a Korean American who spoke eloquently to national television audiences about the targeting of Koreans during the 1992 Los Angeles riots, was appointed to the President's Commission on Race and fought to expand its focus beyond Black-White issues to include Latinos and Asian Pacific Americans. Attorney Mike Yamaki served as the powerful appointments secretary to Governor Gray Davis. His successor, Governor Arnold Schwarzenegger, appointed A.G. Kawamura, a grower and shipper from Orange County whose family grows strawberries and green beans, to head the Department of Food and Agriculture.

Epilogue

The popular culture of contemporary Los Angeles exudes a diverse and pervasive Asian and Pacific Islander profile. Asians are trusted to deliver good and bad news as television anchors and reporters for local newspapers. Fast-food counters dispense teriyaki burgers, curry burritos, and Thai noodles. Sushi bars and restaurants flourish in middle class neighborhoods, and Asian ingredients and culinary techniques are at the core of modern California fusion cuisine. Asian and American themes are reflected in the works of authors like Wakako Yamauchi and Frank Chin. A wide range of musical tastes includes the Hiroshima band, classical violinist Midori, karaoke bars and taiko drummers. Fitness experts promise good health through yoga, acupuncture, tai-chi; and various schools of martial arts attract students of all ages. Entertainers include comedians Margaret Cho and Amy Hill, and performance artists Sandra Tsing Loh and Jude Narita. World-class women's figure skating is dominated by Michelle Kwan, the daughter of immigrants who operated a Chinese restaurant in suburban Torrance. Asian Americans are routinely selected as Rose Parade queens and princesses. Champion professional athletes include Michael Chang in tennis, golf prodigy Tiger Woods, baseball pitcher Hideo Nomo and jockey Corey Nakatani. These positive images attest to the move away from the pre-World War II perception of Asian Pacific Americans as marginal and scorned pariah groups.

From across the Pacific, Asian manufactured automobiles, consumer electronics, household appliances and clothing fill shelves and showrooms; and the names and logos of transnational Asian corporations like Sony, Panasonic, Toyota, Honda, Hyundai, Kia and Nissan are part of the everyday vocabulary of contemporary America. The ancient Japanese art of bonsai is no longer unusual; nor are Buddhist and Hindu temples, Asian landscape gardening, museums dedicated to Asian arts, and traditional celebrations such as Chinese New Year and Vietnamese Tet. The official mandate that May be celebrated annually across the nation as Asian Pacific Heritage month has spawned film festivals, television programs, and special events to educate the general public.

As Asian Pacific Americans grow older, they are increasingly concerned about the need to perpetuate their legacy. Veterans' memorials commemorating the service of Japanese Americans in World War II, Korea, and Vietnam have been constructed in Little Tokyo. In 1994 a huge five-level freeway junction next to Los Angeles International Airport was named the "Sadao S. Munemori Memorial Interchange" for the Nisei recipient of the Congressional Medal of Honor in World War II. The recent creation of the Japanese American National Museum, the Chinese American Museum, and the Korean Cultural Center enrich the multicultural mosaic of themes that pervade Los Angeles' past and present. These new institutions reflect the evolution of once-despised groups who have moved from the margins into the mainstream. Asian Pacific Americans are poised to play a broader variety of roles than ever before in shaping the economy, culture and politics of Los Angeles and Southern California.

On the other hand, while much is made of the cosmopolitan culture of contemporary Los Angeles, diversity is not synonymous with harmony, and little has changed in the tectonic social tensions endemic to the region. The persistence of negative stereotypes and hate crimes against Asians and Pacific Islanders is an ominous reminder of the pervasive appeal of the "Yellow Peril" and the role of Asians and Pacific Islanders as indispensable scapegoats in a time of crisis.

NOTES

[1] Census data has been collected on Chinese since 1860, Japanese since 1870, and Filipinos and Koreans since 1910 albeit intermittently. In 1970 Asian Indians were identified as "White" and Vietnamese were included in the "other race" category. For the first time Census 2000 asked respondents "to report *one or more* races they considered themselves and other members of their household to be," an option which makes the data incompatible with earlier census reports. See "The Asian Population: 2000. Census 2000 Brief," U.S. Census Bureau, Issued February 2002 and "Profile of General Demographic Characteristics: 2000," U.S. Census Bureau. The "other Asian" category includes Asian alone or two or more Asian categories.

[2] In 2000 the Asian Pacific American population in L.A. County was: Chinese (3.5%), Filipino (2.7%), Korean (2.0%), Japanese (1.2%), Vietnamese (0.8%), Asian Indian (0.6%), Other Asian (1.2%), Native Hawaiian and Other Pacific Islander (0.3%). *Ibid.*

[3] James P. Allen and Eugene Turner, *The Ethnic Quilt: Population Diversity in Southern California* (California State University, Northridge: The Center for Geographical Studies, 1997): 129-130, 146-148.

[4] Joe Matthews, "The New Import: Teachers," *Los Angeles Times*, 10 August 2002, sec. A, pp.1, 12. (Hereafter abbreviated as "*LAT*")

[5] Penelope McMillan, "Koreatown: A Struggle for Identity," *LAT*, 17 June 1984, sec. M, p. 4.

[6] Eui-Young Yu and Peter Choe, "Korean Population in the United States as Reflected in the Year 2000 U.S. Census," *Amerasia Journal* 29:3 (2003-2004):14-19.

[7] "Little India in Artesia—Why Not? A community founded by immigrant groups could surely embrace one more," *LAT*, 6 September 1991, sec. M, p. 4; Regine Labossiere, "'Little India' Fights for Recognition," *LAT*, 26 August 2004, sec. B, pp. 1, 8.

[8] Kathleen Day and David Holley, "Vietnamese Create Their Own Saigon," *LAT*, 30 September 1984, pp. 1, 3, 34.

[9] Daniel Akst, "Cruller Fates. Cambodians Find Slim Profits in Doughnuts," *LAT* , 9 March 1993, sec. D, p. 1.

[10] David Haldane, "A Taste of Cambodia. Indochinese Businesses Revitalize Once-Anemic Area in Long Beach," *LAT*, 19 December 1988, sec. IV, pp. 1-2.

[11] See "Census 2000," U.S. Census Bureau. These numbers include the ethnic group alone or in combination with other groups.

[12] Timothy P. Fong, *The First Suburban Chinatown: The Remaking of Monterey Park, California* (Philadelphia: Temple University Press, 1994).

[13] Stephanie Chavez, "New Look Reflects an Old Pattern," *LAT*, 25 July 2004, sec. B, pp. 1, 10.

14 Evelyn Iritani, "Back to His future: Bugle Boy's William Mow is returning to China, the country he fled half a century ago, in a bid to put his apparel firm on the global map," *LAT*, 28 September 1997, sec. D, p. 1.

15 Greg Miller, "Kingston Employees Take Bonus in Stride," *LAT*, 16 December 1996, sec. A, p. 42.

16 Naomi Hirahara, ed., *Greenmakers: Japanese American Gardeners in Southern California* (Los Angeles: Southern California Gardeners' Federation, 2000).

17 See "Census 2000," U.S. Census Bureau.

18 William Petersen, "Success Story, Japanese-American Style," *New York Times Magazine*, 9 January 1966, 20.

19 "Study: Asian Poor Neglected Because of Stereotypes," *Rafu Shimpo*, 2 December 1993, p. 1.

20 Karl Schoenberger, "Escapee Sparked Sweatshop Raid," *LAT*, 11 August 1995, sec. A, p. 1.

21 Susanna McBee, "The Amerasians: Tragic Legacy of Our Far East Wars," *U.S. News and World Report*, 7 May 1984, 49-51; and Dianne Klein, "Vietnam's Lingering Casualties," *LAT*, 30 June 1991, sec. A, p. 1.

22 In June 1982, Vincent Chin, a Chinese American engineering student, was beaten to death by two unemployed White auto workers in Detroit. The judge allowed the defendants to plead guilty to manslaughter rather than murder because they had mistaken Chin for a Japanese whose homeland they held responsible for widespread unemployment in the U.S. auto industry.

23 U.S. Commission on Civil Rights, *Civil Rights Issues Facing Asian Americans in the 1990s* (February 1992), 24.

24 Karl Schoenberger, "Living Off Expatriate Labor," *LAT*, 1 August 1994, sec. A, p. 16.

25 The last documented hate crime of a Filipino American was in 1930 when a mob in Watsonville murdered Filipino lettuce picker Fermin Tobera, and burned and ransacked Filipino farmers' homes and property.

26 Ronald J. Ostrow, "Asian Crime War Rages in L.A. Suburb. 'I Can't Control It' Declares Monterey Park Police Chief," *LAT*, 25 October 1984, sec. II, pp. 1,3; Penelope McMillan and Lenore Look," Monterey Park Chief's Alarm on Gangs Discounted," *LAT*, 26 October 1984, sec. II, p. 1.

27 David Haldane, "Latino and Asian Gangs Engage in Deadly Warfare. Influx of Cambodians into Long Beach has created tension; 'cultural misunderstanding' is blamed by some officials," *LAT*, 15 April 1991, sec. B, p. 1.

28 Marita Hernandez, *LAT*, 18 May 1986, sec. II, p. 1.

29 Paul Ong and Suzanne Hee, *Losses in the Los Angeles Civil Unrest, April 29-May 1, 1992. Lists of the Damaged Properties and the L.A. Riot/ Rebellion and Korean Merchants* (Los Angeles: Center for Pacific Rim Studies, UCLA, 1993), 1-14.

30 Noguchi received nationwide publicity for his autopsy of assassinated presidential candidate Robert Kennedy, and was also known as "the coroner to the stars."

31 Noguchi "was accused of being mentally ill, in need of psychiatric care, and of excessive use of drugs...," *LAT*, 11 July 1969, sec. II, p. 5. In a second case twenty years later, the coroner did not receive widespread community support and lost his position. See Dan Morain, "Supreme Court Refuses to Reinstate Noguchi," *LAT*, 12 March 1987, sec. II, p. 1.

32 California Department of Justice, "Triad: Mafia of the Far East," in *Criminal Justice Bulletin* (July 1973).

33 Attorney Charles Wilson represented Nixon's senior aides H.R. Haldeman and John D. Ehrlichman. See Don and Nadine Hata, "'That Little Jap:' Such Epithets Revive the Old Internment Camp Mentality," *LAT*, 10 August 1973, sec. II, p. 7.

34 Roger Daniels, Sandra C. Taylor, and Harry H.L. Kitano, eds., *Japanese Americans: From Relocation to Redress*, rev. ed. (Seattle: University of Washington Press, 1991), 188-203.

35 Commission on Wartime Relocation and Internment of Civilians, *Personal Justice Denied: Report of the Commission on Wartime Relocation and Internment of Civilians* (1982 and 1983. Reprint. Seattle: University of Washington Press, 1997).

36 In 1942, four young West Coast Nisei who had never met each other— Minoru Yasui, Gordon Hirabayashi, Fred Korematsu, and Mitsuye Endo—challenged the government's policies and pressed their cases to the U.S. Supreme Court. For forty years the Court's rulings in the wartime "Japanese American cases" sanctioned the denial of basic civil rights of U.S. citizens by reason of their race.

37 "It's Official! Reagan Signs Bill. Ex-Internees to Receive $20,000 in Compensation," *Rafu Shimpo*, 10 August 1988, p. 1; also see Mitchell Maki, Harry H.L. Kitano, and S. Megan Berthold, *Achieving the Impossible Dream: How Japanese Americans Obtained Redress* (Urbana, IL: University of Illinois Press, 1999).

38 "Monterey Park: Nation's 1st Suburban Chinatown," *LAT*, 6 April 1987, sec. I, p. 1.

39 Other council members included realtor Paul Bannai, body and fender repairman and insurance agent Mas Fukai, deputy district attorney Vince Okamoto, dentist Paul Tsukahara, and local state college history professor Don Hata who replaced Bannai when he was elected to the State Assembly. Gardena's elected city treasurer slot was filled by appliance dealer George Kobayashi, and elementary school teacher May Doi won perennial elections for city clerk.

40 Fajardo was forced to resign after pleading guilty to a federal charge of collecting attorney's fees even though he was not a lawyer.

[41] S.I. Hayakawa from San Francisco was elected to the U.S. Senate in 1976.

[42] The hearings led to the report *Asian Americans and Pacific Peoples: A Case of Mistaken Identity* (February 1975). Serving as vice chair was Japanese American professor of history Nadine Ishitani Hata.

Chapter 5

A SIMPLE QUEST FOR DIGNITY
African American Los Angeles
Since World War II

Josh Sides

To know the history of African Americans in Los Angeles, one must be willing to think, first, not only historically, but trans-regionally as well; one must be willing to consider the myriad complexities of the westward migration of an historically Southern people; one must also penetrate the often impenetrable meanings of · blackness to African Americans themselves and, no less important, to their neighboring Latinos, Anglos, Asians and Jews in Los Angeles; and one must wrestle with the vast geographical terrain of the greater Los Angeles region, within whose expansive boundaries African Americans have found both Promised Land and Purgatory. Finally, one must nurture a healthy skepticism about reducing the Los Angeles African American experience into simple narratives of either triumphant progress or grinding decline. As has been the case throughout metropolitan America, the postwar history of African Americans in Los Angeles is a story as complex and varied as the personal experiences of its hundreds of thousands of individual participants. Theirs is a story that defies simple classification, but demands simple respect.

The demand for respect is an appropriate place to begin, because this is what lured African Americans to Los Angeles in the first place. Since the late 19th century, when a small number of blacks began migrating to Los Angeles, through the late 1960s when the Great Migration finally began to wane, African American migrants to Los Angeles were on a quest for dignity. They sought, above all, to shed what black poet Paul Laurence Dunbar famously described as "the mask": that veil of racial inferiority and servility brutally mandated by Jim Crow society in the American South. For someone like Sylvester Gibbs, there was nothing more important about migrating to Los Angeles than the opportunity to shed that mask. Gibbs, who was one of the many African American migrants who generously shared their memories with me as I conducted research for my book, *L.A. City Limits*, migrated to Los Angeles from Mississippi in 1948. By virtually any standard, Gibbs was a success, quickly finding career-long, unionized employment as a crane operator in the nation's largest scrap steel yard and purchasing a nice home in the city of Compton, where he and his wife of over fifty years still live as of this printing. Yet, despite all of these material achievements, the most important result of his migration was the quiet dignity it restored. "First thing I remember," Gibbs told me in 1998, "in California you ain't got these folks feeling superior over the blacks." "They may feel that," he conceded, "but they can't go around showing it. You don't go around saying 'sir'. If he don't say 'sir' to you, you don't have to say 'sir' to him." "Out here," Gibbs concluded almost triumphantly, "everybody just called their name."[1]

It was this simple quest for dignity that linked Southern California's pre–World War II community—extensively chronicled in Douglas Flamming's inspirational *Bound For Freedom*—and the postwar African American communities described in this essay. Also connecting them were their strong family ties and their migratory routes out of Texas and Louisiana, where a disproportionate number of migrants came from in both eras. And all were lured by the relative ease of home ownership, the scant history of racial violence toward blacks, and—of course—the fabled climate. Very little, in fact, distinguished the motives, experiences, and economic backgrounds of pre-war migrants from those of wartime and post-war migrants. What, then, changed? Why distinguish between one period of African American migration in Los Angeles and another?[2]

What changed was not so much the people, but the city. World War II changed Los Angeles irrevocably, setting it on its modern economic footing, creating the mega-metropolis and permanently changing the nature of economic, social, and political opportunities for African Americans and all of its other diverse citizenry. Though Los Angeles had already become a regional and national economic powerhouse in the 1920s with a vibrant agricultural, service, and manufacturing base, the war ratcheted the pace of industrial growth.[3] During the war years, Los Angeles became the nation's second largest industrial manufacturing center (outranked only by Detroit), receiving over eleven billion dollars in defense contracts. In the 1950s, Southern California added sophisticated new aerospace and communications industries to the Cold War arsenal, sustaining the region's economic growth even as older "rust belt" cities of the Northeast lost jobs in the 1970s. Since then, the finance, insurance, and real estate sectors have boomed, as have the low-paying service and "sweatshop" manufacturing jobs. And between World War II and the later years of the Cold War, the expansion of employment opportunities in Southern California was complemented by the rapid growth of—until very recently—housing widely affordable to the general population. In these and so many other ways, World War II introduced an era of economic prosperity whose effects are still obvious today.

The generally propitious postwar economy of Southern California made it an unusually popular destination among the approximately 5 million African Americans who left the American South between the 1940s and the late 1960s. Between 1940 and 1970, the black population in Los Angeles grew faster than any other large northern or western city, climbing from 63,744 to almost 763,000. Although this phenomenal growth has slowed considerably since the 1970s, and many African Americans have actually begun to return to the South, Los Angeles now has the seventh largest black population in the country. In their quest for dignity and economic stability, African Americans in Los Angeles, as elsewhere, have found the city to be uneven terrain, bitterly reminiscent of the old South one moment, bursting with opportunity the next. They have often been frustrated by its promises, embittered by what they see as a false-tolerance, captured so well by black novelist Chester Himes in his autobiography, *The Quality of Hurt*. Himes, who had migrated to Los Angeles from Cleveland in 1941 recalled:

> Los Angeles hurt me racially as much as any city I have ever known—much more than any city I remember from the South. It was the lying hypocrisy that hurt me. Black people were treated much the same as they were in any Industrial city of the South ... The difference was that the white people of Los Angeles seemed to be saying, "Nigger, ain't we good to you?"[4]

But African Americans in Los Angeles have also recognized that in a nation, and in an era, in which race still profoundly limited one's opportunities, Los Angeles was about as good as it got. Paradoxical, capricious, and often shockingly brutal and nasty, Los Angeles has also been a city where several generations of African Americans found great prosperity, happiness, and freedom from the racially degrading ritual of Southern life. For many African Americans, Los Angeles was also a preferred destination over the more famous promised lands of Detroit, Chicago, and New York. For those who saw life as a choice between—as one morbid satirist put it earlier in the century—being "gently lynched in Mississippi [or] beaten to death in New York," Los Angeles, with its booming economy and relative racial safety, seemed like a good bet.[5]

Yet by the late 1980s and 1990s, Los Angeles developed a popular national reputation as the *worst* of what metropolitan America had to offer African Americans. Propelled almost single-handedly by the entertainment industry, which recognized the profitability of creating and exploiting the notion of a *uniquely* racially troubled city through hard-core "gansta rap" and a string of dark and violent movies about life in South Central[6], this idea seemed borne out by real events in the early 1990s. The savage beating of motorist Rodney King in 1991, the riots in 1992 which followed the scandalous acquittal of the offending officers, the atrocious murder of Nicole Simpson and Ron Goldman, and the controversial acquittal of African American football and acting star O.J. Simpson, all confirmed the allegedly unique notoriety of either African Americans or race relations in Los Angeles.

What role Los Angeles will play in the imagination of African America in the future—Promised Land or Purgatory—depends to a great extent on the willingness of Angelenos of all races to come to grips with the city's racial past. In particular, it depends on the ability of its citizens to recognize that the African American quest for dignity in Los Angeles has been long and difficult, and, at the time of this writing, still unfinished. Since World War II, the African American quest for dignity has involved the pursuit of at least three central tenets of postwar American citizenship, broadly defined. Most consistently, blacks in Los Angeles have demanded equal access to jobs and equal treatment on the job; they have demanded fair housing policies and the opportunity to choose where they will live and where they will send their kids to school; and they have demanded that their voices be heard, that local political leaders respond to the problems plaguing their communities. Since World War II, these battles have given concrete meaning to the dignity that African Americans have for so long sought, and are, in some cases, still seeking.

THE MIRAGE OF EQUAL EMPLOYMENT

Prior to World War II, employment opportunities for African Americans in Los Angeles were hopelessly circumscribed. With the exception of racial preference for blacks in housekeeping, janitorial work, and some service and menial labor jobs, race almost always worked against black economic aspirations. Racist hiring practices in the city and throughout the nation were so widespread and accepted that they scarcely needed defending. This national pattern was complicated in Los Angeles by intense competition from Mexicans, who were widely viewed as a preferable workforce to blacks. Charles S. Johnson's widely-cited 1926 *Industrial Survey of the Negro Population* confirmed these sobering truths about the impact of race in a region fabled for racial tolerance. Johnson found, for example, that out of 104 manufacturing plants, only 54 hired blacks in any positions, most commonly as janitors, porters, and laborers. More troubling, when asked "If competent Negro workers were available, would you employ them?", 30 flatly stated that they would not do so under any condition. Johnson found opposition to black hiring to be rampant throughout the Alameda Industrial corridor—the city's industrial belt straddling Alameda Street from the Central Manufacturing District some twenty miles south to the Port of Los Angeles—and particularly in apparel, machinery, oil wells, paints and varnishes, furniture, door manufacturers,

manufacturers of electrical goods, and construction companies. Outside in the industrial belt, in the region's suburban aircraft industry, blacks were entirely excluded. According to a 1940 survey of aircraft employers conducted by *Fortune* magazine, there was "an almost universal prejudice against Negroes" in the industry. And, of course, the Great Depression intensified the effects of these restrictive policies. Consequently, 30% of black men and 40% of black women in Los Angeles were unemployed by 1934, half of all black Angelenos were out of work.[7]

But the deepening labor shortage of World War II, coupled with the vast new demand for industrial output, forced the nation's defense manufacturers to look beyond their traditionally white, male, and often skilled, labor pool. Shipbuilding aircraft, steel, and automobile plants retooled for war production, and a host of other large industrial manufacturers were reorganized to speed production by "deskilling" the production process. Lower skill requirements and greater labor demand opened the door of industrial employment to women and African Americans, who had long been denied both the training and experience necessary for such work. In addition, African Americans also benefited from President Franklin Delano Roosevelt's Executive Order 8802, issued in 1941, which forbade discrimination in wartime defense industries and created the Fair Employment Practices Committee (FEPC) to investigate charges of racial discrimination. Los Angeles Urban League director Floyd Covington referred to Executive Order 8802 as the "Second Emancipation for the American Negro" in his 1943 address to the National Urban League. And indeed, the labor shortage coupled with the threat of Federal desegregation resulted in the swift integration of blacks into the region's bustling aircraft, shipbuilding, steel and automobile plants. [8]

Though Covington gave too much credit to the FEPC for improving black employment opportunities, he was right to recognize the revolutionary effect of expanded black employment opportunities, particularly in a city in which they had been so limited. Nor was he alone in his optimism. Charlotta Bass, tireless civil rights crusader and owner/editor of the *California Eagle* sounded a similar note. "Who can deny," she rhetorically asked readers in July of 1942, "that the next six months will see the greatest expansion of opportunities for Negro workers in the history of this nation?" The great social scientists of black America, including Gunnar Myrdal, St. Clair Drake and Horace Cayton, all recognized that World War II represented a critical turning point in the future of African Americans by putting them on equal or near-equal economic footing for whites for the first time in the nation's history. Finally, numerous surveys and studies by the National Urban League confirmed the revolutionary potential of job growth for blacks and one even cited the unique desirability of California for African Americans, ranking Los Angeles and San Francisco as two of the ten best cities for postwar black employment opportunities in 1947.[9]

Covington, Bass, Myrdal, Drake and Cayton were all right. Sort of. Between 1940 and 1960, the proportion of the black male workforce employed as factory operatives in Los Angeles rose from 15% to 24% with most of the growth occurring in metal, automobile, and food industries in assembly, maintenance, welding, and truck-driving positions. Over the same period, the proportion of black men employed as craftsmen rose from 7% to 14%. Similarly the proportion the black female workforce employed as manufacturing operatives rose from 3.9% to 18% in the same period, and black women saw tremendous gains in clerical work and administrative work in the public sector. Beyond these specific occupational gains, the rate of unemployment of African Americans in Los Angeles dipped to its lowest ever in the 1950s, demonstrating that strides made in the city's industrial plants spread well-beyond the shop floor. In an about-face from the pre-war pattern, employers in Los Angeles increasingly recognized that African Americans were a valuable source of labor in the region. But Covington and the others were unable to imagine that these advances could take place even as inequality proceeded unabated. They shared the rather simple dichotomist vision implied in Drake and Cayton's query, posed in *Black Metropolis* in 1945. They asked whether blacks "will remain the marginal workers to be called in only at times of great economic activity, or will become an integral part of the American economy and thus lay the basis for complete social and political integration." What these thinkers and activists all lacked was the cynicism to imagine that there was something woefully in between.[10]

Even as the engine of black opportunity accelerated in postwar Los Angeles, it always strained against overt managerial racism, restrictive seniority rules, white workers' preferences, and deepening competition with Mexican workers. While discrimination in wartime hiring, pay, and shift and job assignments, was rampant, it was most egregious on the docks on the San Pedro and in the shipyards of Terminal Island, where the International Longshoremen's and Warehousemen's Union (ILWU) and the Boilermaker's union sought to retain the all-white (including Mexicans) labor force in their respective industries. Employers, and often unions, in automobile manufacturing, steelmaking, meat packing, and food processing plants rounded out the campaign to limit black industrial gains in the postwar era. It was an open secret in automobile manufacturing, for example, that blacks would always be assigned to the most noxious painting department, while whites would be assigned lighter, cleaner jobs. What would have shocked Covington, Bass, Cayton, Drake, and Myrdal, and what continues to surprise students of Los Angeles history today, is how recently such practices were acceptable.[11]

In most cases, industrial discrimination of this sort continued into the 1970s. It only stopped when African Americans began to avail themselves of legal action they were guaranteed as part of the civil rights legislation of the era. But receiving compensation for years of discrimination took considerable initiative, lots of evidence collection, and lengthy litigation. In many cases, by the time aggrieved black workers were finally compensated, the plants at which they worked were closing down. Clevron Tucker, for example, worked as a truck driver for the Bethlehem Steel company since 1951, and found himself consistently passed over for promotions, assigned to broken-down trucks, and given less pay than both white and Mexican-American workers. Under Title VII of the Civil Rights Act of 1964, Tucker filed several suits against the company and union, but could never prove his case. Under a 1974 consent decree, Tucker and fellow black workers at Bethlehem were given a $200 settlement for twenty four years of mistreatment. Dissatisfied, Tucker and others collectively sued the company in 1980, finally scoring a victory in 1983, just one year after they had permanently lost their jobs when the Bethlehem plant closed down.[12]

The well-documented wave of plant closures that rocked South Los Angeles in the late 1970s and 1980s was devastating to that large stratum of the black population accustomed to stable, moderately well-paying, if emotionally unfulfilling work. The disappearance of these jobs had a measurable effect on the economy of South Los Angeles, undercutting household incomes, pushing black unemployment rates back up and crippling the black business district of Central Avenue, which depended on the patronage of black customers. More abstractly, the disappearance of industrial manufacturing work from South Central Los Angeles was a blow to a dream thirty years in the making: that blacks would achieve full equality in Los Angeles by working hard, doing the same jobs that whites did.[13]

For those aging African Americans who had nurtured the dream only to awaken to the nightmare of pension-free unemployment in old age, there was nothing sanguine about the region's economic shift. But for their children and grandchildren, the shift sometimes portended brighter horizons. In the postwar years, the proportion of African Americans employed in white-collar occupations rose impressively, particularly for women. A small but significant number of African Americans achieved the fabled middle class standard of life in Southern California, moving into communities like West Adams and then Baldwin Hills (discussed below), and sending their children to the city's better schools. Between 1969 and 1989, real earnings for black men in Los Angeles increased faster than those of white, Asian, or Latino men, and black women's real earnings rose and astounding 61%, indicators that African Americans in Los Angeles have made impressive economic strides since the deindustrialization of the 1970s. More impressive, black women's earnings reached parity with white women's earnings in 1979 and exceeded Latina's earnings by 22% in 1989. Yet, signs remain that racial inequality in earnings continues to exist, particularly for black men, and comparisons with other groups make it appear more endemic than one might first assume. For example, although real earnings for black men increased faster than it did for other ethnic groups during the 1969-1989 period, in 1989, black men still made only 72 cents on the dollar compared with whites, 77 cents on the dollar compared with Asians, and 96 cents on the dollar compared with Latinos. More recent national data bears out the logic of this finding: African Americans are still earning far less than whites and even less than Latinos in some instances.[14]

Since World War II, when equality with whites first became conceivable in Los Angeles, complete equality in employment has been a mirage for most African Americans. Yet a combination of African American determination, civil rights legislation, and more racially-enlightened workplace policies, have begun to make African American prosperity a reality. Consequently, a great number of African Americans in Los Angeles have achieved financial comfort and independence than anyone in the 1940s could have imagined, yet Covington, Bass, Myrdal, Drake, and Cayton would likely still be troubled by the disparities in income and earnings between African Americans and other ethnic groups.

MAPPING BLACK LOS ANGELES:
NEIGHBORHOOD CHANGE SINCE WORLD WAR II

African American migrants who had read the NAACP's special May 1942 issue of *Crisis* must have been stunned when they arrived in Los Angeles. The special issue—in honor of the organization's national convention in Los Angeles that year—regaled readers with effusive descriptions of the fabled land of "fun and frolic" and photographs of affluent black households and the city's wide, tree-lined streets. "Few can resist," they wrote, the city's "attractive residential districts with California bungalows and more pretentious mansions flanked by spacious lawns, nestled in shrubbery, and shaded by palm trees. Flowers are everywhere." But for the thousands of migrants who crammed into Little Tokyo, the neighborhoods straddling Central Avenue from downtown to Slauson, and the more remote community of Watts, things looked quite different than they had on the pages of *Crisis*.

Prior to World War II, the majority of African Americans in Los Angeles lived in neighborhoods that were thoroughly multiethnic and multiracial. Most African Americans in Los Angeles lived among and interacted with Mexicans, Japanese, Italians, Jews, and the city's small Chinese population. And, as was the case in most of Los Angeles—a vast city with a famously low population density—African Americans tended to live in small houses with yards rather than cramped tenements. Together, these features mitigated some of the harshest features of ghetto life typical in places like Chicago, Detroit, and Harlem. As one researcher for the Los Angeles Urban League observed in 1933: "The presence of other dark skinned people, Mexicans and Japanese, tends to cause the color line to be drawn more finely." The fineness of this line, many blacks believed, diffused anti-black hostility in Los Angeles. In 1928, black sociologist Charles Johnson observed "the focusing of racial interest upon the Oriental has in large measure overlooked the Negro, and the city, accordingly, has been regarded by them, from a distance, as desirable." Put another way, as the editor of the *Los Angeles Liberator* did in 1911, "[blacks in Los Angeles] have no monopoly of the embarrassing attention and prejudice so often directed mainly at them."[15]

This arrangement changed abruptly during World War II. Despite the immense new burden of overpopulation during the war years, the geographic boundaries of black Los Angeles remained largely unchanged at the end of the war, still bound by Slauson on the South, Broadway on the West, and Alameda on the East. As Mexicans, Japanese and Chinese abruptly left the now increasingly black neighborhoods surrounding Central Avenue and Watts, African Americans found their progress arrested at almost every step by whites aroused into frenzy by the large black population influx. Fearing that the racial covenants which still protected them might fail, white neighborhood groups employed dozens of tactics to scare off prospective black homeowners and relentlessly lobbied the mayor, the Board of Supervisors and the Governor to keep their neighborhoods white. As one white Angeleno named William Ardery indelicately complained to Governor Earl Warren in 1946: "I wish that this state was back to where it was before this scum of the nation came here, before the war." "In southern states," Ardery wrote, "they have laws that keep the niggers in their places, but unfortunately for the white race in this state, there is nothing to control them."[16]

In this case, Ardery's racism was matched only by his ignorance. The reason, of course, that African Americans were still contained in roughly the same geographic area as they had been before the war was precisely *because* the law defended the legitimacy of racially restrictive covenants. But the landmark Supreme Court decisions *Shelley* v. *Kraemer* and *Barrows* v. *Jackson*, handed down in 1948 and 1953 respectively, effectively abolished racially restrictive housing covenants. African Americans in Los Angeles had been challenging racial restrictions since at least 1919, when the California Supreme Court ruled in *Los Angeles Investment Co.* v. *Gary* that it was not legal to restrict sales of property based on race. The court, however, upheld the covenanters' right to keep out non-whites.[17] This created the absurd but oft-occurring scenario in which African Americans could buy property in a racially restricted tract, but could not live there. Thus, by the time of the *Shelley* and *Barrows* decisions, frustration among African Americans had reached its threshold. Finally, they were legally allowed to move into mixed-race or white neighborhoods.

Of course, white homeowners rarely made this an easy process. White resistance to black integration in postwar Los Angeles was always swift and sometimes violent. The Los Angeles Urban League identified no fewer than twenty-six *distinct* techniques—including neighbor payoffs, to vandalism, cross burnings, bombings and death threats—used by white homeowners to exclude blacks. White resistance surfaced in the formerly white neighborhoods of South Central, in the more distant San Fernando Valley, and, most stridently, within the ring of white working class suburbs surrounding South Central, including the cities of Inglewood, Hawthorne, Gardena, Compton, Lynwood, Huntington Park, and South Gate. Within the city of Los Angeles, those "transitional" neighborhoods, in which blacks were slowly buying property, became the front line of white resistance. White residents of Leimert Park, for example, vigorously defended segregation. Located on the western edge of South Central Los Angeles, Leimert Park was created by architect Walter Leimert in 1927 as an upscale white bedroom community. But in the late 1940s, African Americans slowly began purchasing homes in and around the area, provoking growing white hostility. For example, shortly after African American John Caldwell, his wife, and his sixteen-year old daughter moved into their home on 543 Sixth Avenue in 1951, they awoke to the crackling sound of a four foot cross burning on their lawn.[18]

But determined African Americans, black real estate brokers and mortgage lending institutions, a select group of housing tract developers, and white, fear-mongering real estate "blockbusters" all contributed to the effort to push African Americans beyond the traditional racial frontiers and into transitional neighborhoods. Individual black families were the most important players in the transformation of LA's postwar racial geography because it was their intense desire to leave South Central (documented in a 1956 National Urban League survey showing that 84% of Los Angeles African Americans would buy or rent in a "nonminority" neighborhood if they could) that drove the engine of integration.[19] Making that dream of neighborhood migration possible were interracial real estate agencies like the South Los Angeles Realty Investment Company, the all black Consolidated Realty Board, and black-owned/black-serving mortgage lenders like Broadway Federal Savings, Liberty Savings and Loan Association, and Golden State Mutual Life Insurance. And a cabal of cynical white real estate brokers "blockbusted" white neighborhoods by scaring white homeowners into "panic selling," and pocketing a huge profit when they resold to eager and solvent African American families. However it happened, one thing was clear: by the late 1950s, middle class African Americans were on the move.

In the 1950s they fanned east to the once lily-white city of Compton, and northwest to West Adams, which already contained a small but prosperous group of African Americans dating back to the 1930s. As Los Angeles's historic black communities spread southward along Central Avenue in the late 1950s and 1960s— eventually connecting to Watts to make an unbroken "black belt" in Southern California—the city's middle class African Americans also moved southward on a parallel track, from West Adams, down Crenshaw to Leimert Park. After the Watts Riots of 1965, both whites and prosperous African Americans fled the central city and the multiracial Crenshaw community became a safe haven for the black middle class. By the late 1960s, the adjacent communities of Baldwin Hills and View Park became the crown jewels of the black community, a position they still hold today. Baldwin Hills' expansive easterly views, its large homes, and its superior public schools have been clear badges of middle class success among African Americans in Los Angeles. The luster of the Crenshaw business district faded considerably in the 1980s, battered as much

African American families were not welcome in many areas of LA in the 1950s

of South Los Angeles was by sickening gang violence, but since the 1992 riots it is, by all accounts, on the rebound, with a Wal-Mart and an impressive Magic Johnson theater complex anchoring the local economy.

Most African Americans in Southern California, however, have not lived in Baldwin Hills, nor have they lived in West Adams. Since World War II, the vast majority have lived in the historic South Central area, an area that became increasingly isolated and poor beginning in the 1960s. Communities that were once multiracial became solidly black overnight, as Mexicans parlayed their "closer to white" status into suburban opportunities still closed to blacks. Census tract figures reveal a steep decline in Mexican-immigrant and Mexican American population of South Central in the three decades after World War II. For example, at the outbreak of World War II, blacks, Mexicans, and whites represented approximately equal proportions of the Watts community. However, by 1958, blacks represented 95% of the Watts population. Similarly in 1940, the multiracial neighborhood of Avalon, also known as "the Eastside", was about 60% black, the remaining population comprised of Mexican immigrants, Mexican Americans, and whites. By 1960, Avalon was 95% black.[20]

The 1965 Watts Riots further propelled non-blacks, and, as we saw above, much of the African American middle class, out of South Central. The disappearance of the community's business and professional elite, coupled with disappearance of jobs due to deindustrialization contributed mightily to the development of a hard-core "ghetto" in what had once been a hopeful community. Communities like Willowbrook—which had never been model of civic organization—became symbols of the worst sort of racialized blight: unplanned, littered with debris, saturated by liquid industrial runoff, plagued by rodents, and largely invisible to the city government. It was the deplorable conditions in these neighborhoods, the sense of extreme isolation and alienation, and the justified frustration with continuous harassment and violence

Shades of L.A. Archives, Los Angeles Public Library

Children of diverse ethnicity at the Jordan Downs Housing Project in Watts, 1957. White and Mexican families moved out in the 1950s and public housing became mostly black in the 1960s

from local law enforcement agencies, that sparked the bloody melee of 1965 which left at least 34 dead and permanently etched the "Watts" in the minds of a jittery white public.

That jitteriness was again awakened in April of 1992, following the acquittal of the four white police officers who savagely beat black motorist Rodney King. As scenes of looting and killing flashed across television screens worldwide, Angelenos outside of South Central asked "how?", "why?" Yet from within South Central, the devastating riots of 1992 seemed like a natural, even organic, response to the mounting frustration that was plainly visible on the streets. Triggered by the acquittal, the roots of the riot were far deeper. Though they arguably stretched back to the failed promises of the 1960s, they were more immediately connected to the 1980s, a brutal decade during which the California Dream finally died for thousands of African Americans in Los Angeles.

During that decade, the physical deterioration of the poorer black neighborhoods accelerated, and poverty, crime, and social isolation intensified. Two epidemics, crack cocaine addiction and AIDS, ravaged the community. And there was also a deepening distrust of Southern California law enforcement agencies and the legal system in general. For good reason: Between 1975 and 1982, one study found, 16 people died as a result of LAPD and Sheriff's officers applying "choke holds" to suspects: 12 of the 16 were black. Equally shocking, and more directly related to the tension leading up the 1992 riots, was the verdict in the Latasha Harlins case. In March of 1991, less than two weeks after Rodney King was beaten on television, a Korean liquor store owner named Soon Ja Du shot Latasha Harlins, an African American high school freshman, in the back of the head, ostensibly because of a squabble over a $1.79 bottle of orange juice. Judge Joyce Karlin sentenced Mrs. Du to a paltry 5 years of probation and she ultimately served only 6 months of community service. For a goodly number of participants in the 1992 riots, the grim toll of destruction—58 deaths, 2500 injuries, and almost $1 billion in property damage and loss—seemed like appropriate retaliation against a city that appeared to only notice them when they rioted. [21]

As always, however, the majority of African Americans continued to live their daily lives, still finding dignity in their everyday affairs

California national guardsmen restored order in Watts after six days of rioting in August, 1965.
The riot left thirty-four, mostly African Americans, dead, 1,032 wounded and 3,952 arrested

despite the troubled times. Far more enduring than the 1992 riot were the demographic changes taking place under their feet. Most significantly, they began to witness a change in the very thing that gave South Central its identity, its racial composition. Beginning first slowly and then accelerating in the late 1980s and 1990s, Latinos began reclaiming South Central. Of course, these were not the upwardly mobile Mexican Americans who left South Central in the 1960s for neighboring working class suburbs. These, rather, were a diverse lot of Latin Americans, disparate in their national origins but united in their poverty and their determination. Over the last decade, Latinos have been reinvigorating South Central, starting the same sorts of small family businesses that African Americans had before the Watts Riot, and drawing the attention of investors and large retailers who see the untapped potential of what they call the "inner city market."

However, the Latin Americanization of South Central is not without its problems. Many black residents view the transformation of their historic community with considerable ambivalence and often resentment. Having been forced by law into segregated communities during the first half of the twentieth century, blacks made the best of their predicament by investing their time, energy, and their earnings to improve their neighborhoods, their schools, and their institutions. Many within the South Central have retained an unshakable sense of proprietorship over the community, long after the disappearance of *de jure* housing segregation and long after many of their black neighbors have left. But it seems likely that either African American reticence will fade away from South Central, or African Americans will. During the 1990s the Latino population of South Central increased by approximately 78,000 while the black population decreased by almost 70,000. Remarkably, the Census of 2000 revealed that the Latino population of South Central (58%) finally outnumbered the black population (40%).[22]

FROM CIVIL RIGHTS POLITICS TO THE POLITICS OF ETHNIC COMPETITION

Essential to the African American quest for dignity in Los Angeles has been the quest for equal political representation. The simple act of leaving the South had been an important step in that direction: consider that poll-taxes, voter fraud, intimidation, and physical violence rendered most African Americans' technical "right to vote" meaningless in all but the South's biggest cities. For example, African Americans from Shreveport—a small lumber town in northwestern Louisiana from which many African American migrants came in the 1940s and 1950s—remembered the legacy of violence that accompanied attempts to vote. They were raised to know the story of the single black man who dared to vote Republican during Reconstruction and was swiftly executed with impunity. And as children, they watched in horror as the town became a haven for the Ku Klux Klan and as their parish led the state in lynchings. As one NAACP official succinctly put it 1923, "This place is one of the most intolerant in the whole Southland." This brutal campaign almost completely suppressed the black vote, effectively rendering meaningless the 14th and 15th amendments to the United States Constitution.[23]

And then there was Los Angeles, with free and fair elections, and no recent history of voter intimidation. Newly arrived African

American migrants began to register *en masse*. "One thing is certain," African American civil rights and labor leader Revels Cayton said in 1944, "the thousands of Negroes who have come west intend to remain. They are determined to stay, become integrated in their communities and attain full citizenship." Cayton was remarkably prescient: African American migrants, even those voting for the first time, were not content simply to vote. Almost immediately, they asserted their rights to have equal representation and, more pointedly, black candidates. But here, the bright light of Los Angeles democracy seemed a bit dimmer. With the exception of Augustus Hawkins, the light-skinned Louisiana migrant from the multiracial Sixty Second district who ousted African American Fred Roberts in 1934 to become the only African American in the California State Assembly, African Americans in Los Angeles had no elected black leaders. And Hawkins, ambitious though he was, nonetheless lacked the support of fellow Democrats in the capitol and remained powerless to substantively change the conditions on Central Avenue.[24]

Since the 1920s, when African Americans began gaining political power in northern metropolises like Chicago and New York, African Americans in Los Angeles were frustrated by the city's stubborn resistance to African American representation. This was largely a function of the city's unusually large councilmanic districts, the vast size of which eliminated the chance of black near-majorities. In striking contrast to cities like New York and Chicago, both of which were divided by as many as fifty small ward boundaries, Los Angeles only had 15 council districts. Even in a town with district elections, it was hard to get councilmen to listen to the relatively small black population. The large size of the city's districts also made them easily susceptible to racially gerrymandering, a practice which, while never documented, was nonetheless widely recognized in the black community. Until the size of the black population increased, blacks would have to rely on non-black candidates to adequately represent their interests, a dubious arrangement anywhere in the United States before World War II.[25]

During World War II, both Mayor Fletcher Bowron and the County Board of Supervisors became more responsive to the demands of the vastly expanded black community. The Mayor appointed a number of prominent African Americans to blue-ribbon committees and consistently supported the expansion of both public and affordable private, housing. Most intimately connected to the African American community of Los Angeles in the postwar years was Kenneth Hahn, who represented a portion of South Central on the city council from 1947 to 1952 and then continued on County Board of Supervisors until his death in 1997. A white native of South Central, Hahn was one of the few white residents who never left his neighborhood. During his term on the city council, Hahn had worked closely with *Sentinel* editor Leon Washington to identify and fix specific problems faced by black residents of his district. As a Supervisor, Hahn kept those issues close to him, consistently advocating rent control, urban renewal, publicly subsidized childcare, and affirmative action hiring policies. On the Board of Supervisors, Hahn found an ally in fellow supervisor John Anson Ford, a member and staunch advocate for the Los Angeles County Commission on Human Relations. Although they met with bitter resistance, Both Ford and Hahn pushed for the creation of Fair Employment Practices Committees at the city and county levels. Finally, Mexican American councilman Edward Roybal ran for the 9th district—which included parts of Boyle Heights, downtown, Chinatown and Little Tokyo, and Central Avenue—in 1949, working closely with the NAACP for the desegregation of the Fire Department and a number of other critical issues.[26]

Grateful for the efforts of Roybal, Hahn, and Ford on their behalf, African Americans in Los Angeles nonetheless came to view the lack of black representation as intolerable. Thus, in the early 1950s, a group of politically active African Americans met in what became known as the Democratic Minority Conference. The founding members of the organization included well-respected LAPD sergeant Tom Bradley, Vaino Spencer, one of Southwest Law College's first black female graduates, attorney Leo Brantin, and Gilbert Lindsay, a former janitor from Mississippi who became Kenneth Hahn's deputy on the County Board of Supervisors. Members of the Democratic Minority Council had grown weary of the Democratic Party's emphasis on "equal opportunity," pushing instead for affirmative action. They called for community-wide support for black candidates, increased voter registration, and district reapportionment based on race. As one member stated:

> We're beginning to feel that this attitude among white liberals is never
> going to get us anywhere and what we need is not opportunity but power.
> The only way we're going to get that is by drawing the district lines
> to give it to us. You're never going to have a Negro elected anywhere
> from a district that isn't all-Negro. We're just kidding ourselves if we
> think we can get it on any other basis.[27]

Thus, members cultivated black political participation by
canvassing neighborhoods and raising money through church
bazaars, eventually building a membership of over 600. They also
worked in conjunction with the Committee for Representative
Government, led by Leon Washington, which sought two
Congressional seats and four state assembly seats for black Los
Angeles.[28]

Despite being dogged by reapportionment in the mid-1950s, the
Democratic Minortiy Council began to show results by the time
of the 1963 City Council election, which forever changed the face
of local politics in Los Angeles. Shortly before the elections, the
councilman for the tenth district vacated his post, leaving it open
for an interim appointment by the city council. Mayor Sam Yorty
and Roybal urged the council to select a black representative,
and they ultimately appointed Democratic Minority Conference
member Gilbert Lindsay. The popular police-officer turned lawyer
Tom Bradley won in the 10th district and newcomer Billy Mills
won the 8th. Remarkably, 3 of the Los Angeles's 15 council districts
now had African American representatives. No less impressive, the
once staunchly white City of Compton elected its first black city
councilman, an automobile sales manager, Douglas Dollarhide, in
the same year.[29]

These new black leaders not only capably dealt with mundane
issues—like getting traffic lights installed in many of South
Central's most dangerous intersections—but also championed
then-radical agendas like complete school desegregation. Tom
Bradley, Douglas Dollarhide, Gilbert Lindsay and others put
their political careers on the line in 1963 to push for complete
school desegregation under the banner of the United Civil Rights
Council (UCRC). The most dramatic display of UCRC's public
profile was the Freedom March of 1963, organized to protest

continuing school segregation. The front page of the *Los Angeles Times* carried the story under the headline, "L.A. Declared Target for Total Integration." "We are not just asking for a small specific adjustment," influential pastor Maurice Dawkins told the *Times*, "but a total community integration."[30]

Clearly, the most memorable black political victory, however, was the 1973 mayoral election of Tom Bradley. Propelled by the alliance he had developed with the city's liberal Jewish community in his failed 1969 bid for mayor, Bradley returned to defeat Yorty in 1973. Having been entirely shunned from local politics until a decade earlier, African Americans derived great psychological satisfaction from the knowledge that one of their own was now the mayor of a city of almost 3 million. And there were hopeful signs that Bradley, who campaigned as a liberal reformer, could make concrete improvements in city hall. Bradley appointed numerous minorities to his administration, implemented successful Affirmative Action programs in city hiring, and attempted to reign in the LAPD by appointing aggressive civil rights advocates to the Police Commission. Bradley forced the LAPD to eliminate the use of the highly controversial choke hold and limited the department's rampant intelligence-gathering program. Ultimately, however, police reforms under the Bradley administration were quite modest compared to those established in other cities: Los Angeles lacked a civilian review board and the number of police shootings barely changed at all under Bradley's tenure. More troubling for liberal critics was Bradley's deference to downtown business interests in his assignment of urban redevelopment funds. In his unswerving commitment to make Los Angeles a "World Class City," Bradley diverted resources toward downtown redevelopment and away from projects aimed at expanding the affordable housing stock in the city or in improving infrastructure in blighted neighborhoods.[31]

Since the beginning of the Bradley era, African Americans have come to occupy dozens of important posts in Los Angeles city government from the City Council to the Chief of Police. But the simple attainment of these posts, as Bernard Parks' failed bid for reappointment to Chief of Police in 2002 revealed, has not guaranteed smooth sailing. Appointed in 1997, Parks road in on a wave of good feeling, and black voters demonstrated their optimism about City Hall when they helped elect James Hahn—son of the revered County Supervisor from South Central Kenneth Hahn—in 2001. But the honeymoon was short-lived: Dogged by the high profile Rampart police corruption scandal, and citing rising crime, low officer morale, and departmental understaffing, Hahn repudiated Parks' leadership and sought his replacement. As an editorialist for the *Sentinel*, LA's largest and oldest black newspaper, astutely observed:

> The Hahn/Parks dispute represented a traditional black leadership model; African American leaders supported Hahn without really knowing his position regarding Chief Parks and without extracting any specific commitments from him. Hahn's emphatic, high-profile opposition to Parks' reappointment not only shocked black leaders, but exposed their vulnerability and obvious lack of a contingency plan.[32]

The lack of a "contingency plan" has been further complicated by the changing demographics of South Central. The Latin Americanization of South Central, coupled with increased Asian immigration citywide, has created new challenges to traditional black politics in Los Angeles. As Raphael Sonenshein has explained, the black political clout of the Bradley years has steadily eroded over the last decade. Not only has the coalition between white liberals and African Americans in the city suffered in the wake of the 1992 Riots and the infamous O.J. Simpson case, but blacks are losing their place as the most important political minority. Sonenshein argues that there are a growing number of interest conflicts between blacks, Latinos, Asian-Americans and white liberals which threaten black hegemony in the realm of minority politics. As immigration continues, California's African Americans will clearly have to forge creative new political alliances, not an easy task for a group that fought so long to elect their own representatives to address their specific community's needs.

The challenge of this new political milieu has been most evident in Compton, once a bastion of black middle class success and what political scientist Regina Freer has called the "vanguard of black empowerment," and now a majority Latino community. Consequently, the predominantly African American leadership in city government has tended to view "the assertion of Latino demands as a threat to not only their own individual power, but more broadly as threats to African American political empowerment." And as the Latino population surges and makes more demands, the results have become more ironic. For example, in the late 1980s, when Latinos in Compton demanded that the city adopt an affirmative action program to expand municipal employment opportunities for Latinos, African American city leaders flatly rejected the plan, disingenuously arguing that the city's existing affirmative action policy, having incorporated blacks, sufficiently dealt with "minorities." "We do not need affirmative action," John Steward, an African American school board trustee clarified, "the majority of employees are minority." Steward went on to define affirmative action as a form of reparations to black Americans. It was not, he clarified, "based on going back and forth across the border 10 or 15 times a year." The African American response to Latino demands in Compton has dishonored the memory of the region's mid-twentieth century black activists, who sought equal opportunity, not political monopoly and racial exclusionism.[33]

THE END OF AN ERA? THE BEGINNING OF A NEW?

On Wednesday, April 9th, 2003, South Central disappeared. On that day, the Los Angeles City Council voted unanimously to replace "South-Central Los Angeles" with "South Los Angeles" on all city documents and signs. The council was responding to the proposal of a small group of South Central residents led by Helen Johnson, a 72-year-old resident of the historic black community, who wanted to shake off a term that had become virtually synonymous with racial tension, drugs, and gang violence. Angelenos were generally of two minds about the change. For some, it was a long overdue declaration of disassociation from a dark term. Councilwoman Janice Hahn, for example, celebrated the community's detachment from the "false identity" of "South-Central." "This has been a crime," Hahn said, "for many neighborhoods and many communities who have been lumped together under the mostly derogatory term of South-Central Los Angeles." Others were skeptical of the change, arguing somewhat predictably, as numerous editorialists did, that changing the name would not solve the area's problems.[34]

But both positions failed to recognize one salient fact: that changing the name, regardless of its impact on perceptions and realities of the community, was an historically honest act, revealing just how far African Americans had come since the 1940s. Although most Angelenos think that the term South Central refers to the community's general geographic position in the city, it is, in fact, a reference to the once thriving business district on South Central Avenue. When that once-proud business district began to decline in the 1960s, it was both a grim reminder of the deepening poverty of one stratum of the population and a cheerful sign that middle class African Americans and business owners could now move beyond the historic racial borders of the city. Today, "the Avenue", as it was once known, is really *la Avenida*, home to hundreds of small Latino businesses and many scruffy corners. But if the residents of South Los Angeles have shed the name—now little more than an historic relic—they have not shed their continuing quest for dignity in the City of Promise.

NOTES

[1] Sylvester Gibbs, interviewed by author, 2 June 1998. A transcript of this and other interviews that I conducted for *L.A. City Limits*, was donated to the Southern California Library for Social Studies and Research, Los Angeles, California.

[2] On early black Los Angeles, see Douglas Flamming, *Bound For Freedom: Black Los Angeles in Jim Crow America* (Berkeley: University of California Press, 2005); Lawrence B. De Graaf, "The City of Black Angels: Emergence of the Los Angeles Ghetto, 1890-1930." *Pacific Historical Review* 39 (August 1970): 323-352; and various essays in Lawrence B. De Graaf, Kevin Mulroy, and Quintard Taylor, eds. *Seeking El Dorado: African Americas in California* (Seattle: University of Washington Press, 2001).

[3] On the growth of Los Angeles in the 1920s, see Tom Sitton and William Deverell, *Metropolis in the Making: Los Angeles in the 1920s* (Berkeley: University of California Press, 2001).

[4] Chester Himes, *The Quality of Hurt: The Autobiography of Chester Himes, Volume I* (New York: Thunder's Mouth Press, 1971), 74.

[5] Gilbert Osofsky, *Harlem: The Making of a Ghetto—Negro New York, 1890-1930* (New York: Harper and Row, 1968), 11.

[6] The term "South Central"—which I use interchangeably with "South Los Angeles"—describes the broad geographic area of Los Angeles that became increasingly black between the 1940s and the 1970s, the approximate

boundaries of which were Exposition/Jefferson on the North, Alameda on the East, Rosecrans Blvd. on the South, and Crenshaw on the West. Unless otherwise stated, neighborhood data is drawn from the following sources: U. S. Bureau of the Census, *1940: Population and Housing, Statistics for Census Tracts, Los Angeles-Long Beach, Calif.* (Washington: GPO, 1942); *1950: Census Tract Statistics, Los Angeles, California and Adjacent Area, Selected Population and Housing Characteristics* (Washington: GPO, 1952); *1960: Census Tracts, Los Angeles-Long Beach, Calif., Standard Metropolitan Statistical Area* (Washington: GPO, 1962.

[7] For an example of preference for Mexicans, see *California Eagle,* 30 October 1931; Charles Johnson, "Industrial Survey of the Negro Population in Los Angeles, California, Made by the Department of Research and Investigations of the National Urban League" (1926), 20, 23, 28, 32, 55. See also, James M. Ervin, *The Participation of the Negro in the Community Life of Los Angeles* (M.A. thesis, University of Southern California, 1931), 18. On aircraft employment, see "Half a Million Workers," *Fortune* 23 (March 1943), 98. Depression unemployment figures from, Leonard Leader, *Los Angeles and the Great Depression* (New York: Garland, 1991), 6,11,14.

[8] "Los Angeles Biennial Report of the Executive Director," 1 March, 1943, pg. 12, box 19, National Urban League Papers, Library of Congress, Washington, D.C.

[9] Bass quote from the front page of *California Eagle,* 16 July 1942. Survey from Lawrence de Graaf and Quintard Taylor, "Introduction: African Americans in California History, California in African American History," in eds. de Graaf, Mulroy, Taylor, *Seeking El Dorado,* 33.

[10] Unless otherwise stated, author's employment calculations are based on the following documents from the U.S. Bureau of the Census: *Sixteenth Census of the United States: 1940, Population vol. 3, The Labor Force, pt. 2, Alabama-Indiana* (Washington, DC: GPO, 1943), 244-250; *Census of Population: 1950, vol. 2, Characteristics of Population, pt. 5, California* (Washington D.C.: GPO, 1952), 350-351; *Census of the Population, 1960, vol. 1, Characteristics of the Population, pt. 6, California* (Washington, D.C.: GPO, 1963), 705-707.

[11] On racial discrimination in Los Angeles automobile plants, see Myrna Cherkoss Donahoe, *Resolving Discriminatory Practices Against Minorities and Women in Steel and Auto: Los Angeles, California, 1936-1982* (Los Angeles: Center for Labor Research and Education, Institute of Industrial Relations, University of California, Los Angeles, 1991).

[12] *Charles H. Bratton, et al v. Bethlehem Steel Corporation and Local 1845 United Steel Workers of America,* 649 F. 2d 658.

[13] On American deindustrialization in general, see Barry Bluestone and Bennet Harrison, *The Deindustrialization of America: Plant Closings, Community Abandonment, and the Dismantling of Basic Industry* (New York: Basic Books, 1982). On the selective deindustrialization of Los Angeles, see

Edward Soja, Rebecca Morales, and Goetz Wolff, "Urban Restructuring: An Analysis of Social and Spatial Change in Los Angeles." *Economic Geography* 59 (1983): 195-230. On its impact on the Los Angeles black community, see California Senate, Committee on Industrial Relations, *In the Matter of Senate Bill 1494, Plant Closures* (Sacramento, 1980), 124-126.

[14] David M. Grant, Melvin L. Oliver, and Angela D. James, "African Americans: Social and Economic Bifurcation," in ed. Roger Waldinger and Mehdi Bozorgmehr, *Ethnic Los Angeles* (New York: Russell Sage Foundation, 1996) 382, 384. "Blacks Still Trail in Wages," The Sacramento Bee, 30 April 1995, A7.

[15] Charles S. Johnson, "Negro Workers in Los Angeles Industries," *Opportunity* (August 1928), 234. *Los Angeles Liberator*, 21 April 1911, as cited in Bunche, "A Past Not Necessarily Prologue," 104.

[16] See, Los Angeles City Planning Commission, "Distribution of Negroes: U.S. Census Data, 1940," "Distribution of Negroes: U.S. Census Data, 1946," in box 104, National Urban League Papers, Library of Congress; William C. Ardery, to Governor Earl Warren, 17 July 1946, F3640:3677, Earl Warren Papers, California State Archive, Sacramento, California.

[17] D.O. McGovney, "Racial Residential Segregation by State Court Enforcement of Restrictive Agreement, Covenants, or Conditions in Deeds is Unconstitutional," *California Law Review* 33 (1945), 8.

[18] *Hearings Before the United States Commission on Civil Rights: Hearings Held in Los Angeles and San Francisco, January 25-28, 1960* (Washington: Government Printing Office, 1960), 158-159. *Daily Peoples' World*, 7 Sept. 1951; 4 Oct. 1951.

[19] *Hearings Before the United States Commission on Civil Rights* (Washington: GPO, 1960), 203

[20] South Central Area Welfare Planning Council, *Watts Area Study: 1959*. The Avalon neighborhood was bound by Main on the west, Jefferson north, Alameda on the east and Slauson on the south.

[21] James H. Johnson Jr. and Walter C. Farrell Jr., "The Fire This Time: The Genesis of the Los Angeles Rebellion of 1992," in ed. John Charles Boger and Judith Welch Wegner, *Race, Poverty, and American Cities* (Chapel Hill: University of North Carolina Press, 1996): 166-185. See also, James H. Johnson, Jr., Walter C. Farrell Jr. and Melvin L. Oliver, "Seeds of the Los Angeles Rebellion of 1992" *International Journal of Urban and Regional Research*, 17, 1: 115-118; Allen J. Scott and E. Richard Brown, *South-Central Los Angeles: Anatomy of an Urban Crisis* (Los Angeles: Lewis Center for Regional Policy Studies, University of California, Los Angeles, 1993); Brenda Stevenson, "Latasha Harlins, Soon Ja Du, and Joyce Karlin: A Case Study of Multicultural Female Violence and Justice on the Urban Frontier," *Journal of African American History* 89 (Spring 2004): 152-176.

[22] See the following reports by Dowell Myers, both published by the Population Dynamics Research Group, School of Policy, Planning, and Development, University of Southern California, Los Angeles: "Special

Report: Demographic and Housing Transitions in South Central Los
Angeles, 1990 to 2000" (22 April 2002) and "Actual Percentage Growth
for Non-Hispanic Blacks by County, 1990-2000" (April 2001).

[23] Adam Fairclough, *Race and Democracy: The Civil Rights Struggle in
Louisiana, 1915-1972* (Athens: University of Georgia Press, 1995), 8.

[24] Cayton quote from *Chicago Defender*, 23 September 1944; On Augustus
Hawkins, see Douglas Flamming, "Becoming Democrats: Liberal Politics
and the African American Community in Los Angeles, 1930-1965," in
Seeking El Dorado, 286-287. For a list of bills proposed by assemblyman
Hawkins, see "Assembly Bills," box 99, folder 1, Augustus Hawkins
Papers, Department of Special Collections, University Research Library,
University of California, Los Angeles.

[25] On suspected gerrymandering, see *California Eagle*, 10 November 1960; On
comparisons between black politics in Los Angeles and other cities see,
James Q. Wilson, *Negro Politics: The Search for Leadership* (Glencoe, Ill.:
Free Press, 1960); *The Amateur Democrat: Club Politics in Three Cities*
(Chicago: University of Chicago Press, 1962).

[26] On Hahn's record, see: "Newsclippings," box 392, Kenneth Hahn Papers,
Huntington Library, San Marino, California. On Fire department see
California Eagle, 24 Dec. 1953. See Katherine Underwood, "Pioneering
Minority Representation: Edward Roybal and the Los Angeles City
Council, 1949-1962," *Pacific Historical Review* 66 (August, 1997): 399-425.

[27] James Q. Wilson, *The Amateur Democrat: Club Politics in Three Cities*
(Chicago: University of Chicago Press, 1962), 283.

[28] Wendell Green, "Join the Fight for Our New Frontiers: 2 Negro
Congressmen, 4 Negro Assemblymen: A Position paper given to the
Interim Committee on Elections and Reapportionment, December 17,
1960," NAACP, West Coast Region Papers, Bancroft Library, UC Berkeley.

[29] Steven V. Roberts, "Compton, Calif., 65% Negro, Believes in Integration
and in Peaceful Change," *New York Times*, 8 June 1969, 65.

[30] "L.A. Declared Target for Total Integration," *Los Angeles Times*, 31 May
1963, 1.

[31] Raphael J. Sonenshein, Politics *in Black and White: Race and Power in Los
Angeles* (Princeton: Princeton University Press, 1993), 139-175, 159-161.

[32] Larry Aubry, "Black Leadership: Still Navigating a Turbulent Future,"
Sentinel, Dec 11-17, 2003, pg. A7.

[33] Regina Freer, "Black Brown Cities: Black Urban Regimes and the Challenge
of Changing Demographics," presented at the Annual Meeting of the
Western Political Science Association, Denver, Colorado, March 27-29,
2003.

[34] Matea Gold and Greg Braxton, "Considering South-Central By Another
Name," *Los Angeles Times*, 10 April 2003, B3; Roy Rivenburg, "As If: A
Spin By Any Other Name...." *Los Angeles Times*, 14 April 2003, E13;
"What's in a Name? South Los Angeles Will Still Be South Central,"
Daily News, 11 April 2003, N14.

Chapter 6

BEHIND THE SHIELD
Social Discontent and the
Los Angeles Police Since 1950

Martin Schiesl

F ew public agencies have received more attention and criticism in the development of Los Angeles since 1950 than has the Los Angeles Police Department. Several television series over the years, such as *Dragnet, Adam-12*, and *Police Story*, have generally portrayed the LAPD as a peaceful and impartial protector of law and order in the city. The actual conduct and performance of the department, however, rarely conformed to this positive image. Operating in periods of extensive social and political change, the LAPD advanced a very partisan system of law enforcement which, while serving well the needs of the white population, caused much discomfort and suffering for the city's minority groups. The department also showed little tolerance for political activism and organized dissent. Various community leaders and organizations strongly protested against these conditions and sought to drastically change the policies and practices of the LAPD. This led to much controversy and conflict over questions of the use of force, police accountability, citizen control, and preservation of fundamental individual liberties. Resolving these critical issues led eventually to the enactment of major police reforms designed to guarantee that law enforcement was carried out in an impartial and fair manner for all residents of Los Angeles.

The LAPD experienced major changes in policy and procedure under William H. Parker. Parker joined the LAPD in 1927, attained the rank of captain in 1939, moved up to the position of inspector in 1947, and won promotion to deputy chief two years later. The Police Commission appointed him to chief's post in the summer of 1950.[1] He launched a tough selection and training program which included comprehensive examinations and a long probation period, placed special emphasis on science and technology in crime prevention, and created a planning and research division to analyze crime patterns and department resources. Parker relied heavily on the managerial philosophy of Orlando W. Wilson, a widely respected police administrator and scholar. Wilson advocated that police departments be arranged along semimilitary lines so as to maintain strict command and control. Communication and responsibility flowed up and down the organization, but all lines eventually led back to Parker, who spelled out the duties of each administrative level and defined the limits of authority and discretion. The result was a highly centralized, impersonal, and very arrest-conscious department.[2]

Such reform brought a different kind of law enforcement. In the 1940s the police had patrolled city streets on foot and knew personally the residents of the area. They developed neighborhood connections and often used selective judgment in making arrests. Parker took the police off the beat, put them in radio-equipped cars, and ordered around the clock surveillance to discourage criminal activity. He also insisted that all laws be strictly enforced and without exception.[3] These "preventive" patrols seldom caused problems in white communities; few of the residents used the streets in ways that aroused police suspicion. In black neighborhoods, where teenagers and young adults spent a good deal of their time on the streets, preventive patrols meant continual harassment and intimidation. Also, most policemen were white and came from working-class backgrounds that had fostered the belief of racial supremacy. They rarely distinguished between innocent and troublesome residents and treated most ghetto dwellers as potential criminals. Many middle-income adults were often stopped for interrogation and sometimes rousted because their prosperous appearance led the officers to suspect that they might be engaged in bookmaking and drug trafficking.[4]

More disturbing were incidents of physical brutality. "The technique is the same," Everette R. Porter, a member of the legal redress committee of the National Association for the Advancement of Colored People (NAACP), noted. "After a citizen has been brutally beaten by the policemen, they book him on some trumped up charge, usually drunkenness and resisting arrest."[5] Similar abuse was occasionally meted out to Mexican American residents. Especially nasty was the "Bloody Christmas" incident in December 1951. Two patrolmen entered a downtown bar to break up a brawl and were attacked by several patrons, one so badly that he had to be taken to the hospital. Several officers arrived later, arrested seven young Chicanos, and took them to Central Station where the police were celebrating Christmas Eve. A rumor spread through the station that the hospitalized officer was going to lose an eye. Angry and drunk policemen hauled the boys out of their cells and beat them viciously. The assault prompted Mexican American councilman Edward Roybal to charge the LAPD with systematic brutality. While Chief Parker denied the allegation, some 300 officers were interrogated, with 200 taking lie detector tests. Parker turned over their testimony to a police board of rights and the county grand jury. Eight officers were indicted, two others were dropped from the force, and another thirty-six received official reprimands.[6]

These actions, however, did little to discourage the mistreatment of minority citizens. Jimmy Witherspoon, a famous blues singer, was stopped by two officers for drunk driving in early 1952. He asked them for a sobriety test but instead they handcuffed the singer, threw him into their car, and pounded him in the stomach and the knees.[7] The police commission decided to hold a public hearing on law enforcement in nonwhite neighborhoods. "We suspect that there are altogether too many police officers who are persuaded that some groups in Los Angeles must be kept in line," the committee of the Los Angeles County Conference on Community Relations, an organization representing different ethnic groups, churches, and various civic associations, bluntly observed, "and that some others believe that the people of certain groups ought to be struck regularly, like gangs." Complaints about

such behavior brought little redress. The committee reported that
the department's internal affairs division did not allow complainants
to have counsel and usually interrogated them in an antagonistic
manner. It recommended that one police commissioner be present
at every division hearing to ensure fair and objective review of
citizen complaints and proposed the establishment of police-citizen
committees in nonwhite neighborhoods.[8]

None of this won support from Chief Parker who believed that
effective law enforcement in the ghetto required a concentration
of police power to cope with high levels of criminal activity. Police
work in a big city, Parker told a meeting of the National Council
of Christians and Jews in 1955, was heaviest in minority areas
because "certain racial groups" accounted for a "disproportionate
share" of the total crimes. "In deploying to suppress crime, we
[LAPD] are not interested in why a certain group tends toward
crime, we are interested in maintaining order," stated Parker.[9]
Many patrol officers, however, acted like an occupation army.
Street gang members experienced much abuse. One member of
the Businessmen recalled that the police often used racial slurs
and sometimes put a pistol to his head to exact compliance. If
arrested, he and his comrades would be taken to damp cells with
little ventilation and no showers.[10]

Black residents also suffered unprovoked police assaults. In 1957
Hosie Tenner and his pregnant wife, along with some other people,
left the home of a friend and stopped on their way to their cars
to watch two officers cite a motorist for a traffic violation. As the
cops were leaving the scene, someone in the group made critical
remarks. The police returned and placed Tenner under arrest. When
his wife protested that he was merely an on-looker and had not
said anything, she was knocked to the ground and later suffered
a miscarriage. The NAACP held a mass meeting to focus critical
attention on law enforcement in the ghetto. Several people described
their experiences as victims of police harassment and brutality.
Reverend Maurice A. Dawkins, local NAACP president, told the
audience that it was time to "get off the dime and get a plan to change
police practices in Los Angeles."[11] The police commission could do
little to help the NAACP, however. It did not have the authority to
investigate personnel matters believed to be discriminatory.

Police conduct remained a hot public issue. In the 1961 mayoral election, Samuel Yorty, former member of the state legislature and the U.S. House of Representatives, charged that Mayor Norris Poulson was a tool of downtown business elites and that Chief Parker and the police commission were insensitive to minority group problems. He promised the city's nonwhite citizens a change in police management. Shortly before the election, a riot involving 75 policemen and 200 black teenagers took place at Griffith Park and ended with four policemen injured and three blacks arrested. The African American community saw the disturbance as one more example of police abuse and their votes, in combination with a large turnout in the East Los Angeles barrio, gave Yorty a comfortable victory.[12] Seeking to give Chief Parker "a lot of schooling" in police-minority relations, he appointed a black attorney, a Mexican American physician, and a professor of public administration from the University of Southern California to the police commission. The commissioners respected Parker, apart from his insensitivity to racial issues, and did not want a major confrontation over the character of local policing.[13]

Such deference gave Parker little incentive to change the department's policies toward black residents. He stepped up patrols in the ghetto to undermine the growing influence of militant groups who he saw, without any real evidence, as enemies of the state. His major target was the local Black Muslim sect that advocated black pride and black power through the development of autonomous institutions, such as businesses, churches, and schools. It also stressed paramilitary training and threatened armed resistance to police repression. An opportunity for the latter came tragically in April of 1962. Several patrolmen stopped two burglary suspects near the Muslim Temple, exchanged gunfire with some militants, and then entered the building, shooting wildly. When the smoke cleared, one black was dead, another was permanently disabled, and four others were seriously wounded.[14]

The shootout aroused Malcolm X, a fiery Muslim preacher, who accused the police of murder and claimed that Parker was fostering racial hatred. The United Clergymen of Central Los Angeles called Parker "anti-Negro" and requested an independent civilian review board. They also asked that Mayor Yorty personally investigate the complaints of black residents against certain patrol officers. He turned down their request, blamed Black Muslims and subversive groups for the brutality charges, and saw publicizing minority grievances as a communist plot to "secure endless publicity for every charge brought against the police department, no matter how frivolous."[15]

The California Advisory Committee to the U.S. Civil Rights Commission visited Los Angeles in the fall of 1962 to investigate law enforcement practices in nonwhite communities. Chief Parker assured the committee that no "difficult problem" existed between his officers and minority residents. Several civil rights activists, however, provided the committee with evidence of much discriminatory law enforcement in the ghetto and in local barrios. The police often scolded residents with discourteous and derogatory language, arrested blacks and Mexican Americans for minor offenses (ignored when committed by white people), and used excessive force in a large number of arrests.[16]

Complaints about these practices seldom found redress. "When I first became involved in police brutality cases in Los Angeles in the mid-1960s, it often was a pretty lonely fight," noted civil rights attorney Johnnie Cochran recalled. "Just a victim and his family, me, and sometimes a few community activists against an entrenched bureaucracy confident the police could do no wrong."[17] The local chapter of the American Civil Liberties Union (ACLU) reported that the internal affairs division continued to be unsympathetic to stories of racial abuse, harassed minority citizens at their homes and jobs, and threatened them with criminal prosecution if their complaints were not sustained.[18]

In the spring of 1963, the ACLU and NAACP teamed up with the local branch of the Congress of Racial Equality to establish the United Civil Rights Committee. Headed by Reverend H. H. Brookins, one of the city's most respected black ministers, the committee organized a conference with leading white officials and business executives to discuss the serious inadequacies .in housing, employment, and education. Police attitudes and conduct were also on the agenda. "Negroes do not receive equal treatment at the hands of law enforcement officers in the city and county," Thomas G. Neusom, a prominent black attorney, bluntly stated. "Persons guilty of this conduct may be a small minority, but unchecked as they are, except in very flagrant cases, the community continues to suffer and long smoldering resentment continues." He and other civil rights activists demanded a civilian review board. Chief Parker expressed strong opposition to outside supervision of police conduct and told the audience that the internal affairs division provided adequate redress on those unfortunate occasions when a citizen suffered police mistreatment.[19]

The United Civil Rights Committee organized several demonstrations in the summer of 1963, demanding an end to racial discrimination in public schools, private business, and various municipal agencies, including the LAPD. Parker's intelligence division had compiled dossiers on alleged radicals and subversives and supposedly found such people in the civil rights movement. Inspector Edward Davis claimed to know of a number of a "second generation communists on the racial picket lines."[20] Furthermore, a relatively low turnout of black residents in the demonstrations convinced Parker that civil rights activists were out of touch with the ghetto population. Los Angeles, he assured a group of local journalists in the fall of 1963, would never become "part of the battleground of the racial conflict that is raging in the United States today." He told them that the city was "ten years ahead of other major metropolitan areas in assimilating the Negro minority."[21]

Daily life in Watts revealed a far different situation. The number of blacks in Los Angeles County had grown to 650,000 in 1965, most of them crowded into the south central part of the city, including the Watts area. Unemployment, after the 1961 recession, rose to 30 percent by 1965. Four out of ten families lived below the poverty level.[22] Housing and transportation were also serious problems. Most of the homes were owned by absentee landlords and badly needed sanitary and structural improvements. Savings and loan associations involved in mortgage finance refused to provide loans to families wanting to live outside the ghetto. The people who found work spent hours on overcrowded, expensive buses in order to get to their jobs. Police violence also rose dramatically in ghetto neighborhoods. Sixty blacks were killed by patrolmen from 1963 to 1965, of whom twenty-five were unarmed and twenty-seven were shot in the back.[23]

All of these conditions contributed to the outbreak of massive rioting in the Watts district. On the sweltering evening of August 11, 1965, a highway patrol motorcycle officer stopped a young black named Marquette Frye for speeding and reckless driving on a main thoroughfare near Watts. He ordered him to get out of the car and take a sobriety test. Frye failed the examination and was placed under arrest for drunk driving. As a patrol car arrived to carry the youth to jail, several people gathered around the vehicles, including Frye's brother and mother. They scuffled with the police and were also arrested. A growing crowd prevented the patrol car's departure, forcing the officers to summon reinforcements. Local and state police left the intersection surrounded by an angry mob of about 1,000 persons. The mob then proceeded to throw rocks and bottles at unsuspecting whites driving through the area. More rioting, accompanied by arson and looting, occurred in other parts of Watts the following day. Formerly hostile gangs, like the Gladiators and the Slausons, forgot old grudges and participated with other blacks in burning and looting numerous businesses, many owned by whites. The police could not penetrate to the center of the disturbance and failed to restore order. California national guardsmen arrived on the scene, moved en masse through the district, and started clearing the streets of rioters and looters. By August 17 the riot was over. It had covered about 46 square miles and left thirty-four persons, mostly blacks, dead, 1,032 wounded, and 3,952 arrested. Property damage amounted $40 million, with over 600 buildings damaged or destroyed.[24]

Much of the immediate reaction centered on the role of the LAPD. Black leaders blamed Chief Parker, not only for previous police brutality, but for his intemperate language and conduct during the disturbance. He had branded the rioters as "monkeys in a zoo" and refused to consult with local black ministers and officials, claiming that they had little power to alleviate the situation. Civil rights leader Martin Luther King, Jr., after a tense meeting with Parker, declared that he showed a "blind intransigence and ignorance of the social forces involved." Parker accused the Black Muslims of provoking racial hostility and keeping the riots going when they might have died out with little bloodshed. He also claimed, in a meeting with the city council, that two agitators with loudspeaking bullhorns kept inciting the rioters. Councilman Tom Bradley, a 21-year veteran of the LAPD, wanted some evidence of this activity and demanded that Parker identify any outside agitators in the ghetto. The chief resented Bradley's request and charged that he and other minority leaders were "trying to put the blame" on his department by engaging in a "sham" discussion of police brutality.[25]

Los Angeles County Fire Department
Police brutality greatly contributed to the eruption of violence in Watts in August 1965. Almost every store in this block of 103rd Street was severely damaged

Governor Edmund G. "Pat" Brown worried about the possibility of more racial violence in Los Angeles. He appointed a commission to investigate the riots and named former CIA director John McCone to head it. The McCone Commission consulted numerous experts in the field of race relations and heard testimony from over 500 witnesses, a few of whom had participated in the rioting. Its final report, entitled *Violence in the City: An End or a Beginning?*, documented serious economic and social deprivation suffered by the ghetto and recommended a large increase in public spending on jobs, schools, and. transportation. The commission, however, minimized the extent of riot participation in the black community and portrayed most of the rioters as members of a criminal class.[26] It dismissed the charges of systematic police brutality as highly exaggerated and naively concluded that the problems in police-minority relations were mostly the result of misunderstanding rather than mistreatment. "Despite the depth of feeling against Chief Parker expressed to us by so many witnesses," declared the commission, "he is recognized, even by many of his vocal critics, as a capable Chief who directs an efficient police force that serves well this entire community." However, the commission did point out that there was a "deep and long standing schism between a substantial portion of the Negro community and the Police Department." It advocated the strengthening of the police commission to improve its ability to supervise the department and proposed the establishment of an independent inspector general's office to review citizen complaints. It also called for an expansion of the department's community relations program and recommended the hiring of more black and Mexican American officers who, taken together, constituted less than eight percent of the police force.[27]

Parker paid little attention to these proposals. The city's white majority, shaken by the Watts uprising, supported the chief and expected him to keep a tight lid on any suspicious activity in the ghetto. His intelligence division discovered some members of the Communist party working with activist groups and concluded that they were behind most of the ghetto hostility. Armed with this information, Parker asked an unconvinced city council to double the police force and demanded more shotguns and antiriot equipment. When Parker died suddenly of a heart attack on July 16, 1966, civil rights activists and black politicians joined with white officials and newspaper editors in praise of the chief and stressed his personal integrity and strong devotion to the city.[28] Few of the former group, however, were sorry to see him go.

The police commission appointed Deputy Chief Thomas Reddin to the chief's post. Reddin was determined to ameliorate the LAPD's unpleasant relationship with black residents and sought to provide them with more flexible and sensitive policing. He increased the community relations unit from four persons to 120 and instructed it to establish citizen councils in all of the department's seventeen divisions. From the councils came some recommendation which won the support of Reddin. He instructed his officers to issue warnings instead of citations for minor mechanical violations of the vehicle code, an important concession in poor black neighborhoods. Reddin also put cops back on foot patrol, reinstituted youth-related programs, and stepped up the recruitment of black and Mexican American officers. In addition, he created the office of inspector-general to supervise the internal affairs division and report directly to the chief.[29]

These reforms, while admirable and long overdue, accomplished little change in the attitude and behavior of the police toward black residents. ACLU officials had opened a police malpractice complaint center in Watts in late 1966. Anyone who suffered police mistreatment was urged to get assistance for lodging grievances with the LAPD. By the end of the next year, the center had received and filed numerous complaints charging certain patrol officers with verbal harassment and occasional physical abuse.[30] Police shootings also increased in black neighborhoods. Twenty-five blacks were shot and killed by officers in 1967 and 1968, of whom three were shot in the back.[31]

A new militancy arose in the ghetto. Most resentful of the police was the Black Panther Party (BPP) founded in Oakland, California, in 1966, by Huey Newton and Bobby Seale. The BPP promoted revolutionary nationalism and organized a system of patrol cars filled with law books and guns to contain police activity. Whenever black people were stopped by the police, armed Panthers appeared on the scene, making sure that their constitutional rights not being violated.[32] The next stop was the Los Angeles ghetto and charismatic Alprentice "Bunchy" Carter. "Everybody had heard of Bunchy," Panther leader Elaine Brown later recalled. "He was a lion from the streets of L.A., the former head of the Slauson gang, five-thousand strong, originator of its feared hard-core, the Slauson Renegades."[33] Carter did time in Soledad Prison, where he became a Muslim. After his release from Soledad, Carter returned to Los Angeles and established the southern California chapter of the BPP in late 1967. He recruited gang members and transformed them into soldiers against police repression. Each of them was required to have a gun and enough ammunition to protect themselves and their homes. One former gang member recalled that he joined the Panthers "to stop police harassment, to unite, to hold our ground."[34]

The police saw the Panthers as a major threat to their authority on the streets. They kept Panther leaders under constant surveillance, sometimes entered their homes without search warrants, and often stopped their cars in search of alleged stolen goods.[35] Patrol officers also looked for the least little opportunity to provoke a confrontation with the militants. One gun battle in August of 1968 left two officers wounded, three Panthers dead, and segments of the black population in an uproar.[36]

The late 1960s also saw growing ethnic consciousness and activism in the East Los Angeles barrio. The civil rights movement and black nationalist program made many Mexican Americans cognizant that they shared similar problems with the black community and suggested how change could be pursued through mass mobilization. From this recognition came new social and political organizations strongly committed to racial pride and solidarity. Particularly influential was the Young Citizens for Community Action (YCCA) founded by a group of Chicano high school students in early 1967, YCCA, among other things, helped elect Julian Nava, a Mexican American professor at San Fernando Valley State College, to the Los Angeles Board of Education. It also opened a coffee house in East Los Angeles called La Piranya and held discussions and classes in Mexican culture and history. As Los Angeles County Sheriff's deputies routinely harassed the group, YCAA grew more belligerent, adopted military garb, and changed its name to the Brown Berets. The Berets strongly promoted cultural nationalism and threatened

Courtesy of *Its About Time: Black Panther Party Legacy & Alumni*
Former head of the fearsome Slauson gang in Los Angeles, Alprentice "Bunchy" Carter established the southern California chapter of the Black Panther Party in 1967. He recruited gang members and transformed them into revolutionary soldiers against police repression

armed resistance against any unwarranted police action against Latino residents. The sheriff's department and the LAPD believed that the group was capable of inspiring violent behavior in other barrio organizations, authorized raids on the Berets' headquarters, planted informers in their ranks, and worked to discredit them in the eyes of the Mexican American community.[37]

Racial activism became the leading issue in the 1969 mayoral race. Tom Bradley, a critic of police mistreatment in minority areas since his election to the council in 1963, talked about problems of urban renewal, rapid transit, ecology, and business expansion. Mayor Yorty linked Bradley to the Black Panthers and contended his election would persuade many police officers to quit. Chief Reddin's decision to resign provided timely justification for the mayor's warning. Yorty's shameless appeal to the fears of white voters won him the election by a comfortable margin. The police commission appointed Edward Davis to the chief's post.[38]

Chief Davis had little patience with any militant group and attributed their activities to communist propaganda and infiltration. Any major disruption of the peace, he warned, would be met with swift and forceful resistance. An antiwar protest in response to President Richard M. Nixon's decision to invade Cambodia in 1970 set off demonstrations on colleges and university campuses across the nation, including one at the University of California at Los Angeles. Adding to the tension on the campus were the demands of Chicano students for the expansion of Mexican American programs and early implementation. School authorities chose not to meet with the students. Their decision led some militant Chicanos to join forces with a number of white activists and smash the glass doors of two classroom buildings, break many windows, and destroy several display cases. Two hundred Los Angeles police officers marched onto the campus to restore order and took 74 persons into custody. Chief Davis congratulated his men on their performance in a "pressurized situation" and declared that they rendered "an excellent service to the citizens of Los Angeles."[39]

Many students and faculty members charged that the police had used excessive force and arrested people indiscriminately. Chancellor Charles C. Young shared their concerns and appointed a commission to investigate the disturbance. The commission reported that student violence was dying out by the time the police arrived on the scene, however, and officers wandered about the campus, physically attacked innocent persons, and arrested people who had not damaged any school property. Among them were several blacks, Chicanos, and other minority students. The police, in this instance, went well beyond their instructions, personalized the issues, and graphically showed partisanship.[40]

In the Eastside barrio, the public schools were overcrowded, employed few Chicano teachers, and paid little attention to the cultural heritage of Mexican people. Students at Roosevelt High School walked out in June of 1970 in protest against these conditions. The Brown Berets helped them organize several demonstrations. School authorities called upon the Los Angeles police to maintain order. KMEX, the local Spanish-language television station, filmed the beating of many students, and several officers stormed into the station in an effort to keep the pictures off the air. The behavior of the sheriff's department was equally repressive, especially unprovoked assaults by deputies on prisoners in custody. Six Mexican Americans died at the East Los Angeles sheriff's station in the first five months of 1970, three of whom hung themselves. Their deaths aroused concern among community residents and led to demonstrations against police brutality. One took place in front of the sheriff's station on the Fourth of July and ended with one Chicano shot and 21 others arrested.[41]

The war in Vietnam joined police repression as another issue that brought the community closer together. Chicanos accounted for some nineteen per cent of all servicemen from the Southwest killed in action from 1967 to 1970, although they comprised only about twelve percent of the total population. The National Chicano Moratorium, a coalition of groups opposed to the Vietnam war, conducted huge protest marches in Los Angeles in December of 1969 and in February of 1970. Many members of rival barrio gangs participated in the marches. Former gang member Luis J. Rodriguez remembered that "for a most productive and wonderful time, gang violence stood at a standstill." The gangs, he continues, had "something more important to fight for."[42] Another demonstration occurred on August 29 in Laguna Park and attracted between twenty and thirty thousand people. During the afternoon some trouble broke out at a liquor store across the street. The incident turned into an assault by sheriff's deputies on the people in the park and ended in a major riot. Many people were seriously injured and three deaths occurred, the most controversial being the slaying of Ruben Salazar, a well-known reporter for the *Los Angeles Times* and news director at station KMEX. He and his T.V. crew had captured some of the action on film and retired to the Silver Dollar Cafe located a few blocks away. A group of deputies surrounded the bar, supposedly looking for a man rumored to have a rifle. One of them fired a tear gas projectile into the bar and it struck Salazar in the head, killing him instantly. District Attorney Evelle Younger, after reviewing the verdict of a coroner's jury in which only three of nine jurors voted in favor of accidental death, decided not to indict the deputy. His decision led to several demonstrations. The biggest one took place in front of Parker Center and resulted in a police riot and the arrests of 32 people.[43]

The BPP also felt police repression as the party attracted many young blacks with a mixture of Marxist-Maoist dogma and advocacy of resistance to the police and other symbols of white authority. By the end of 1968 it had twelve hundred members in chapters throughout the country. Seeing the BPP as an alleged threat to the internal security of the nation, FBI director J. Edgar Hoover established a secret operation named COINTELPRO ('Counter Intelligence Program') and instructed his field agents to destroy the party. FBI agents exacerbated the rivalry between the BPP and United Slaves, a black nationalist group, by sending fabricated letters, leaflets, and cartoons to both organizations. This literature, purporting to be from one group, ridiculed and defamed the other group, leading to bloody confrontations which culminated in a shootout at UCLA in January of 1969 that left Panther leaders Bunchy Carter and John Huggins dead in a dispute over the head of the school's proposed Afro-American Studies Center.[44] Later in the year numerous LAPD officers raided the Panther headquarters and exchanged gunfire with eleven militants for four hours. When the smoke cleared, some Panthers were wounded, the office destroyed, and the local Panther movement left in shambles.[45]

The collapse of the BPP chapter led some black youth to organize new street gangs. One of them, Raymond Washington, a 15-year old student at Fremont High School, formed a gang in late 1969 named Baby Avenues, which later became the Cribs. The Cribs intended to continue the revolutionary ideology of the Panthers, but lacked the political skills to develop an agenda for social change. Dressed in black leather jackets and usually carrying canes, the gang drifted into criminal activity. Local newspapers gave some attention to the Cribs and often referred to the group as the Crips. The Crips gradually spread to Inglewood and Compton and numbered eight separate gangs in 1972. Many youngsters chose to form their own gangs but, encountering continual intimidation from the Crips, organized a federation known as the Bloods. The Bloods and Crips staked out territories in the ghetto and periodically engaged in shootings and street fights.[46]

Alarmed, Chief Davis formed an anti-gang task force to crack down on gang violence. They regularly broke up gatherings of gangs on street corners and in parks, discouraged them from loitering around schools, and occasionally stopped cars carrying suspected gang members. Davis also added intelligence officers to the department's juvenile crime unit and ordered regular surveillance of neighborhoods inhabited by gangs. The police often failed to distinguish between innocent and troublesome youth, however, and treated the majority of black youngsters as actual or potential members of gangs. They routinely stopped groups of young people on the streets, asked them for identification, and detained those who were not cooperative.[47]

Political activism attracted heavier police surveillance. Davis in 1970 replaced the old intelligence unit with the Public Disorder Intelligence Division (PDID) and staffed it with a large number of officers experienced in undercover operations. PDID investigated and collected files on a wide range of activists and organizations in the city, including minority leaders critical of police conduct, with little or no supervision from the police commission.[48] The 1973 mayoral election ended the practice of secrecy when Tom Bradley, running on a law and order platform, defeated incumbent Sam Yorty. To ensure that city residents received the best possible law enforcement and to recapture a measure of community control over LAPD operations, Bradley appointed five liberal-minded minded professionals to the police commission. The commission discovered that PDID's intelligence-gathering net extended beyond private political groups to elective officials, civic-minded organizations, and even members of the police commission. It enacted detailed rules for the collection and maintenance of intelligence materials. PDID could only investigate potential criminal acts that might result in physical or property damage. Two commissioners would audit the division on a regular basis and review major sources of intelligence information. Names were also to be removed from PDID files after five years if there was no evidence of involvement in criminal operations.[49]

An escalation of police violence gave the commission another opportunity to expand its authority. Eighty-seven people were shot to death by patrolmen from 1975 to 1977, of whom a large number were unarmed black residents. Mayor Bradley, upset with the killings, asked the police commission to hold public hearings on the LAPD's firearms policy. Members of the Coalition Against Police Abuse testified that suspects were often shot if they appeared to be reaching for weapons or fled from the scene of the crime. The latter criteria, in the commission's opinion, was too harsh. It drafted new rules on the use of guns and ordered that they be integrated into the department's training programs. One rule forbid an officer to shoot at a fleeing felon unless the person had committed a violent crime and presented a "substantial risk of death or serious bodily injury to others." Another authorized the use of deadly force only when "all reasonable alternatives" had been exhausted. Chief

Davis strongly objected to these restrictions and charged that his officers would be "walking into situations with their guns in their holsters and bullets in their heads." Commissioner Stephen Reinhardt disagreed. He praised the new guidelines as "reasonable and moderate" and contended that the chief was inflaming the police force unnecessarily. He and his colleagues rejected requests from Davis to modify certain parts of the rules and instructed him to make sure that they were being fully implemented throughout the department.[50]

Such actions, coupled with the new restrictions on intelligence gathering, convinced Davis that the commission had moved in the direction of being master of the LAPD rather than its booster. He decided to retire in 1978 and was succeeded by Daryl F. Gates. Gates had joined the LAPD in 1949 and rose rapidly through the ranks to assistant chief at the time of his appointment. Crime in the ghetto was of particular concern to him. "South Central Los Angeles has never been easy to police," he declared in an editorial in the *Los Angeles Times*. "It has always required an aggressive effort by the department in order to cope with a crime level that is a plague upon those who live in the area."[51] The killing of Eulia Love did not exactly fit his description. On January 3, 1979, an employee of the Southern California Gas Company presented Love with an unpaid $22 bill and proceeded to shut off the gas at the side of the house. She became upset and hit him with a shovel. He went to a company office nearby and telephoned the police. Two officers accompanied the man's supervisor to Love's house and stood by while he turned off the gas. In a fit of anger, she threw a kitchen knife at the officers and they opened fire, emptying twelve rounds into her body. Anticipating controversy, Gates instructed the department's shooting review board to investigate the incident. It justified the shooting on the grounds that the policemen were confronted with a "life-threatening situation" and concluded that their actions complied in "all respects" with department policies concerning the use of deadly force.[52]

These findings did not satisfy the city's black leadership. Councilman Robert C. Farrell, in whose district Eulia Love had lived, persuaded the police commission to hold a public hearing on the shooting. At the hearing Farrell, other minority officials, and several black ministers and civil rights activists denounced the LAPD defense of the killing as a "whitewash" and demanded the creation of an independent civilian review board. Mayor Bradley described the woman's death as a "terrible tragedy" and asked the police commission to reassess the department's firearm policies. The commission closely investigated the shooting and put its findings in a detailed report that discredited the department's evaluation. Commissioner Reinhardt, reading parts of the report at a meeting attended by LAPD executives, top city officials, and black leaders, pointed out that the conclusions of the shooting board were based on "erroneous and misconstrued facts." The two officers, he noted, made "serious errors in judgment" and drew their guns "before all reasonable alternatives had been exhausted." The commission renamed the shooting review unit as the Use of Force Review Board and ordered that its reports be submitted to the chief. He, in turn, had to review the board's findings and provide the commission with his own explanation and evaluation of a particular shooting. The commission would then either adopt the chief's findings and recommendations or conduct an independent review to make sure that important evidence was not being overlooked.[53]

Concern with intelligence operations flared again. PDID personnel usually ignored the police commission's guidelines on surveillance and sought to undermine a number of politically active organizations. Members of the Coalition Against Police Abuse came across a partial list of PDID personnel and discovered that one of them had served for a time as the group's secretary. They gave the list to the Citizens Committee on Police Repression who, in turn, gave it to the Alliance for Survival, an anti-nuclear group, the Young Workers Liberation League, and the Campaign for Democratic Freedoms, which sponsored forums on abuses in federal law enforcement. When some of their members were revealed to be PDID officers experienced in undercover work, leaders of the latter three groups requested the ACLU in 1978 to file a lawsuit in their behalf against the LAPD for illegal spying and invasion of privacy.[54]

Joining them as co-defendants were several local radical groups and minority organizations. They filed lawsuits against the department in 1981 and 1982 charging that certain officers and civilian informants had infiltrated their activities and unlawfully collected information on private meetings. The court ordered the LAPD to release 6,000 pages of intelligence documents which revealed that PDID officers kept close tabs on campaigns calling for a civilian review board, infiltrated black and Chicano organizations on college campuses, and reported on the appearances of city council members at meetings critical of local law enforcement. This indiscriminate surveillance exhausted the patience of the police commissioners; they disbanded PDID in 1983 and replaced it with a new Anti-Terrorist Division (ATD) with the chief held accountable for its conduct. The spying lawsuit was resolved in an out-of-court accord designed to provide more civilian control of undercover operations. The city council approved the accord in 1984 and agreed to pay $1.8 million in damages to 131 plaintiffs, including 23 organizations. The stringent guidelines on police intelligence gathering required the police commissioners to authorize any ATD undercover operation. In addition, they would periodically audit the records of the division and make certain that information on its activity was available to the public.[55]

Gang violence in South Central Los Angeles was more troublesome for the LAPD, particularly the brutal conflict among different Crips gangs or "sets." They turned streets into armed camps and battled each other ferociously. "The idea was to drop enough bodies, cause enough terror and suffering," Kody Scott, former member of the Eight-Tray Gangster Crips, writes in his graphic autobiography, "so that they [rival gangs] would come to their senses and realize that we were the wrong set to fuck with. Their goal, I'm sure, was the same."[56] As gang-related homicides rose dramatically from 167 to 1981 to 512 by 1984, Chief Gates added more personnel to the department's Community Resources Against Street Hoodlums (CRASH) units and instructed them to remind gang members that they, in the words of one officer, "don't rule the streets." CRASH officers stepped up surveillance of places where gangs hung out, randomly stopped and frisked gang members, and often arrested them for minor violations, such as loitering and swearing in public.[57]

Despite these actions, South Central experienced a major increase in gang membership in the mid-1980s, due largely to major

512 pa. gang deaths by 1984.

dislocations in the region's economy. Some 131 plants shut down permanently and many local manufacturers moved to new facilities in Orange County, San Gabriel Valley and the San Fernando Valley, closing off resident's access to formerly well paying jobs. Unemployment rose to 45 percent among young blacks.[58] During the same period, the Medellin Cartel moved an enormous amount of cocaine or "crack" into the city offering unprecedented economic opportunities for street gangs. Prominent criminologist Jeffrey Fagan points out that "crack distribution became a major part of the informal economy" in which unemployed gang members "could achieve economic returns well beyond the returns of low-wage jobs."[59] The number of black gangs jumped from 74 in 1982 to 138 by 1990. They claimed specific neighborhoods in a manner unthinkable in the 1970s and furiously fought each other over who sold drugs and where, resulting in a large increase of gang killings.[60]

One death sparked a police assault on the gangs. On the night of January 30, 1988, Karen Yoshima was walking in Westwood, an upscale shopping and entertainment center, when outside a theater members of two rival Crips gangs exchanged gunfire and accidentally shot Yoshima. Angry with this senseless killing, Chief Gates instructed the Gang Related Active Trafficker Suppression program (GRATS) to conduct raids on "drug gangs" in South Central. Two to three hundred GRATS officers organized nine sweeps in February and March, impounded five hundred automobiles, and took nearly fifteen hundred people into custody.[61] Shortly after the sweeps, some Crips fired at a crowd on a street corner in South Central, killing a 19 year-old woman. Gates ordered additional crackdowns on the gangs. Dubbed Operation Hammer, 1000 policemen, on weekends in April, swept through black neighborhoods and detained thousands of alleged gang members congregating in public places. Forty-five percent of those arrested did not belong gangs, while many were picked up for minor offenses, such as curfew violations and delinquent parking tickets. Raymond L. Johnson, president of the local NAACP chapter, criticized the officers for stopping young blacks just because they wore clothing in gang colors and demanded that the police exercise more caution in making arrests. Even gang members themselves, he added, "have constitutional rights that must be protected."[62] The sweeps continued into 1989, although with smaller groups of one hundred to three hundred officers.[63]

There were other serious problems in South Central prompted by large numbers of poor Latino workers and their families settling in the region during the mid-1980s. By 1990 Latinos constituted roughly 50 percent of South Central's population. They, like most black residents, were isolated from employment opportunities that paid good wages, could only find menial jobs, and were unable to maintain reasonable living standards. Thirty-three percent of the area's population lived below the poverty level, compared to 18 percent of all city residents.[64] There was also growing tension between blacks and Korean merchants who owned some 350 stores in South Central. Black patrons regularly complained that the merchants overcharged them and were often disrespectful. The tragic death of fifteen-year old Latasha Harlins in March of 1991 added some credibility to these complaints. Korean grocer Soon Ja Du shot Harlins, apparently in an argument over a bottle of orange juice. Judge Joyce Karlin let Mrs. Du off with a $500 fine and four hundred hours of community service. Her decision aroused anger in the black community and left them more resentful of Korean store owners.[65] *What did the Koreans think?*

The Rodney King affair created new and bitter controversy for the LAPD. On March 3, 1991, King, an African American, was out on the town driving with some friends when a California Highway Patrol car observed King speeding and tried to pull him over. King, on parole for second degree robbery, panicked and exited the freeway with the CHP chasing him through the city streets, joined by a LAPD patrol car. King finally stopped, got out of his car, and received a vicious beating from four LAPD officers. One delivered two stun gun blasts, another stomped him, and two others struck him with their batons fifty-six times, producing a concussion, multiple skull fractures, nerve injuries, and a broken leg. A tenant in a nearby apartment building videotaped the beating, and it soon played continuously on television stations in the city and throughout the world. The officers were arrested and charged with assault with a deadly weapon and the use of excessive force.[66]

After the beating, Mayor Bradley appointed a commission to investigate the LAPD and named Warren Christopher, a prominent

King didn't charge the officers?
Drunk + drugged?

lawyer and future Secretary of State, to head it. The Christopher Commission reviewed a large number of messages on police computers, closely examined the department's handling of citizen complaints, and conducted five public hearings at different locations around the city. Its final report identified dozens of policemen who regularly used brutal force, discovered numerous racist messages on police computers, and found the department's complaint and disciplinary system to be inadequate. It recommended, among other things, improved training procedures, the tracking of problem officers to reduce incidents of police abuse, and an Inspector General to monitor officer disciplinary investigations.[67]

Meanwhile, the four officers indicted for the Rodney King beating secured a change of venue for the trial to Simi Valley in Ventura County, a suburban community where many policemen resided. On April 29, 1992, after hearing the evidence, the jury, composed mostly of white persons, acquitted all of the officers and ignited a bloody uprising in South Central Los Angeles. A mob assaulted a police station, motorists were yanked from their cars and beaten, and arsonists set numerous businesses on fire. Forty-two percent of the rioters were African Americans, and forty-four percent were Latino, as economic deprivation fueled much of their rage. They also remembered the killing of Latasha Harlins and torched a large number of Korean-owned stores as the uprising spread from Korea Town to the mid-Wilshire area. California national guardsmen joined forces with thousands of highway patrol officers and local policemen to clear the streets. By May 5, the rioting was over. It left 58 dead, more than 2,000 injured, and 17,000 people were arrested, of whom two-thirds were unemployed. Property damage amounted to over $1 billion, with 1,200 buildings destroyed.[68]

The riot marked a turning point for the LAPD. Charging that the department was partly responsible for the rioting, the Citizens Committee for Law Enforcement and Reform, a group consisting of representatives from churches, various civic associations, and minority organizations, campaigned vigorously for civilian control of the LAPD. It persuaded the city council to hold public hearings on the Christopher Commission reform proposals and, after lengthy debate, the council incorporated some proposals into Charter Amendment F and placed it on the June ballot. Bill

Fires rage through the buildings at 3rd Street and New Hampshire Avenue during the 1992 riots. Total property damage from the riots exceeded $1 billion, and 1,200 buildings were destroyed

Violante, president of the Los Angeles Police Protective League, described the measure as "a sham, a bunch of garbage." Shortly before the election, a *Los Angeles Times* poll found widespread disillusionment with the management of the LAPD largely as a result of the department's slow response and lack of effectiveness to the rioting. Supporters of Charter Amendment F blamed this situation on Chief Gates and also charged that he and other LAPD officials had failed to deal with racism and the use of excessive force by officers. The measure won by 2 to 1, with a majority in every part of the city and among all ethnic and racial groups. It dramatically changed the LAPD's power structure and made it more accountable to the community. It limited a police chief to two terms, allowed the mayor to select a chief with the consent of the council, and provided civilian review of officer misconduct.[69]

Chief Gates rightly saw the election as a repudiation of his leadership and retired on June 25. The police commission had already chosen Philadelphia Police Commissioner Willie L. Williams, an African American, to replace him.[70] Community policing was of particular importance to Williams. The Christopher Commission had emphasized it as a way to improve the image of the LAPD and repair trust between the police and the public, especially in minority neighborhoods. The focus would be on crime prevention, with officers cooperating with residents in solving problems rather than just arresting criminals. Williams devoted specific attention to the Basic Car Plan, instituted by Chief Davis in the 1970s, that assigned officers to the same patrol district for extended periods of time and instructed them to interact with citizens. Williams reassigned 144 additional officers to the program. He also established Community Policy Advisory Boards in all of the department's 18 divisions and put a captain and civilian in charge of each of them. The Christopher Commission reforms were slow to come, however. The department in 1993 found many of them not in place and cited a lack of financial resources for the delay. By 1996 it reported progress in some areas as the number of use of force incidents had declined considerably and there was improvement in the quality of adjudication in the complaint and discipline areas.[71]

The conduct of the LAPD toward street gangs remained the same. Leaders of the Crips and Bloods had grown tired of gang killings in the ghetto and they declared a truce in the spring of 1992. "Instead of shooting each other," one member of the Hoover Crips asserted, "we decided to fight together for black power."[72] The truce effort spread beyond South Central to include Latino gangs as far away as the San Fernando Valley. Luis Rodriguez recalled that gang members "were feeling a heavy weight lifted off them . . . . For the first time a semblance of calm and even hope visited these streets."[73] None of this mattered to the police. They believed, without any evidence, that the truces were simply an excuse for the gangs to join forces against them. They regularly harassed gang members, occasionally broke up unity rallies among the gangs, and sometimes arrested truce leaders when they had done nothing wrong.[74]

Chief Williams assigned additional officers to CRASH units and ordered a crackdown on street gangs. One of them was the Blythe Street gang, a Latino clique located in Panorama City. City authorities in early 1993 filed an injunction against the gang, the first of its kind in the city's history, outlawing activities already forbidden by law and barring other activities, such as carrying on conversations or visiting with friends. Armed with this legal weapon, the police blocked off several streets in the neighborhood, raided suspected gang hangouts, and arrested a large number of gang members mostly for minor offenses. ACLU officials denounced the injunction, charging that it was an inexcusable violation of "fundamental constitutional rights." Chief Williams also authorized raids on gangs in South Central. A raid in early 1995 on a neighborhood inhabited by the Eight-Tray Gangster Crips, dubbed Operation Sunrise, saw several hundred officers, accompanied by FBI agents, storm into 135 homes, ransack the premises, and confiscate numerous weapons and a small amount of cocaine. Sixty-three people were taken into custody, of whom only one was charged with a violent felony. Many residents protested the raid and accused the police of casting to broad a net over African American youth. "You [the police] don't know our community; we do," a mother told a group of officers. "And to call our kids all gang members is wrong. I am not saying everyone is innocent, but it is unfair."[75]

The leadership of the LAPD also came under scrutiny. In December, 1994, Stephen Downing, former deputy police chief, informed the police commission that Chief Williams, in direct violation of department policy, had accepted free meals and rooms from Las Vegas hotels. Williams denied he had done so. The commission confirmed the allegation and officially reprimanded the chief. Mayor Richard Riordan upheld the reprimand, declaring that the commissioners "merit the gratitude of our city." City council members did not agree for fear that the commission's action might arouse racial discord as Williams had the support of most of the city's black leaders. Even though the council voted 12 to 1 to overturn the reprimand, the commission, after several meetings with LAPD officers, public officials, and community groups, voted unanimously to deny Williams a second term and appointed Bernard Parks, a black department veteran with over 30 years on the force, to the chief's post.[76]

Developments in the Ramparts division presented Parks with the worst scandal in the history of the LAPD. The Ramparts neighborhood was home to the powerful 18th Street gang and, when authorities in 1996 filed an injunction against the group,

Officer Raphael Perez, a member of the Rampart division CRASH unit, provided important evidence in support. Two years later Perez was caught stealing eight pounds of cocaine from a police evidence locker. In exchange for leniency in his sentencing, he turned state's evidence and implicated himself and more than 30 current and former Ramparts CRASH officers in misconduct and criminal activities. They included beatings, the planting of evidence, theft of money and drugs, police murder, unauthorized searches, and false imprisonment. One officer planted rock cocaine on unsuspecting victims, another liked to "thump people," and still another planted guns on suspects. A particularly brutal case involved Juan Francisco Ovando, a member of the 18th Street gang. After picking Ovando up for questioning about a burglary, Perez and his partner took him to an abandoned apartment building, shot him in the neck, and charged him with assaulting a police officer. Paralyzed from the waist down from his injury, he was convicted and received a sentence of 23 years.[77]

These revelations ended the careers of more than a dozen officers in the Ramparts division. Some were fired and others resigned from the department.[78] A Board of Inquiry examined the distribution of formal authority and blamed managerial incompetence and a breakdown in supervision of the gang unit for the corruption and misconduct. Chief Parks disbanded all of the department's CRASH units and replaced them with antigang squads with tighter supervision.[79] This action, while long overdue, was not enough for political activists in the city who believed that police abuse existed in many of the LAPD's divisions. The influential Coalition for Police Accountability, a collection of over forty community and civil rights groups, sought "to improve the policies and practices of the LAPD and restore the legitimacy of the people's faith and trust" in the police. Building upon the earlier work of reform organizations, such as the Coalition Against Police Abuse, the group conducted public protests and press conferences and pushed for a number of changes in LAPD operations, including the tracking of problem officers, increased response to citizen complaints, and civilian control of the department.[80]

Several leading professionals and public figures felt that major reforms could only be enacted with federal intervention. Among them were Paul Hoffman, former legal director of the ACLU Foundation of Southern California, Robert Garcia, a longtime civil rights attorney, and Tom Hayden, a member of the California State Senate. They complained to U.S. Assistant Attorney General Bill Lann Lee, head of the Justice Department's civil rights division, about a "pattern and practice" of violations in the LAPD and urged swift action against the department.[81] Lee and his staff reviewed reports on officer-involved shootings and numerous files of misconduct complaints and civil suits against individual officers. "As a result of our investigation," Lee wrote in a letter to City Attorney James K. Hahn in May of 2000, "we have determined that the LAPD is engaging in a pattern or practice of excessive force, false arrests, and unreasonable searches and seizures in violation of the Fourth and Fourteenth Amendments to the Constitution." He insisted that city authorities sign a legal agreement with the Justice Department in the form of a consent decree to ensure that meaningful and permanent police reform would take place.[82]

Hahn concluded that the city had no choice but to accept Lee's demand. "The whole Rampart issue brought to light that there are still officers who feel that they can do anything they want and their colleagues will keep a code of silence," he stated.[83] Mayor Riordan, Chief Parks, and a few council members, however, rejected the proposed decree. They believed that the LAPD was capable of reforming itself without any outside intervention. When Lee threatened federal legal action against the city, the council reluctantly approved the Justice Department's consent decree in the fall of 2000. The agreement, among other items, proposed the establishment of a computerized system to track the activities of all officers, the creation of a specially trained unit to investigate officer-involved shootings and other major uses of force, and an expansion of the authority and responsibilities of the police commission and the inspector general. The decree provided for an outside official, appointed by a federal judge, to monitor the department's compliance with these and other reform measures.[84]

In the mayoral election of 2001, James Hahn ran on a platform strongly committed to police reform and defeated Antonio Villaraigosa, former member of the California State Assembly, by a comfortable margin. Parks' leadership was of much concern to the Hahn, who felt that the chief was moving too slowly in implementing certain reforms prescribed in the consent decree. Hahn also pointed to low morale and understaffing in the LAPD. He announced, to the anger of the city's black leaders, that he was opposed to Parks' gaining a second term.[85] The police commissioners, too, were unhappy when Parks tried to circumvent a commission decision on police work schedules. Furthermore, the crime rate had risen in the city since the late 1990s for which the commissioners held Parks partly responsible. They voted 4 to 1 to deny his request for a second term. Hahn appointed William J. Bratton, former Police Commissioner of New York City, to the post.[86]

Chief Bratton devoted a great deal of attention to the LAPD's long and troubled relationship with the African American community. He promised black citizens that the police would be more sensitive to minority feelings and assured them that they would not employ paramilitary tactics. "We do not want to come in as an invading army, a platoon of strangers," Bratton told a large gathering of black residents in late 2002. "We want to come in with authorization. We want to come in respectfully."[87] Declaring that gangs "are the head that needs to be cut off," Bratton targeted a number of black neighborhoods in South Los Angeles and ordered a crackdown on gang-related violence. Several raids occurred in the summer of 2003. LAPD officers, joined by sheriff's deputies, arrested sixty-seven people mostly on drug charges. One resident complained about the police "pulling people out of houses" and added that they should "at least ask a couple of questions first."[88] The biggest raid took place in Nickerson Gardens, the state's largest public housing project, in early 2004. Several hundred LAPD officers and FBI agents stormed through the project, ripped doors off their hinges, and rousted many residents. Forty-one gang members were arrested, of whom most had committed minor violations. "It was a nightmare, something I thought I'd only see on television," a worker told a *Los Angeles Times* reporter shortly after the raid. "I saw mothers and kids sitting on the ground shivering."[89]

Police abuse of individual minority residents also occurred occasionally. On June 23, 2004, LAPD officers spotted Stanley Miller, an African American, driving through a stop sign. They checked the license plate and learned that the car had been reported stolen. They followed Miller onto the freeway and attempted to pull him over. He exited the freeway and led the police on a chase along the streets of South Los Angeles and Compton. Miller stopped the car and tried to escape on foot. Out of breath, he surrendered to an officer who tackled him. Two other cops arrived, one of whom kicked Miller, struck him eleven times in the upper body with a metal flashlight, and kneed him five times. Television crews in helicopters recorded the beating. Chief Bratton described the assault as "a mess" and added that it was "not what we teach at the [police] academy."[90] The NAACP called the arrest " an ugly case of police brutality" and urged that the officers be brought to justice. Day of Dialogue, a group of civic leaders and community activists that promoted popular discussion of socially divisive issues, organized several forums to focus critical attention on law enforcement in the city. Some minority residents attended the meetings and complained about being harassed and intimidated by the police.[91]

More upsetting was the death of Devon Brown, a 13-year old black youth. In the early morning of February 6, 2005, two LAPD officers saw Brown run a red light, followed him onto the freeway, and tried to pull him over. He left the freeway, lost control of the car, and drove onto the sidewalk. The police parked behind vehicle and when Brown backed into the patrol car, one officer fired 10 times, killing the boy instantly. The shooting angered leaders of the African American community. "They [police] are supposed to protect and serve, and they got it wrong," stated Geraldine Washington, president of the local NAACP chapter. John Mack, president of the Los Angeles chapter of the Urban League, spoke more candidly. "The residents are very disturbed over this tragic and needless shooting," he declared. "We have a pattern here [South Los Angeles] where some police officers don't value the lives of young African American males. There is a frustration here that's building up and makes it hard to build a partnership with the police."[92]

The years since 1950 saw the development of social discontent and much protest in Los Angeles. In the face of this turbulence, many police officers, under the direction of strong-willed and imposing chiefs, confused professional obligations with the unrestrained use of power and undermined the civil liberties of racial minorities and politically active groups. Reform-minded police commissioners and LAPD officials, in response to constant pressure from community organizations, set down new and tough regulations which stressed the use of minimal force and ensured impartial and equitable policing for all city residents regardless of their political views or racial background. The consent decree between the city and the federal government provided additional assurance that these egalitarian standards remained a dominant part of LAPD operations.

The recent beating of Stanley Miller and the killing of Devon Brown, however, serve as reminders that some police officers have not gotten the message. Furthermore, police raids in minority neighborhoods, while intended to reduce gang violence, have also brought discomfort and humiliation to law abiding residents. The police will always be part of any program of gang control, but they cannot alone stem the problem of gang violence because the problem has deep roots. A successful antigang strategy requires less use of police suppression, more cooperation between the community and the police, and greater emphasis upon gang prevention and intervention programs. *Liberal solution,*

NOTES

[1] Dean Jennings, "Portrait of a Police Chief," *Saturday Evening Post* 232 (7 May 1960): 87, 89.

[2] James A. Gazell, "William H. Parker, Police Professionalization and the Public: An Assessment," *Journal of Police Science and Administration* 4 (Mar. 1976): 31-32; Joseph G. Woods, "The Progressives and the Police: Urban Reform and the Professionalization of the Los Angeles Police," Ph.D. diss., University of California, Los Angeles, 1973, 425-29, 434-35.

[3] Los Angeles Police Department, *Annual Report, 1952*, 12; idem, *Annual Report, 1955*, 13.

[4] Woods, "Progressives and the Police," 457; Gazell, "William H. Parker," 35.

[5] George M. O'Connor, "The Negro and the Police in Los Angeles," M.A. thesis, University of Southern California, 1955, 136.

[6] Jennings, "Police Chief," 89; Woods, "Progressives and the Police," 437-38.

[7] O'Connor, "The Negro and the Police," 135.

[8] Los Angeles County Conference on Human Relations, Police Relations Committee, "Report to the Los Angeles Police Commission," 17 March 1952, Edward Roybal Papers, University of California, Los Angeles, box 29, 2, 4-6.

[9] William H. Parker, "The Police Role in Community Relations," address before the National Conference of Christians and Jews, East Lansing, MI, 19 May 1955, Roybal Papers, box 29, 25-26.

[10] Gerald Horne, *Fire This Time: The Watts Uprising and the 1960s* (Charlottesville, VA: University Press of Virginia, 1995), 194.

[11] "Pregnant Mom Says Officer Mauled Her," *Los Angeles Sentinel*, 6 June 1957; "NAACP Demands End of Brutality in Area," *Ibid.*, 20 June 1957.

[12] "75 Policemen Quell Riot in Griffith Park," *Los Angeles Times*, 31 May 1961; John C. Bollens and Grant B. Geyer, *Yorty: Politics of a Constant Candidate* (Pacific Palisades, CA: Palisades Publishers, 1973), 122-23, 132-34.

[13] Howard Kennedy, "Yorty Pledges Clean Sweep for City Hall," *Los Angeles Times*, 2 June 1961; Woods, "Progressives and the Police," 467-68.

[14] "Special Muslim Report," Los Angeles Fire and Police Protective League, *News* 11 (May 1962): 1-2; Ed Cray, *The Big Blue Line: Police Power vs. Human Rights* (New York: Coward-McCann, 1962), 130-31.

[15] Woods, "Progressives and the Police," 476.

[16] U. S. Commission on Civil Rights, California Advisory Committee, *Police Minority Group Relations in Los Angeles and the San Francisco Bay Area*, August, 1963, 8-9; also see Hugh R. Manes, *A Report on Law Enforcement and the Negro Citizen* (Los Angeles, 1963), 9-31.

[17] Johnnie Cochran with David Fisher, *A Lawyer's Life* (New York: Thomas Dunne Books, 2002), 173.

[18] California Advisory Committee, *Police-Minority Group Relations,* 13, 17-18.

[19] Eason Monroe, "Safeguarding Civil Liberties," Oral History Collection, University of California, Los Angeles, 1972, 146-47; Paul Weeks, "Law Enforcement Hit by Negroes," *Los Angeles Times*, 25 June 1963.

[20] Monroe, "Safeguarding Civil Liberties," pp. 147-49; Los Angeles Police Department, *Annual Report, 1963*, 7; Woods, "Progressives and the Police," 455, 477.

[21] "Ruling on Delinquency Asked in Bias March," *Los Angeles Times*, 21 September 1963.

[22] Robert Gottlieb and Irene Wolt, *Thinking Big: The Story of the Los Angeles Times, its Publishers, and their Influence on Southern California* (New York: Putnam, 1977), 376; Institute of Industrial Relations, University of California, Los Angeles, *Hard-Core Unemployment and Poverty in Los Angeles* (Washington, D.C.: Area Development Administration, U. S. Department of Commerce, 1965), 9, 240.

[23] Gottlieb and Wolt, *Thinking Big*, 376-77.

[24] Horne, *Fire This Time*, 3, 195-96; Governor's Commission on the Los Angeles Riots, *Violence in the City: An End or a Beginning?* (Los Angeles, n.p., 1965), 10-24.

[25] Woods, "Progressives and the Police," 485-87.

[26] Governor's Commission, *Violence in the City*, 4-7, 40-42, 54-58, 78-80; Robert M. Fogelson, *Violence as Protest: A Study of Riots and Ghettos* (New York: Anchor, 1971), 182-86.

[27] Governor's Commission, *Violence in the City*, 27-28, 30-37; Fogelson, *Violence as Protest*, 187-88.

[28] Woods, "Progressives and the Police," 491-93.

[29] Robert Conot, "The Superchief," *Los Angeles Times West Magazine*, June 9, 1968, 14-15; Linda McVeigh Matthews, "Chief Reddin: New Style at the Top," *Atlantic* 223 (March 1969): 91-92.

[30] Monroe, "Safeguarding Civil Liberties," 155-57.

[31] "Black Brothers Killed by the Police," (1969), in folder entitled "Black Panther Party, Flyers/Literature," Black Panther Party Collection, Southern California Library for Social Sciences and Research, 1-2.

[32] Robert O. Self, *American Babylon: Race and the Struggle for Postwar Oakland* (Princeton: Princeton University Press, 2003), 224, 226-27;

[33] Elaine Brown, *A Taste of Power: A Black Woman's Story* (New York: Pantheon, 1992), 118.

[34] *The Black Panther* 5 (October 17, 1970), 1; Alejandro A. Alonso, "Los Angeles Gang Regions," a paper presented to the Association of American Geographers, Boston, March 26, 1998, 6, copy in author's possession; Bob Baker, "Modern Gangs have Roots in Racial Turmoil of the '60s," *Los Angeles Times*, 26 June, 1988.

[35] "Defend the Black Panther Party Against Racist Police" (ca. 1968), in folder entitled "Black Panther Party, Flyers/Literature," Black Panther Party Collection, Southern California Library for Social Studies and Research; "General Repression of the Black Panther Party Nationally," (1968), *Ibid.*, 2.

[36] Phil Fradkin and Dial Torgerson, "Negro Leaders Urge Suspect in Police Shootout to Give Up," *Los Angeles Times*, 7 August 1968.

[37] Sylvia Guerrero, "The Political Development of the Mexican-American Community, 1950-1978," M.A. thesis, California State University, Los Angeles, 1985, 87-88; Rodolfo Acuna, *Occupied America: A History of Chicanos*, 4th ed. (New York: Longman, 2000), 364.

[38] J. Gregory Payne and Scott C. Ratzan, *Tom Bradley: The Impossible Dream* (Santa Monica, CA: Roundtable, 1986), 99, 102-03, 108; Woods, "Progressives and the Police," 504-05.

[39] University of California, Los Angeles, Chancellor's Commission, *Violence at UCLA: May 5, 1970*, a report by the Chancellor's Commission on the Events of May 5, 1970, 1-12; Noel Greenwood, "Calm Returns to UCLA after Violent Eruption," *Los Angeles Times*, 7 May 1970.

[40] Chancellor's Commission, *Violence at UCLA*, 25.

[41] Rodolfo Acuna, *A Community under Siege: A Chronicle of Chicanos East of the Los Angeles River, 1945-1975* (Los Angeles: Chicano Studies Research Center Publications, University of California, Los Angeles, 1975), 198, 200, 202.

[42] Acuna, *Occupied America*, 377-78; Luis J. Rodriguez, *Always Running: La Vida Loca: Gang Days in L.A.* (Willimantic, CT: Curbstone Press, 1993), 166.

[43] Acuna, *Occupied America*, 378-80.

[44] Quintard Taylor, *In Search of the Racial Frontier: African Americans in the American West* (New York: W. W. Norton, 1998), 303-07; U. S. Congress, Senate, Select Committee to Study Governmental Operations with Respect to Intelligence Activities, "The FBI's Covert Action Program to Destroy the Black Panther Party," *Final Report of the Select Committee to Study Governmental Operations* (Washington, D.C.: GPO, 1976), 187-95.

[45] Angela Davis, *An Autobiography* (New York: Random House, 1974), 227-31.

[46] Jerry Cohen, "Black Youth Gangs: Is Threat Overestimated?" *Los Angeles Times*, 19 March 1972; Baker, "Modern Gangs"; Alejandro A. Alonso, "Territoriality Among African-American Street Gangs," M.A. thesis, University of Southern California, 1999, 89-95.

[47] David Rosenzweig, "Gang Violence Linked to Desire for Notoriety," *Los Angeles Times*, 24 December 1972; Los Angeles Police Department, *Annual Report, 1973*, 10-11.

[48] Jerry Belcher and David Rozenweig, "Politics and the Police Department," *Los Angeles Times*, 18 December 1977; Paul Hoffman and Robert Newman, "The Police Spying Settlement," *Los Angeles Lawyer* 7 (May 1984): 20.

[49] Payne and Ratzan, *Tom Bradley*, 127-31; Doug Shuit, "Bradley names 140 to Commissions, Retains 21 of Yorty's Appointees," *Los Angeles Times*, 8 August 1973; "New Guidelines for Review of Police Intelligence Unit Okayed," *Ibid.*,17 December 1976.

[50] Myrna Oliver, "Police Policy on Gun Use Being Revised," *Los Angeles Times*, 28 August 1977; Dale Fetherling and Michael A. Levett, "Value of Life Must be Guide, Commission Says," *Ibid.*, 9 September 1977; Dale Fetherling, "Police Board Upholds New Firearms Policy," *Ibid.*, 30 September 1977.

[51] *Los Angeles Times*, 20 August 1978.

[52] Los Angeles Board of Police Commissioners, *The Report of the Board of Police Commissioners Concerning the Shooting of Eulia Love and the Use of Deadly Force: Part I: The Shooting of Eulia Love*, October, 1979, 1-9.

[53] Doug Shuit and Penelope McMillan, "Police Board Cites Errors in Love Shooting," *Los Angeles Times*, 25 April, 1979; Los Angeles Board of Police Commissioners, *The Report of the Board of Police Commissioners concerning the Shooting of Eulia Love and the Use of Deadly Force: Part 2: Investigation and Adjudication of Use of Force Incidents*, October 1979, 2, 5-6.

[54] American Friends Service Committee, *The Police Threat to Political Liberty* (Philadelphia: American Friends Service Committee, 1979), 41-42.

[55] Roxanne Arnold and Joel Sappell, "Decree Leaves L.A. with Toughest Police-Spy Rules," *Los Angeles Times*, 23 February 1983; Joel Sappell, "Police Intelligence Given to New Unit," *Ibid.*, 10 May 1983; Hoffman and Newman, "Police Spying Settlement," 23-24.

[56] Kody Scott (aka Sanyika Shakur and Monster Kody Scott), *Monster: The Autobiography of an L.A. Gang Member* (New York: Atlantic Monthly Press, 1993), 55-56; also see Baker, "Modern Gangs."

57 David Freed, "Policing Gangs: Case of Contrasting Styles," *Los Angeles Times*, 19 January 1986.

58 James H. Johnson, Jr., et al., "The Los Angeles Rebellion: A Retrospective View," *Economic Development Quarterly* 6 (November 1992): 362; James H. Johnson, Jr. and Walter C. Farrell, Jr., "The Fire This Time: The Genesis of Los Angeles Rebellion of 1992," *North Carolina Law Review* 71 (June 1993): 1411; Mike Davis, *City of Quartz: Excavating the Future in Los Angeles* (New York: Verso, 1990), 305.

59 Jeffrey Fagan, "Gangs, Drugs, and Neighborhood Change," in *Gangs in America*, ed. C. Ronald Huff, 2nd ed. (Thousand Oaks, CA: Sage Publications, 1996), 58; also see James Diego Vigil, *A Rainbow of Gangs: Street Cultures in the Mega-City* (Austin: University of Texas Press, 2002), 82.

60 Davis, *City of Quartz*, 311-13; Alonzo, "African-American Street Gangs," 95.

61 Bob Baker, "With No New Ideas on Gangs, War is Lost," *Los Angeles Times*, 30 January 1989; Davis, *City of Quartz*, 272-73.

62 Eric Malnic and Mark Arax, "1,000 Officers Stage Assault Against Violent Gangs," *Los Angeles Times*, 9 April, 1988; Bob Pool, "Police Call Gang Sweep a Success; 1,453 are Arrested," *Ibid.*, 12 April 1988; David Ferrell, "NAACP Raps Police Over Gang Sweeps," *Ibid.*, 15 April 1988.

63 John Johnson, "Night of the 'Hammer': Retaking the Streets of South L.A.," *Ibid.*, July 1989.

64 Johnson and Farrell, "The Fire This Time," 1407, 1412-13; California, Assembly Special Committee on the Los Angeles Crisis, *To Rebuild is not Enough: Final Report and Recommendations of the Assembly Special Committee on the Los Angeles Crisis*, Sacramento, September 28, 1992, 11.

65 Lou Cannon, *Official Negligence: How Rodney King and the Riots Changed Los Angeles and the LAPD* (New York: Times Books, 1997), 108-09, 113-15, 169.

66 Independent Commission on the Los Angeles Police Department, *Report of the Independent Commission on the Los Angeles Police Department*, July 9, 1991, 4-7; Robert W. Cherny, Gretchen Lemke-Santangelo, and Richard Griswold del Castillo, *Competing Visions: A History of California* (Boston: Houghton Mifflin, 2005), 412-13.

67 Independent Commission, *Report*, ii-iii, 39-46, 62, 71-77, 104-05, 134-35 158-60, 165-68, 173.

68 Cherny, Lemke-Santangelo, and Griswold del Castilllo, *Competing Visions*, 413; James J. Rawls and Walton Bean, *California: An Interpretive History*, 8th ed. (New York: McGraw-Hill, 2003), 546. Shortly after the verdict of the Simi Valley jury, President George Bush ordered a federal investigation of the four officers for violating Rodney King's civil rights. Tried on federal charges, two of them were found guilty in April 1993 and sentenced to thirty months in federal correctional facilities. Cannon, *Official Negligence*, 374-75, 485-86.

[69] Louis Sahagun and John Schwada, "Measure to Reform LAPD wins Decisively," *Los Angeles Times*, 3 June 1992; Cannon, *Official Negligence*, 356.

[70] Cannon, *Official Negligence*, 356.

[71] *Ibid.*, 588-89; Merrick J. Bobb et al., *Five Years Later: A Report to the Los Angeles Police Commission on the Los Angeles Police Department's Implementation of the Independent Commission's Recommendations*, May, 1996, 3-4, 33-34, 52.

[72] Louis Sahagun and Leslie Berger, "Some Gang Members Agreeing to a Truce," *Los Angeles Times*, May 1992; Robert Gottlieb et al., *The Next Los Angeles: The Struggle for a Livable City* (Berkeley: University of California Press, 2005), 126.

[73] Richard Lee Colvin, "Valley Gangs's Peace is Strained but Holding," *Los Angeles Times*, 26 December 1993; Luis J. Rodriguez, *Hearts and Hands: Creating Community in Violent Times* (New York: Seven Stories Press, 2001), 169-70.

[74] Luis J. Rodriguez, Cle Sloan, and Kerhaun Scott, "Gangs: The New Political Force," *Los Angeles Times*, 13 September 2002; Gottlieb et al., *Next Los Angeles*, 126.

[75] Willie L. Williams with Bruce B. Henderson, *Taking Back Our Streets: Fighting Crime in America* (New York: Lisa Drew/Scribner, 1996), 210; ACLU Foundation of Southern California, *False Premise, False Promise: The Blythe Street Gang Injunction and its Aftermath*, May 1993, 1-2; Paul Feldman and Edward J. Boyer, "Street Gang Crackdown Producing Mixed Results," *Los Angeles Times*, 20 April 1995.

[76] Cannon, *Official Negligence*, 540-43, 562-63, 595.

[77] Scott Glover and Matt Lait, "Police in Secret Group Broke Law Routinely, Transcripts Say," *Los Angeles Times*, 10 February 2000; Lou Cannon, "One Bad Cop," *New York Times Magazine*, October 1, 2000, 34-35. Ovando's conviction was overturned in 1999. The city council paid him $15 million, the single largest police misconduct settlement in Los Angeles's history. See Tina Daunt, "City Okays $15 million to Victim of Alleged LAPD Shooting," *Los Angeles Times*, 22 November 2000.

[78] "Anatomy of a Scandal," *Los Angeles Times*, 8 November 2001. The legal fallout from the Ramparts scandal was enormous. More than 100 criminal convictions were overturned. Thirty people sued the city, charging violations of their civil rights. The city settled the lawsuits for a total of $70 million. See Scott Glover and Matt Lait, "LAPD Settling Police Abuse Scandal," *Ibid.*, 31 March 2005.

[79] Los Angeles Police Department, *Board of Inquiry into the Rampart Area Corruption Incident*, March 1, 2000, 56-61; Cannon, "One Bad Cop," 37.

[80] Gottlieb et al., *Next Los Angeles*, 127.

[81] Tom Hayden, *Street Wars: Gangs and the Future of Violence* (New York: The New Press, 2004), 103-04.

[82] Bill Lann Lee to James K. Hahn, May 8, 2000,1, copy of letter in author's possession.

[83] Tina Daunt, "Council will Try to End LAPD Stalemate," *Los Angeles Times*, 9 September, 2000.

[84] Tina Daunt, "U.S. Underlies its Determination on Police Reform," *Ibid.*, 14 September 2000; Tina Daunt and Jim Newton, "LAPD Reform Deal Okayed by City Council," *Ibid.*, 3 November, 2000.

[85] Matea Gold, "Hahn Sworn in as Mayor, Lays out Course of Action," *Ibid.*, 3 July 2001; Matea Gold and Jill Leovy, "Hahn Explains Stance on Chief; Many Express Anger," *Ibid.*, 6 February 2002.

[86] Jill Leovy and Mitchell Landsberg, "Police Commission Rejects Parks," *Ibid.*, 10 April 2002; Tina Daunt and Geoffrey Mohan, "Hahn Picks Bratton to Lead Police Force," *Ibid.*, 3 October 2002.

[87] Megan Garvey and Daniel Hernandez, "Chief Shares Ideas, Hears Concerns in South L.A.," *Ibid.*, 26 November 2002.

[88] Megan Garvey and Richard Winton, "City Declares War on Gangs," *Ibid.*, 4 November 2002; Jill Leovy, "LAPD Tries New Tack in Policing Gangs," *Ibid.*, 14 July 2003.

[89] Richard Winton and Michael Krikorian, "41 Arrested in L.A. Housing Project, " *Ibid.*, 22 January 2004.

[90] Richard Winton, Jill Leovy and Andrew Blankstein, "Beating by LAPD Officer Airs on TV," *Ibid.*, 24 June 2004; Richard Winton, "Bratton Calls Beating 'a Mess'," *Ibid.*, 1 July 2004. The police commission, after meeting with LAPD officials and community leaders, adopted a new policy restricting the use of flashlights as weapons to emergencies only. The policy requires written explanations by officers and extensive review whenever a flashlight is used to subdue a suspect. Richard Winton, "Police Panel Sharply Limits Flashlight Use," *Ibid.*, 12 January 2005.

[91] Jason Felch and James Ricci, "Policing in L.A. Comes under Fire," *Ibid.*, 7 July 2004. A LAPD disciplinary panel recently completed an investigation of the beating of Stanley Miller. It concluded that officer John Hatfield used unnecessary force on Miller and recommended that Hatfield be fired from the department. See Jill Leovy, "Firing of Officer in Taped Beating is Urged," *Ibid.*, 30 July 2005.

[92] Natasha Lee and Richard Winton, "L.A. Boy's Death Prompts Outcry," *Ibid.*, 8 February 2005. The officer told police investigators that he felt in danger as Devin Brown backed his car toward him, leaving him no choice but to shoot. The LAPD recently reenacted the shooting and concluded that the officer was standing to the side of Brown's car when he fired 10 rounds into the vehicle. See Richard Winton and Andrew Blankstein, "Police Slaying Re-Creation Stirs Doubt," *Ibid.*, 27 July 2005.

Chapter 7

LATINO LOS ANGELES
THE PROMISE OF POLITICS

Kenneth C. Burt

REMEMBER—how we used to ask for street lights, bus transportation, play grounds, side walks, street repairs, for help in getting equal treatment in housing and employment?

REMEMBER—how they used to cup their hands to their ears and say, "Speak louder, please. We only hear about one-fifth of what you are saying"?

That is because only one-fifth of us had registered and voted. That is why we always ended up with one-fifth of the neighborhood improvements we needed.

—Community Service Organization
Get-Out-The-Vote flyer, 1948[1]

This 1948 Community Service Organization flier was emphatic in its message that the best way to make government responsive to the people was for the people to vote. Five decades later, history has repeated itself as a new generation of immigrants and their children experienced the consequences of powerlessness and being ignored, or worse, being blamed as scapegoats for larger socio-economic ills. In 1943, during the Zoot Suit Riots, uniformed military personnel attacked young Latinos on the streets of Los Angeles. In 1994, Governor Pete Wilson led the campaign to pass Proposition 187, a voter initiative to deny millions of Latino children access to a public education and medical care. In both cases, the marginalized population was a group of significant size—people (by and large) whose first language was Spanish and who was not part of the political system. Each of these events also served as a catalyst that generated an intense and passionate reaction from the largely disenfranchised Latino community. Substantial numbers of eligible voters were motivated to enter the political arena (many for the first time) and elected new leaders, which in turn, resulted in the emergence of powerful new alliances. Energized by the voters' mandate, the new Latino elected leaders sought more than just ending the attacks on the community; they sought to use the power of government to improve the lives of ordinary people.

There are many similarities between the political activism of the 1940s and 1990s. The young activists of the 1940s were the children of those who had fled the violence of the Mexican Revolution of 1910 to 1917, a period during which 10 percent of population in Mexico emigrated to the United States. The size of the community grew with additional migration and a high rate of childbirth so that in the 1940s Los Angeles was roughly 10 percent Mexican American. Comparatively, during the 1990s many of the activists were from families escaping poverty in Mexico and the civil wars in Central America, especially El Salvador. The most notable difference is in the size of the two groups. During the Mexican Revolution, the numbers of immigrants measured in the tens of thousands. However, the wave of those escaping the poverty and civil wars of Mexico and Central America numbers in the millions. This has had a dramatic impact on Los Angeles in terms of race, class, and culture; demographic changes have corresponded to an economic restructuring as well as an outbound migration of Anglo Saxon Protestants who for decades dominated the region in terms of government and commerce. These migratory trends—into and out of Los Angeles—led to the rapid "Latinoization" of many smaller cities in Los Angeles County, effectively unseating the power from traditionally elected Anglo leaders to Latino leaders. The largest municipality, the City of Los Angeles, itself is roughly one-half Latino.

Finally, the growth among Los Angeles Latinos has occurred within the context of continued growth in California, in both total population and relative size to the rest of the United States. The growth of the state's congressional delegation illustrates these dramatic changes as well as the state's increased importance. In 1910, at the start of the Mexican Revolution, Latinos comprised only 2.4 percent of the state and California had only eight of the 435 members in the U.S. House of Representatives. The California delegation was the same as Kansas and Mississippi, and less than Minnesota. By the 1930s, when this story starts, California claimed twenty seats, the sixth largest total. In 1960, California surpassed New York to become the most populated state and was awarded 38 seats, and Latinos were roughly 10 percent of the state. Today the state's delegation has 52 seats, and Latinos are more than a third of the population.[2]

VOTES, COALITIONS, AND LEADERSHIP

Latino Los Angeles became active in electoral politics during the 1930s, but the number of voters was small due to low rates of naturalization and the fact that only a few of the American-born children had reached voting age, which was then 21. During this era, three men captured the community's imagination: the President, Franklin D. Roosevelt, first elected in 1932; then the gubernatorial campaigns of Upton Sinclair (1934) and Culbert Olson (1938). Roosevelt's appeal was based on the fact that he "seemed to care about the poor."[3] The national Democratic Party put an emphasis on organizing the poor, blue-collar workers, and the foreign-born and their children (which then included about 25 percent of the country, mostly from Europe).

"After the 1932 election, the Democrats possessed a relatively vast coalition, in which Mexicans were numerically a modest part."[4] For this, Los Angeles Latinos were rewarded a few symbolic appointments to boards and commissions. Still, the number of eligible Mexican American voters was not sufficient to elect one of their own to the State Assembly or to the Los Angeles City Council. Even by the end of World War II, Latinos had not yet organized a collective voice comparable to the National Association for the Advancement of Colored People (NAACP), in the African American community, or the Japanese American Citizens League (JACL).

Nonetheless, with the absence of an organizational voice, in 1947 a handful of Latino businessmen encouraged 29-year-old Edward R. Roybal to run for the city council in the Ninth District. Despite his age, Roybal seemed older and more established than most other

World War II veterans. Roybal was born in Albuquerque to a family that traced its roots back 400 years to the founding of Santa Fe. His parents moved to Boyle Heights from New Mexico in 1922 to start a new life following a railroad strike that had left Roybal's father unemployed. Edward Roybal graduated from Roosevelt High School, joined the New Deal Civilian Conservation Corps, and attended the University of California at Los Angeles and then worked for the Los Angeles County Tuberculosis and Health Association. Roybal, his wife, and two children lived in "the flats" located on the southern edge of Boyle Heights.[5]

Roybal would run against an aging incumbent, Parley P. Christensen. Like most Angelenos of the day, Christensen was a native of another state. He became a national figure of the American Left in 1920 as the presidential candidate of the Farmer-Labor Party. In Los Angeles, Christensen successfully used progressive ideology and support from organized labor to cut across ethnic and racial lines to maintain a progressive coalition. This strategy worked for years because the Ninth District was progressive and multicultural in what was then a mostly white, Protestant, and politically moderate Los Angeles. Based in Boyle Heights, the Ninth District served as the entry point for immigrants, particularly Jews from Eastern Europe and smaller numbers of Latinos from Mexico. The district extended downtown, and included numerous residents in large older homes on Bunker Hill to the more cramped quarters in Little Tokyo. In addition, the Ninth District had a thriving commercial, entertainment, and office center. As the district turned south it took in part of Central Avenue, the center of segregated African American life in Los Angeles. This area had exploded in growth due to the arrival of Blacks who had escaped the serfdom of the "Jim Crow" American South. The cosmopolitan Ninth District was a cauldron of leftist political activity, residents radicalized by events in their home countries (including the Russian Revolution and the Mexican Revolution) and by the upsurge in political and labor activism during the Great Depression.[6]

In the campaign of 1947, Christensen once again utilized his labor and minority coalition to emerge victorious. Roybal finished third out of the five candidates, earning just 16 percent of the votes. However, after the election, Roybal and his small band of campaigners decided to stay together to form the Community Political Organization.

Over the next few months, a convergence of events, interests, and individuals began to unfold. Two participants from outside the community focused on helping the young activists organize into a stronger community voice. The first was Fred Ross, a talented young Anglo organizer who had previously worked with Mexican Americans in several surrounding communities and wanted to organize in Los Angeles. He sought to combine his strategic vision with the raw talent of the young activists, most of whom had learned leadership skills through service in World War II, or in unionized factories on the home front during the war. However, the main problem was money as the new group did not have the funds to hire Ross. About the same time, Saul Alinsky, the head of the Chicago-based Industrial Areas Foundation (IAF), wanted to start a new organizing project and heard of Ross. Alinsky, a Jew, had organized one of Chicago's multi-ethnic neighborhoods in conjunction with the Catholic Church and the United Packinghouse Workers union. This confluence of interests was to have an historic result. The Latino group broadened its goals beyond politics, changed its name to the Community Service Organization (CSO), and became a non-profit affiliated with the IAF. Alinsky agreed to undertake this first project focused on Latinos and to pay Ross' salary for the next year; Ross agreed to become the CSO organizer.[7]

One of the first tasks was to formalize CSO's structure. Roybal became chairman, in large part because he was widely known in the Mexican American community due to his recent campaign. He was also representative of World War II veterans and the emerging middle class. Jaime Gonzalez, a labor leader-turned-YMCA youth counselor, filled the slot of vice chairman. Emigrant Maria Duran, then a member of the executive board of the ILGWU Dressmakers Union, accepted the post of treasurer. The board also included steelworker Tony Rios and X-ray technician Henry Nava. Nava, the son of a barber, grew up in a local Spanish-speaking Presbyterian Church. Most of the twenty people coming to the CSO meetings were, like Rios and Nava, friends or co-workers of Roybal or, like Manuel, Roybal's uncle, part of the extended family.[8]

CSO decided to build from the ground up. It utilized nightly "house meetings," then an innovative process whereby members invited friends and family to their home to talk about their frustrations and to learn how by working together, through CSO, they could collectively address these concerns. Interested individuals were put to work on a committee or agreed to host a meeting of their own. At the same time, Ross moved to obtain the institutional support from the groups with the largest number of Latinos: organized labor and the Catholic Church. CSO established ties to two strategically situated unions in which core group members were already active: the AFL International Ladies Garment Workers Union (ILGWU) and CIO United Steel Workers. Each had ten to fifteen thousand members in Los Angeles and believed in organizing around labor and community issues. The Roman Catholic Church also embraced CSO. At the request of Monsignor Thomas O'Dwyer, Father William J. Barry, then an assistant pastor at St. Mary's Church in Boyle Heights, joined the CSO board. CSO also reached out to the Protestant churches, small business people, and to the large Jewish community.[9]

It became clear that elected officials were not motivated to address community concerns put forward by CSO because most of the people it represented were not registered to vote. So CSO began to focus its attention on voter registration. "All of us were voter registrars," recalled Margarita Duran, then enrolled at the University of California at Los Angeles. "That's how I met my husband. We registered people to vote. Fred [Ross] would pick you up at the house. He'd drop you off in a neighborhood. Then he'd pick you up after a few hours of work."[10] Those who agreed to register had to decide which political party to join. "Mexican Americans didn't really know the difference between the Democratic Party and the Republican Party," lamented ILGWU organizer Hope Mendoza, a World War II "Rosie the Riveter." "They would ask, 'What was Roosevelt?' You'd say, 'Democrat.' 'That's what I want to be.'"[11]

The results were phenomenal. "In a 3 1/2 month campaign by the Community Services Organization, more than 11,000 voters were registered in Los Angeles' eastside communities," announced the weekly *Belvedere Citizen* in April of 1948.[12] CSO celebrated its success in registering thousands of new voters in Boyle Heights and Belvedere by sponsoring a dance at St. Mary's Church. CSO followed this up by running a non-partisan get-out-the-vote drive in June and November 1948. The goal was to inculcate the

CSO members are sworn-in as deputy registrars of voters in early 1948 at St. Mary's Catholic Church in Boyle Heights. This was the beginning of the first large-scale voter registration drive within the Latino community

importance of voting in the newly registered. There was also a second motive: those who did not vote in the 1948 presidential elections would be purged from the election rolls prior to the spring municipal contests.

In January 1949, Edward Roybal officially made the transition from CSO President to candidate for the 9th district city council seat. The campaign was based on two fundamental strategies: mobilizing Latino voters, and then forming coalitions with other groups, most notable Jews, and segments of organized labor, but also smaller numbers of Irish-American, Japanese-American, and African-American voters. Roybal beat out the other challenges and forced the incumbent into a runoff election. When the polls closed and the votes were counted, the extent of CSO's operation and the larger Roybal campaign became clear. Roybal received over 20,000 votes. This was more than double the *total* votes cast in the entire 1947 election. Roybal's margins were greatest in the Latino and Jewish sections of Boyle Heights.[13] The CSO-registered voters had turned out at the unbelievably high rate of 87 percent.[14] In July 1949, Roybal was sworn in as Los Angeles' first Latino City Councilman since 1881.[15]

THE 1950S: BEYOND BOYLE HEIGHTS

Councilman Roybal authored several fair employment ordinances, delivered dozens of streetlights and sidewalks to his district, and took on the issue of police brutality, which came to a head when CSO's third president, steelworker Tony Rios, was beaten by members of the Los Angeles Police Department in 1952.[16] In all these efforts, Roybal continued to closely work with CSO, and with Jewish, Black, labor, liberal and religious allies.[17]

The new power at the ballot box was infectious and exhilarating. CSO took its message—voting makes a difference—to marginalized Latino neighborhoods around Los Angeles County. The total number of CSO registered voters climbed to 35,000 prior to the November 1950 election. CSO's influence now reached way beyond the Eastside, into the San Fernando Valley, the San Gabriel Valley, the Southeast portion of the County, and the Westside. CSO had effectively mobilized Latinos to vote.[18]

The most dramatic election was in the City of San Fernando, northwest of downtown. The city had grown up around a Spanish Mission, but was now part of the developing suburbs. Led by Hope Mendoza, CSO activists went door to door and registered hundreds in the segregated Latino sections of town. Then in April 1950, Latino activists turned out the Latino vote for a young Mexican American businessman, Albert G. "Frank" Padilla. Padilla not only became that city's first Latino councilman, but he came in first in a multi-candidate field for two seats.[19]

In the early fifties, as CSO expanded to other cities (Cesar Chávez joined in San Jose in 1952,) while in Los Angeles and the organization enjoyed expanded political influence even as many activists started to focus on to other aspects of their lives. This included getting married and having children, attending college and buying a home, usually in a developing suburb. "Housing was real scarce," recalled social worker Margarita Duran Mendez. "We had thought we'd buy a house in the City Terrace or East L.A. and stay close to the neighborhood. We couldn't find anything. And these houses [in southeast L.A. County] came really cheap. $100 down. Naturally we moved down here [to Norwalk]."[20] She added that her situation was similar to many of her friends. CSO's second president, Henry Nava, bought a house in Monterey Park. Hope Mendoza Schechter moved to the San Fernando Valley, as did Henry's brother, Julian Nava.[21]

The increasingly dispersed Los Angeles Latino community leaders began to play even more important roles in civic life as they concentrated on careers and families. This included garnering appointments to local and state boards and commissions. One of the most celebrated victories was Republican Governor Goodwin Knight's appointment of Carlos Teran to the East Los Angeles Municipal court. This made him the first Spanish-speaking judge in modern Los Angeles. Judge Teran is representative of the upwardly mobile members of the Mexican American Generation. The child of an immigrant, he was a company commander in World War II. Upon returning to the states, he used the GI Bill to go to college, graduating from the University of Southern California Law School. He was also active in the community, serving as President of the Board of Directors of the Council of Mexican-American Affairs, and a member of the American GI Forum, a Latino veterans group.[22]

CSO spearheaded the movement that had profound and lasting consequence in Los Angeles and the state for generations to come; it successfully worked to change federal immigration law to make it easier for Latinos to become naturalized citizens, by expanding eligibility and allowing the test to be taken in Spanish. In 1952 Senator Pat McCarran of Nevada was moving a major immigration bill through Congress. Hope Mendoza Schechter, the Latino liaison to Congressman Chet Holifield (D-East Los Angeles), said that Holifield persuaded McCarran to amend the bill, by using the phrase "it's politically important." Holifield also "flattered" McCarran, saying that the senator "would go down in history and this doesn't change the essence of the Act."[23] Soon thereafter, CSO also undertook organizing the first large-scale citizenship classes. In the fall of 1955, CSO sponsored a mass swearing in of 3,000 new citizens at the Hollywood Bowl.[24]

While still only a small portion of the city's population, Los Angeles Latinos continued to register voters in a city still dominated by Anglos throughout the fifties. On the city council, the only other "minority" was Roz Wyman, who was Jewish and female; there were no African or Asian American, or other women on the council. Councilman Roybal (whose district had never been majority Latino) continued to show leadership within his own ethnic community while maintaining cross-cultural, and class-based coalitions to advance the interests of his lower income constituents.

By 1958, the Mexican American generation stood on the cusp of another major breakthrough. Councilman Roybal, one of the most popular elected officials in Los Angeles, was running the open seat on the Los Angeles County Board of Supervisors. He enjoyed a broad coalition and the support of the retiring supervisor, John Anson Ford. At the same time, Los Angeles attorney Henry P. Lopez won the Democratic Party nomination for Secretary of State. The son of a Colorado beet farmer, Lopez had served in World War II, and was one of the first Latinos to graduate from Harvard Law School. He was active in the California Democratic Council (CDC), CSO, and the American GI Forum. [25]

Roybal and Lopez ended their symbolically powerful campaigns at Brooklyn (now Cesar Chávez) and Soto, in the heart of Boyle Heights, where the young Roybal had first won his city council seat nine years earlier. Despite well-run campaigns, the two lost in a cloud of scandal and anger that was to having last effects within the ethnic community. It initially appeared that Roybal had won the race for supervisor, but after days of recounting, and the discovery of additional voting boxes, he was declared the loser. Lopez lost his statewide race by a narrow 50,000-vote margin. It was particularly painful because he was the only statewide candidate to lose in what was otherwise a Democratic sweep. Some activists, like fellow attorney Herman Sillas, speculated his loss was due to anti-Latino bias. Lopez believed that it was the presence of a third party candidate that took anti-incumbent voters away from him. [26]

THE 1960s: CONGRESS AND THE STATE LEGISLATURE

Despite these setbacks, the Latino community experienced unprecedented victories over the next five years. In 1960, Mexican

Americans played a major role in the presidential campaign of John F. Kennedy, and emerged from the experience with heightened expectations for the Latino role in politics at all levels of government. In 1961, for the first time, Latinos made the critical difference in the election of Sam Yorty as the new Mayor of Los Angeles. Mayor Poulson explained his defeat, saying, "In the districts where I won, there was a light turnout but in the Negro and Mexican districts the turnout was larger."[27] The victory was particularly sweet because *Newsweek* magazine gave Los Angeles Latinos credit for Yorty's win.[28] Sweeter still, Mayor Yorty quickly rewarded Latinos for their critical support. Yorty placed Dr. Francisco Bravo on the important Police Commission. He put Professor Julian Nava on the Civil Service Commission. More important still, Yorty placed Richard Tafoya on his personal staff where he functioned as a deputy mayor, a first for Mexican Americans.[29]

Latinos retained their momentum as 1961 rolled into 1962. Roybal was elected to Congress and Phil Soto and John Moreno were elected to the State Assembly, which was then a part-time job. Roybal, Soto and Moreno benefited from post-Census reapportionment that created districts without incumbents. Each could campaign partly on their service as veterans of World War Two, and on their city council records. All three received volunteers by virtue of their being part of the newly established Mexican American Political Association (MAPA).[30] Roybal and Soto won in districts without a majority of Latino voters. Roybal's urban district started in Boyle Heights and moved onto Hollywood. Soto, a small businessman and councilman in La Puente, represented the post-war movement of Latinos to the Southeastern Los Angeles County. He estimated that his district was 10 percent Latino. Schoolteacher Moreno was the Mayor of Sante Fe Springs and represented greater East Los Angeles. It was a majority Latino district, and should have been politically safe. However, Moreno would last only one term due to a drunken driving scandal that led Dionicio Morales to challenge him. A number of suburban elected officials backed Morales, such as Pico Rivera Councilman Frank Terrazas and Sante Fe Councilman Ernest Flores. This divide in Latino voters allowed an Anglo to beat them both in the primary. For his part, Soto survived two terms. He lost his "swing district" to a Republican as part of the landslide for Ronald Reagan in 1966.[31]

Congressmen Edward R. Roybal, Joseph Montoya (New Mexico), and Henry B. Gonzalez (Texas)
with President John F. Kennedy at the White House in 1963. For the first time, Los Angeles
Latinos enjoyed access to power at the highest levels in Washington, D.C.

The following year, 1967, Julian Nava, became the first Los
Angeles Latino to win a seat on the Los Angeles School Board, then
a citywide race. Nava grew up on the Eastside, worked in an auto
plant, and then earned a doctorate at Harvard University. Back in
Los Angeles, he involved himself in the community and served
as a Mayor Yorty appointee to the Civil Service Commission and
helped found the American Federation of Teachers at California
State College, Northridge. The campaign leadership represented
his broad political support. African American City Councilman
Tom Bradley, Jewish AFL-CIO head Sigmund Arywitz, and Judge
Leopoldo Sanchez served as campaign co-chairs. Hollywood

celebrities Steve Allan and Gregory Peck lent their name, as did a host of present and former Democratic elected officials, including Senator Robert Kennedy.[32] Nava assembled a board coalition and campaigned vigorously. The San Fernando resident recalled that "University lecturing, in addition to the CSO experience, had prepared me very well to speak to all groups across town."[33]

In 1968, the Latino community played a huge role in the presidential primary victory of Senator Robert F. Kennedy. That election brought Latinos into the national spotlight as never before, in part because of Kennedy's champion of the farmworkers' cause, and a massive voter registration and turnout by MAPA and the United Farm Workers. However, the election of Roybal aide Alex Garcia to represent the Boyle Heights-based Assembly District was nearly forgotten in the anguish over the assassination of Senator Kennedy. "Roybal called me and asked me to help," recalled Hank Lacayo, president of the 30,000 member United Auto Workers Local 887. "We won with Garcia because we went in with heavy fire power, with money, and all that."[34] Garcia subsequently moved to the State Senate and Richard Alatorre and Art Torres won seats in East Los Angeles, while Joseph Montoya won in the suburbs of Southeast Los Angeles in the early 1970s.[35]

From Washington, Congressman Roybal delivered federal job training programs to improve the lot of Los Angeles Latinos. He authored the amendment that created the first federal support for bilingual education, and signed by President Lyndon Johnson in 1968. Roybal also helped place Latinos in appointed and civil service posts within the federal government. Likewise, Roybal helped to pass the 1965 immigration reform bill to increase the number of people from Mexico and Latin America who could enter into the United States. While no one then knew the full impact of this bill (which was the first major change in federal law since 1924), there was a definite sense of its historic value. In an image that captures both the past and the future, Roybal flew with Johnson on Air Force One to New York where, against the backdrop of the Statue of Liberty, he signed the new immigration bill that would help reshape California and the nation.

The upward trajectory of Latino political empowerment in the State Legislature, Congress, and in presidential politics was not

matched on the Los Angeles City Council. The 1963 election
to replace Roybal on the Los Angeles City Council exposed the
weaknesses created within the Latino community by the passage
of time and the demographic shifts in Los Angeles. Roybal sought
to increase the chances that a Mexican American would replace
him. He addressed a large gathering of activists at a MAPA called
meeting at the Alexandria Hotel. "Many of you are under the false
impression that the Mexican-American lives in the greater majority
in this district," said Roybal. "In the last 10 years the Mexican-
American population has been less than the Negro community!"[36]
Holding on to the seat would require, as Roybal laid out, both
Latino unity and an understanding with the African American
community leaders. This might be possible because, despite the
intense desire that Gilbert Lindsay get the seat, and thus become
the first African American on the city council. There were also
strong coalition campaigns underway for the spring 1963 municipal
elections. Tom Bradley and Billy Mills were running with liberal
white support in two other districts with a significant percentage
of black voters. Roybal sought another meeting to decide upon a
sole community representative; he could also use the time to talk
with Black leaders to see if there was a Latino candidate whom they
could coalesce. To Roybal the lesson from his 1949 election was
clear: that in a cosmopolitan district where Latinos were a minority
of the voters, they must unite behind a single candidate who had
the ability to work with other groups. Unfortunately, it was not so
clear to a majority of those present who proceed to endorse three
Latinos, ensuring a Latino divided electorate, and opposition from
the African American community united behind former janitor
Gilbert Lindsay.[37]

The problem was complicated by the fact that the strongest
candidate, Richard Tafoya, Roybal's cousin, was a polarizing figure.
The majority of the city council and key liberals strongly opposed
his patron, Mayor Yorty, who had also angered the African American
community by not following through on his promise to fire Chief
of Police Parker. Moreover, Tafoya was not seen as liberal enough
for the progressive district. Meanwhile, absent an effort to find a
Latino candidate agreeable to Black voters, a consensus developed
among African Americans for Gilbert Lindsay, an aide to Supervisor

Kenneth Hahn and a former CIO activist. Lindsay's supporters did not wait for the special election, instead getting allies on the city council to push through his interim appointment. Lindsay immediately reached out to the Latino community by hiring one of the candidates, Felix Ontiveros, to serve as his chief deputy.[38]

In the runoff, Roybal and other Eastside activists endorsed Tafoya.[39] These endorsements appear to have solidified the Latino support for Tafoya, but the candidate emphasized the reduced number of Spanish-speaking voters in the district due to the building of freeways, urban renewal, and the movement to the suburbs. "Mexican Americans went into Pico Rivera, Whittier, and Montebello. The Jewish population, which was very liberal and which could have voted for a Mexican, moved out," said Tafoya. "Who moved in? Mexicans from Mexico, primarily, who didn't vote."[40]

The anger within the Latino community over Tafoya's defeat only intensified because Lindsay's 1963 election coincided with the election of two other African Americans, Tom Bradley and Billy Mills. There were three Blacks, one Jew, and eleven Anglos on the fifteen-member city council. A sense of shock and then depression set in among Latino activists who never really considered they could lose the city council seat that for so long was emblematic of the community's political empowerment.[41]

The problem was painfully clear—there was no organization in Latino Los Angeles in the mid-sixties with the muscle exhibited by CSO in 1948-1952. Under the leadership of organizer Fred Ross, CSO made sure that Roybal was the only Latino would appear on the ballot, it registered voters and then mobilized them with the assistance of the progressive elements of organized labor and the Catholic Church. At the same time, Roybal and CSO build alliances with non-Latinos to form a majority coalition. In response, a new form of organization would emerge: the Latino political machine, that depended not on social movements, but on money and connections, in a way had more in common with political traditions in New York and Chicago than Los Angeles.

Finally, understanding the development of California Latino politics requires a look at strategies in light of shifting demographics and changing rules. The post-Mexican American era can be broken down into three district periods: the rise of political machines in Los Angeles, the statewide Latino-business alliance, and the present Latino-labor alliance. These developments are unique to California, which never had the ethnic political machines so typical of the white ethnic immigrant period on the East Coast and Midwest. As Carey McWilliams and others noted in the 1940s, political parties in California are weak and campaigns are candidate centered. The state's decision to place the party label on legislative candidates helped the Democrats come to power in 1958 and undoubtedly helped Latinos win seats in Congress and in the part-time State Legislature in 1962. The part-time nature of the Legislature also meant very limited staff and limited budgets to mail to constituents, making it harder to solidify a political base, and thus harder to hold on to newly won seats.

LATINO POLITICAL MACHINES

The move to a full-time Legislature with large staffs was designed to enhance the power of the legislature relative to that of the governor and the lobbyists. But it also had major political implications because it quickened the trend toward concentration of power in Sacramento, which was possible because of the decline of volunteer-driven groups like Mexican American Political Association and the California Democratic Council. This made possible the creation of Latino political organizations with the ability to recruit candidates, direct financial and political support, and disciple members. Members of the Chicano Generation, who came to power in the early seventies, would lead these organizations. These new political forms were designed to take control politically of—and to hold on to—vast neighborhoods in Los Angeles with large numbers of Latino residents but small number of voters, like Boyle Heights and East Los Angeles. Assemblyman Richard Alatorre was the architect of this new organization, which also became identified with Art Torres.[42]

Alatorre became a close ally of Assembly Speaker Willie L. Brown, who developed the most powerful Speakership in modern state history. Key to the operation was Brown's ability to centralize power. This allowed Brown to raise huge amounts of campaign funds from a wide range of economic interests. One year he induced the United

Farm Workers to turn over it's half-million dollar war chest for his distribution. Brown spent liberally to protect incumbents against primary challengers as well as Republicans. He also aided legislators interested in moving up the political ladder. This was achieved, in part, through the newly created unit known as the Speaker's Office of Majority Services. For example, this unit organized an Alatorre-sponsored community event where volunteers painted over graffiti. To maximize the political benefits, they arranged for the press to cover the event and then sent copies of the resultant article, along with a letter from Alatorre, to district voters. At election time, Majority Services staff often transferred to the Speaker's campaign payroll to work on targeted legislative races. An assembly member's career was thus protected in return for his loyalty to the Speaker.[43]

Inside the Capitol, Speaker Brown named Alatorre to chair the powerful Reapportionment Committee to oversee the redrawing of the legislative boundaries following the 1980 Census. In this capacity, he helped Brown further consolidate power and he represented Latino participation in the ruling coalition. During the 1970s, the statewide Latino population had grown due to immigration and childbirth by 92 percent, from 2.37 million to 4.54 millions. Latinos now constituted 20 percent of the state population but held few legislative or congressional seats. Alatorre was limited in his ability to draw districts favorable to Latinos because of the importance of votes and coalition politics. The most notable achievement of the redistricting was the creation of a second Latino congressional seat in Los Angeles County. The longtime United Auto Worker staffer and President Carter appointee, Esteban Torres, won the seat in the San Gabriel Valley. Mid-year Assemblyman Marty Martinez won an election to fill a third seat of an Anglo Congressman in Southeast Los Angeles who retired early. The general inclination to protect incumbents combined with the vested interests of other minority machines to reduce possibilities for new "Latino seats," especially in the State Legislature. Equally important, however, was the reality that few Latinos voted—and voters, not residents, decided elections. The low point was in Assemblywoman Gloria Molina's Boyle Heights-based district, where only seventeen percent were registered! This small number of voters made it difficult for Latinos to compete in areas where their proportion of residents would have otherwise made them a powerful force. Stated Brown: "They are fine people, but if they're not registered to vote they can't help you much."[44]

LEGAL STRATEGIES DRIVE POLITICS

Beginning in the late 1980s a fundamental transition began to take place in the Latino community. Faced with the reality of perilously low voter participation, Latino activists sought to change the rules of the game as the best way to gain advantage at the ballot box. The most successful was the creation of "majority minority" districts that all but guaranteed Latinos election. This was achieved through a combination of federal intervention and legal action. Congress amended the 1965 Voting Rights Act and the U.S. Justice Department's subsequent interpretation had far reaching consequences. The federal government had long held that state and local government could not gerrymander district boundaries to prevent the election of a minority candidate. Now they decided that government at all levels now had the affirmative responsibility to create districts dominated by minorities even if it involved piecing together non-contiguous areas. Legal advocates pushed for district elections in cities, counties, and school districts where Latinos were having trouble winning in an at-large system. This would give Boyle Heights its own school board member, for example, reducing the need for extraordinary candidates like Julian Nava who could stitch together a citywide coalition. The strategy also reflected a dependence on an elite, top down legalism that had grown out of the later stages of the civil rights movement. It stood in stark contrast to CSO's earlier bottom-up strategy of mobilizing the masses and forming alliances with other communities. It did dovetailed with the operation of the Alatorre-Torres machine then seeking to leverage its power in Sacramento to break into Los Angeles politics.[45]

The U.S. Department of Justice sued the City of Los Angeles for not creating a council district in which a Latino could be assured of winning. As a by-product of this suit, Boyle Heights City Councilman Art Snyder resigned in 1985. Assemblyman Alatorre was elected to the post with the help of Speaker Brown. Alatorre thus became the first Latino on the city council since Roybal resigned to take his seat in Congress some twenty-three years earlier. On the council, Alatorre became an ally of Mayor Tom Bradley, the city's first and only African American mayor.[46] Soon thereafter, Richard Alarcon broke another barrier and was elected to represent the eastern portion of the San Fernando Valley, giving Latinos a second councilman for the first time. The Civil Rights Act were also used as the basis of challenging at large elections. This led the Los Angeles School Board to adopt district elections, making it easier to elect a Latino.[47]

Attention then turned to the five-member Los Angeles County Board of Supervisors. In 1988, the Mexican American Legal Defense Fund (MALDEF), the ACLU of Southern California, and the U.S. Department of Justice sued, claiming that the board had purposely drawn the lines to prevent the election of a Latino. After extensive maneuvering, the board created a largely Mexican American district. Assemblywoman Gloria Molina, now head of her own political machine, won, becoming the first Latina on the Los Angeles Board of Supervisors, just as she had been the first Latina in the state legislature. At her swearing-in, Molina stating that she should not have been the first Spanish-speaking supervisor. "This victory should have been celebrated 30 years ago. That is why I want to dedicate this victory to Congressman Ed Roybal. They stole the election from him 30 years ago."[48]

Changes in the Voting Rights Act had a similarly dramatic impact on the state legislative races following the 1990 census, despite an acknowledged undercount of minorities. This was due to a second decade of unprecedented growth in the Latino population. Latinos now comprised 37.8 percent of Los Angeles County and more than a quarter of the state. When Republican Governor Pete Wilson and the Democratic-controlled Legislature failed to agree on a reapportionment plan, the issue went to the State Supreme Court. The Court—using the new interpretation of the Voting Rights Act—exaggerated the effects of the demographic changes by reducing the number of politically moderate, mixed suburban-urban districts in favor of Democratic-oriented, urban, majority-minority districts, and Republican-oriented, Anglo dominated suburban districts. Race based reapportionment thus served to reduce the lag-time between demographic change and political representation by radically changing the districts on the incumbents. The effort to create Latino districts resulted in a fourth Latino seat in Congress and the addition of legislative seats in the Eastern and Southeast portions of the county. Among those who would win a congressional seat was Assemblywoman Lucille Roybal-Allard who took her father's seat. In so doing she became the first Latina of Mexican heritage to be elected to Congress.[49] Another Latina with ties to the past was Nell Soto. She won a seat in the state legislature where her husband, Phil Soto, had served from 1963 to 1967.[50]

The 1990 statewide reapportionment also produced the first large number of Latino legislators outside of Los Angeles. One Los Angeles Latino, Assemblyman Richard Polanco, an Alatorre ally, did more than anyone else to elect Latinos to the Legislature.[51] He recognized that there was a basic organizational void in the Latino community; and labor had stopped being a major political player. The opportunity rested, as Polanco saw it, in raising large sums of money from business and then using it to run consultant driven and mail oriented election campaigns in targeted seats. This Latino-business alliance produced generally conventional and moderate public policy and focused on existing voters. Moreover and there was a growing gap in thinking between more affluent third generation Latinos and the working class immigrants. Political columnist Dan Walters put it succinctly: "Anglo voters and middle-to-upper income Asians and Hispanics are identifying more strongly with the Republican Party. And while they may be outnumbered in the general population, they are the most likely to be politically active—to register and vote."[52]

PROPOSITION 187

The Republican Party appears to have taken its growing share of the upwardly mobile Latino vote for granted as it moved to scapegoat immigrants for the state's economic malaise in 1994. Eighteen points behind in the polls just weeks before his reelection, Governor Wilson made the aforementioned Proposition 187, to deny public services to undocumented immigrants, the centerpiece of his campaign. The pro-187 campaign spent millions of dollars to air television commercials showed Mexicans illegally crossing the border while an announcer intoned, "And they keep coming." The Proposition 187 campaign served Wilson's short-term political needs because it allowed him to win reelection and for the Republicans to take control of the State Assembly and come close to winning control of the State Senate. Also dashed in the election was hope of Senator Art Torres, the best known Latino in the state, who had sought to become the first statewide elected official. He narrowly lost the race for Insurance Commissioner.[53]

Governor Wilson had shocked the Latino community more violently than at anytime since soldiers and sailors attacked unarmed Latinos in the Zoot Suit Riots during World War II. This traumatized the immigrant community and angered deep-rooted Mexican Americans. The loudest voices of support for the immigrant community came from Cardinal Roger Mahony and the Catholic Church, and a number of AFL-CIO unions. (Only a majority of Asians, Jews, and Latinos vote against the initiative.[54]) Among Latinos, Proposition 187 led to an unprecedented level of pre-election mobilization, with 100,000 people marching through the streets. But neither Proposition 187 nor Torres on the ballot substantially increased turnout. "The forecast is for rain, but there is sun behind those clouds," stated Congressman Xavier Becerra.[55]

The Republican Party continued its anti-Latino drumbeat into 1995 and 1996. This further engrained Proposition 187 in the collective memory even as it was appealed in the courts (and eventually overturned). With the November 1994 Republican takeover of Congress, Speaker Newt Gingrich adopted the anti-immigrant agenda: "House GOP Charts California Agenda," read one headline in the *Los Angeles Times*.[56] Congress proceeded to deny benefits to legal residents to undocumented and legal non-citizen residents alike. In response, an unprecedented number of Latinos—including some who had been in California for decades—completed the process to become citizens and to register to vote. The number grew rapidly because President Clinton, recognizing the value of Latino voters, cut the time it took the federal government to process citizenship applications from two years to six months.[57]

In California, the Republicans in 1996 underscored the importance of voting for Latinos by backing Proposition 209 to end affirmative action, reducing opportunities for college and employment.[58] Worse yet, the 1996 Republican Dole for President campaign openly appealed to racial antagonisms and linked affirmative action to immigration issues. "The significance of Dole's endorsement of California's Proposition 209 is not that it was a new political strategy, but rather, by openly appealing to white racial resentment for political gain, it revived a tactic that had been considered off-limits in American politics since the [pro-segregationist] George Wallace presidential campaign in 1968."[59] As a result, 80 percent of California Latinos voted for Clinton, the best performance for any Democrat since President Johnson in 1964. Moreover, a third of the Latino voters "either naturalized or turned 18 years of age since the last election."[60] There were also changes among Anglo voters. Los Angeles County, which had voted for Ronald Reagan for president in 1980 and 1984, voted for Clinton in 1992 and 1996, allowing the Democrats to carry the state in a presidential election for the first time since 1964.[61] The increased Latino civic engagement combined with the intensity of the anti-Latino attacks produced a new interest in the plight of immigrants by progressive non-Latinos, organized labor, the Catholic Church, and by the Democratic Party. The time was ripe for a reemergence of a more activist style of Latino coalition politics as practiced by Roybal and CSO and segments of organized labor in the late 1940s.

LATINO-LABOR ALLIANCE

Yet another unpredictable event was to shape the modern history of California Latino politics. James Wood, the executive secretary of the Los Angeles County Federation of Labor died in mid-1995 (about the same time as the national AFL-CIO elected new, more aggressive leadership). This opened the door to a Latino to head the Los Angeles Federation more than a decade before it would otherwise have occurred in the seniority driven institution. Miguel Contreras, the County Federation's Political Director, emerged victorious, earning the right to speak for 600,000 union members in Los Angeles County. He had assets that uniquely positioned him to tap into the political developments within the state, the labor movement, and the immigrant community.

Born into a farmworker family in Dinuba, a small town south of Fresno, in the Central Valley, Contreras saw the confluence of labor and culture and politics and its impact on workers and their families. He first met Cesar Chávez when the labor leader came to town to rally workers to campaign for Robert Kennedy in the 1968 presidential primary. After Kennedy's assassination, Contreras joined the UFW's Ranch Committee and then in 1973 moved to Toronto, Canada to help organize the grape boycott. There he learned the art of Alinsky-style organizing that would underpin the rest of his life. He worked with labor unionists, housewives, students, as well as ministers, priests, and rabbis. Returning to California, he became an organizer for the Hotel Employees and Restaurant Employees, taking on tough projects in San Francisco and Los Angeles, and other cities. In these jobs he worked with a multi-racial workforce, but his knowledge of Spanish was instrumental in organizing the increasingly large number of immigrants in the hospitality industry (and some, like himself, who had started as farmworkers). During these and other jobs, he worked with some of the best organizers of his time, including Cesar Chávez, Dolores Huerta, and their mentor, Fred Ross.[62]

Contreras immediately began to look for political opportunities. The goal for organized labor was, like for Latino Los Angeles, to demonstrate that it was relevant politically. That it could go beyond backroom deal making to mobilize its members to walk precincts and to vote in ways that it had not done for years. Contreras found a place where there were low expectations, but a high level of rewards if victory was achieved: the 1996 legislative elections. "Assembly Democrats are saying, we will win in the Salinas area…, we will win in Orange County…, but don't think we can win in Los Angeles," Contreras said afterwards. "We said, no, we are targeted and we are focused and we are working in conjunction with the national AFL-CIO. So we are going to put all the unions on the same page when it came to politics in November 1996."[63] The new labor movement in Los Angeles focused on "kitchen table economics" and delivered the message by mail and with 3,500 union volunteers. At the same time, SEIU and the education unions utilized their Opportunity PAC, which spent hundreds of thousands of dollars on these races. On Election Day, Los Angeles labor helped Democrats win in historically Republican suburbs, including a Latina community college teacher, Sally Havice, and to thereby take back the majority in the State Assembly. This led to the election of Cruz Bustamante as the first Latino speaker. One of his major achievements was the restoration of some programs used by immigrants that were cut by Newt Gingrich and the House Republicans in Washington, D.C.

With Los Angeles labor having demonstrated that they could deliver the winning margin between two self-selecting candidates, Contreras then sought to prove that new labor movement could elect one of its own. The opportunity presented itself the next year in a special election for the assembly seat based in Boyle Heights, the birthplace of CSO and the historic center of the progressive Latino politics. But those days seemed so far way. Louis Caldera had occupied the seat. He was a talented man, Harvard and West Point educated, but a self-identified moderate largely seen as a "business Democrat." The air apparent was Vickie Castro, a school board member and protégé of Supervisor Molina. Labor's candidate was union organizer Gilbert Cedillo. He was a product of the Eastside, with ties to the old CSO and Jewish labor. Most importantly, as the leader of SEIU union representing county workers, he had played a pivotal role in saving the County General Hospital, where the largely uninsured Eastside residents obtain health care. He did this by putting thousand of protesters in the streets and by having national union leaders pressure President Clinton to provide a partial bailout. That campaign set a new tone for labor and community alliance.

Cedillo, the crusading labor leader started the campaign far behind Castro, the entrenched politician, who enjoyed a huge lead in the polls, ample financing, and a traditional résumé. Had Cedillo run a standard campaign he would have lost badly, as Roybal had against Christensen in 1947. He could win only if the campaign because a cause, and labor and its allies dramatically enlarged the number of voters. There would be three parallel and reinforcing efforts. Cedillo's campaign made the case that he would be the best person for the job. The Los Angeles County Federation of Labor had its campaign, based on economic issues, with its own mail program, and a dozen full-time organizers, who mobilized hundreds of others to communicate with AFL-CIO members. Equally important was the "new voter" program, led by the immigrant unions, and community allies, such as Hermandad Mexicana Nacional, led by the aging labor and Latino activist Bert Corona. This was possible because he had mentored a number of the new labor leaders, including Maria Elena Durazo, and dreamed of building a new social movement. Their message was clear and passionate: immigrants needed to vote as a way to fight the attacks their families and on their community. In their fight, Cedillo would stand and fight with them. The Latino Caucus added to Cedillo's margin when it arranged for some business groups to back Cedillo.[64]

This "new style" of campaigning was reminiscent of Roybal's initial win in 1949, when CSO brought thousands of new voters to the polls—and it worked. Cedillo won big, sending shock waves through the political establishment. (For his part, Cedillo would keep faith with the immigrant community in his fight for a drivers license bill for non-citizens.) Politics in Latino Los Angeles had changed course. In the succeeding years the County Federation of Labor has become a political machine, consciously constructing a Latino-labor alliance, as well becoming a force in other ethnic and minority communities. This is due to its unique ability to deliver thousands of campaign volunteers at a time when activists are absent from many campaigns. It is also due to the ability of organized labor to target large sums of money, spent wisely with the aid of top-flight political consultants. The ability to exercise such influence is due, in part, to the huge influx of Latinos into Los Angeles and the corresponding flight of Anglos and much of the traditional business elite. It also reflects labor's ever-present attempts to speak for working families and for immigrants beyond its own membership, and its partnerships with the faith community. Contreras and new labor received generally positive mark form the *Los Angeles Times,* for which Frank Del Olmo provided a Latino voice.[65]

The changing of the formal political rules in California and in Los Angeles also contributed to the lessening of the power of incumbent politicians. For the Latino community it represented both a threat to existing Latino held seats while holding the promise for Latino victories in Anglo held seats.[66] Under voter-approved term limits (yet another conservative voter initiative, this one designed to drive African American Speaker Willie Brown from power), elected officials may serve only three two-year terms in the Assembly, and two four-year terms in the Senate. Los Angeles voters followed suit and imposed limits of two four-year terms on their city councilmembers. These limits have led to constant turnover in the ranks of the once entrenched politicians. Up-and-coming elected officials still need to establish name identification and to develop a fund raising base, and those in office still influence their replacement. However, there has been a fundamental shift in power away form politicians and towards the constituency groups who participate in this game of musical chairs.[67]

The new Los Angeles-based Latino-labor alliance came into its own in Sacramento with the election of Antonio Villaraigosa as the second Latino speaker, and the first from Los Angeles. A smart and charismatic leader, Villaraigosa was a former organizer for United Teachers Los Angeles. When forced out by term limits, he decided to run for Mayor of Los Angeles. Early polls gave him only 4 percent support, a measure of how little press state legislators receive in the celebrity and crime oriented Los Angeles media, far behind a number of other contestants. The County Federation of Labor decided to go all out and Villaraigosa sought to construct a coalition based on the Roybal model. In one of the memorable rises in local politics, the coalition carried Villaraigosa into the runoff and into a 47 to 47 tie in the polls just days before the runoff. "Labor, the constituency that is the linchpin of his coalition, is the single most potent anti-nationalist force in the city. Time and again over the past five years, the County Federation of Labor has opposed ethnocentric candidates backed by Polanco with class-oriented candidates of its own," opined *L.A. Weekly*'s Herald Meyerson.[68] In the end, Villaraigosa came up short, but it was a dramatic event, with the defeated candidate's party outnumbering that of the victorious Jimmy Hahn. Shortly thereafter, Villaraigosa gambled again: he defeated a city council incumbent from Boyle Heights by dramatically increasing voter turnout with the help of labor.

Cedillo and Villaraigosa were not the only ones to emerge from the ranks of Latino-labor alliance. In 2002, Cedillo moved to the State Senate, filling the seat occupied by Richard Polanco, who was forced out by term limits. This opened up the Boyle Heights-based seat in the State Assembly. The progressive candidate was Fabian Nuñez. The twelfth son born to a maid and a gardener, the 35-year-old Nuñez attended college and became a labor organizer. Nuñez came to prominence in East Los Angeles fighting the passage of Proposition 187. Soon thereafter Nuñez assumed the post as political director of the Los Angeles County Federation of Labor, AFL-CIO, where he worked with Miguel Contreras to forge a Latino-labor alliance. Nuñez then headed the governmental relations unit for the Los Angeles Unified School District.

Nuñez was opposed by a more conventional Latino candidate, Pedro Carrillo, aide to Congresswoman Lucille Roybal-Allard, and was backed by forces close to the California Chamber of Commerce. The business interests pumped resources into both his formal campaign, which was very nasty, and into a series of "independent expenditures" on behalf of their candidate. However, this was a fight that labor was determined to win. The Los Angeles County Federation of Labor and the Opportunity PAC spent $500,000 on their own "independent expenditures" that included precinct walkers on release time and Spanish-language TV ads. Nuñez won and in his freshman year was elected Speaker of the Assembly by his new colleagues. His election as Speaker was supported and encouraged by two important mentors—City Councilman Antonio Villaraigosa and AFL-CIO head Miguel Contreras.

Mayor Antonio Villaraigosa

Antonio Villaraigosa soon eclipsed Nuñez by being elected as the first Latino Mayor of Los Angeles in since Cristobal Aguilar left office in 1872. Villaraigosa's election in 2005 drew national and international coverage. In its cover story, entitled "Latino Power," *Newsweek* emphasized that Villaraigosa's dramatic defeat of an incumbent mayor in the nation's second largest city was emblematic of the rise of Latinos within the political arena.[69] In this they are correct. There is no question that Villaraigosa represents a major electoral breakthrough. But even as Villaraigosa's election is an historic milestone, he is also representative of a long tradition of coalition politics in Los Angeles. For the first time, Latinos accounted for a quarter of the city's electorate. While this is a huge jump over previous years, it still necessitates an electoral alliance. Villaraigosa won with a coalition that included Jews, African Americans, Asians, organized labor, and the liberal-left. It is not a coincidence that just such an alliance elected Edward R. Roybal as the first Latino to the Los Angeles City Council back in 1949 from a district in which Latino voters were likewise a minority. It was a matter of philosophy and strategy that led Villaraigosa to make history as a Latino candidate by campaigning to be the mayor "for all of Los Angeles."

Villaraigosa thematically stressed bringing the city together and injecting new energy into municipal government. He also benefited enormously from an engaging personality, government experience, and his years as a coalition builder and fund raiser and the high name identification from that previous mayor campaign that had catapulted him to celebrity status rare for politicians. The endorsement of U.S. Senator John Kerry (for whom Villaraigosa was as a national co-chair of his 2004 presidential campaign) served to reinforce the councilman' momentum and helped secure votes in the more politically moderate San Fernando Valley. In the final days the both the city's newspapers endorsed. "Villaraigosa's drive, people skills and knack for coalition-building earned our endorsement in 2001," noted the *Los Angeles Times*, before concluding: "He is the best choice to lead Los Angeles."[70]

The most fundamental change in the city's politics that made victory possible, in addition to the growing number of Latino voters, was the creation a labor-based, progressive and multi-cultural network of organizations, donors, and elected officials. The architect of this new Los Angeles was labor leader Miguel Contreras, who died, at age 52, two weeks prior to Villaraigosa's triumphant election. While the Los Angeles County Federation of Labor did not campaign for the Villaraigosa as it had in all his previous races (because the incumbent, Mayor Hahn, had delivered for labor), the majority of labor's dollars and votes went to the former teachers' union organizer. Contreras, more than anyone else, had helped construct the foundation for victory by increasing Latino voter registration and by restitching the pieces of progressive Los Angeles. He led the movement that redefined the role of local government to helping create a livable city for immigrants and working families.[71]

On Election Day, Villaraigosa decisively defeated Mayor Hahn. The 59 to 41 percent margin represented a victory for his coalition strategy of reaching out to every group and every geographic region of the city. Latino elected officials, such as Assemblywoman Cindy Montañez of San Fernando, partnered with hundreds of farmworkers and hotel workers who helped turnout the Latino vote in the Northeast San Fernando Valley. The Villaraigosa campaign oversaw a parallel operation in its base in East Los Angeles, the political birthplace of California Latino politics. These turnout efforts reinforced the desire by many Latinos to elect one of their own. For the first time, Latinos represented 25 percent of the total city electorate; an overwhelming 84 percent voted for Villaraigosa. According to the *Los Angeles Times'* exit poll, he also enjoyed majority support from three important groups: Jewish voters, union members, and liberals, and split white voters. Among identified ethnic and racial groups, Villaraigosa won 55 percent of the Jewish voters (17 percent of the total), 48 percent of African Americans (15 percent of the electorate), and 44 percent of the Asian voter (5 percent of the total). Even though Villaraigosa narrowly missed receiving the majority of African American votes, he ran strong with Blacks under 45 years of age, which is seen as an important step in healing historic tensions. Celebrating the victory, the rainbow of multicultural Los Angeles joined Villaraigosa on stage.[72]

THE PROMISE OF POLITICS

The search for a Latino political voice expressed in the 1948 CSO leaflet has been realized many times over. Today, Latinos are omnipresent in Los Angeles City Hall. The large and growing number of Latino voters is a reality in many districts. The number of Latino elected and appointed officials—beginning with Mayor Antonio Villaraigosa—provides a level of influence in the corridors of power unknown in previous generations. The politically powerful Los Angeles County Federation of Labor has served an important role in electing councilmembers and in advocating for policies that benefit immigrants and working class families. Organized labor also serves as a bridge to other minority, religious, and political organizations that helped reduce the political isolation and parochialism that is more prevalent with ethno-centric candidates.

Los Angeles Latinos also benefit from the statewide Latino population growth, and the fact that the Latino Caucus is now the largest group within the majority party within the State Legislature. Moreover, close to half of the Latino Caucus are from Los Angeles County. This helps account for the fact that three of the last five Assembly Speakers have been Latinos, and two of the three—Villaraigosa and Nuñez—are from Los Angeles. Likewise, five of the seven Latino Members of Congress are from Los Angeles County; moreover, four the five are Latinas: Grace Napolitano, Lucille Roybal-Allard, Linda Sanchez, and Hilda Solis. There are also a growing number of women and men serving in local government. Gloria Molina is the County Supervisor, Rocky Delgadillo is the City Attorney, and Alex Padilla is the City Council President. The fifteen-member city council includes four Latinos (27 percent), and 82 of the 344 board and commissioners are Latino (24 percent).[73] Many of the county's smaller cities are now entirely Latino-led, from San Fernando to Southgate.

The demographic and political changes over the last sixty years since the end of World War II are profound. Never again will the Latino community be so highly dependent on a single elected official, as it was when Edward Roybal was the only major elected official in the city and the state. Yet his election and public service was an important milestone in the community's political awakening and development. Moreover, the political pioneers' realization—that votes count, coalitions matter, and leadership makes a difference—is a timeless truism. Still, politics occurs within a larger political context. This may also help explain the timing of the two big breakthroughs. The Roosevelt New Deal Democratic Party coalition and World War II changed the way Latinos saw themselves and the way the community was approached by potential allies. So today, Latinos have decided to stand up for their rights at the same time the sixties values of civil rights and equal opportunity have come to dominate cities like Los Angeles. "Today's Democrats are the party of the transition from urban industrialism to a new postindustrial metropolitan order in when men and women play equal roles and in which white America is supplanted by multiracial, multiethnic America."[74]

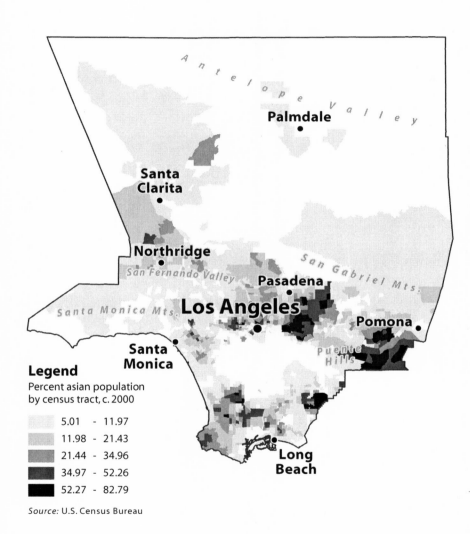

Legend

Percent asian population
by census tract, c. 2000

	5.01 - 11.97
	11.98 - 21.43
	21.44 - 34.96
	34.97 - 52.26
	52.27 - 82.79

Source: U.S. Census Bureau

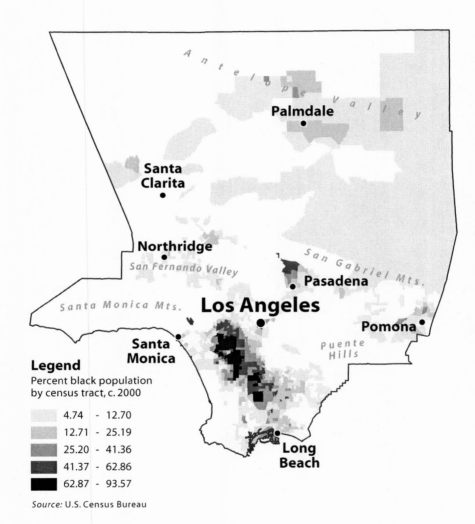

Palmdale

Santa
Clarita

Northridge

Pasadena

Los Angeles

Pomona

Santa
Monica

Legend
Percent black population
by census tract, c. 2000

4.74 - 12.70
12.71 - 25.19
25.20 - 41.36
41.37 - 62.86
62.87 - 93.57

Long
Beach

Source: U.S. Census Bureau

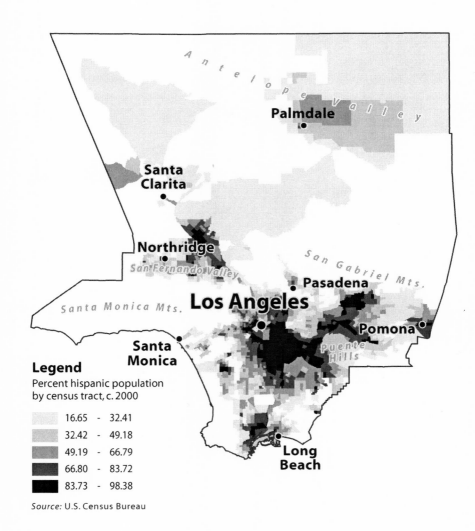

Legend

Percent hispanic population
by census tract, c. 2000

16.65 -	32.41
32.42 -	49.18
49.19 -	66.79
66.80 -	83.72
83.73 -	98.38

Source: U.S. Census Bureau

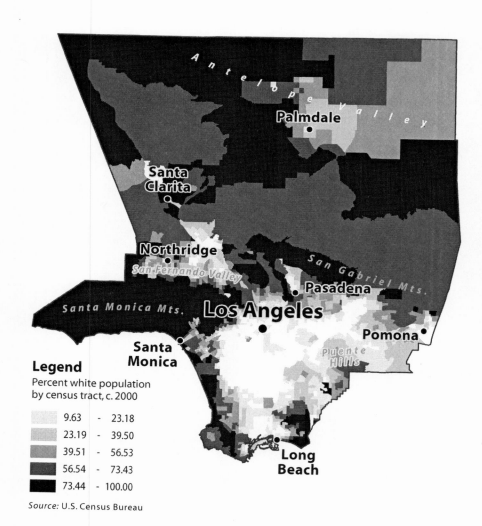

Legend

Percent white population
by census tract, c. 2000

9.63   - 23.18
23.19 - 39.50
39.51 - 56.53
56.54 - 73.43
73.44 - 100.00

Source: U.S. Census Bureau

Favorable context alone may not be enough to trigger a large increase in civic engagement. It may require a catalyst. This helps to explain why the two largest jumps in the percentage of Latino voter registration in California history occurred in the years following traumatic attacks on the community. In Los Angeles, five years after the Zoot Suit Riots, the 1948 CSO driven voter registration drive netted 15,000 new voters that more than doubled the size of the Latino electorate. The momentum continued and by 1950 the number of new Latino voters had grown to 35,000. So, too, in 2000, five years after Proposition 187, the number of new voters had doubled. In Los Angeles, this translated to 500,000 new Latino voters. What differentiates the two periods is the size of the Latino community. However, the number of residents is not enough. What counts is the number of voters, activists and elected officials. At least in the City of Los Angeles, the need for Latino civic engagement and for coalition politics will continue as people from varied backgrounds continue to seek the promise of politics—and a fulfilling life—in a diverse metropolitan community.

NOTES

[1] CSO, "Attention Voters, We Are 16,000 Strong," 15/Mexican Groups, 1948, Jewish Community Relations Council Papers, Urban Archives Center, California State University, Northridge.

[2] Mark Baldassare, *California in the New Millennium: The Changing Social and Political Landscape* (Berkeley: University of California Press, in conjunction with the Public Policy Institute of California, 2000), p. 3; David Hayes-Bautista, La Nueva California: Latinos in the Golden State (Berkeley: University of California Press, 2004), 16-17. *California Statistical Abstract*, (Sacramento: State of California, 1970), p. 11; *California Statistical Abstract*, (Sacramento: Department of Finance, State of California, 2001), p. 11; *Democracy At Work, The Official Report of the Democratic National Convention, 1948* (Philadelphia: Local Democratic Political committee of Pennsylvania, 1948), p 553.

[3] Rodolfo Acuña, *Occupied America: A History of Chicanos*, Fourth Edition (New York: Longman, 2000), p. 216.

[4] Juan Gomez-Quiñones, *Roots of Chicano Politics, 1960-1940* (Albuquerque: University of New Mexico Press, 1994), pp. 400-401.

[5] Author's interview with Edward Roybal, Pasadena, March 10, 1995; Author's interview with Roger Johnson, Hollywood, December 19, 1981; Himilce Hovas, *The Hispanic 100: A Ranking of the Latino Men and Women Who Have Most Influenced American Thought and Culture* (New York: A Citadel Press Book, 1995), pp. 81-85.

6 Author's interview with Leo Frumkin, for Japanese American National Museum, Tarzana, December 19, 2001; Roger Johnson interview; Author's interview with Margarita Duran Mendez, Norwalk, March 11, 1995; Author's interview with Hope Mendoza Schechter, Sherman Oaks, September 3, 1994; Author's interview with Tony Rios, Los Angeles, 1992-2002; Edward Roybal interview; "Parley P. Christensen," *Who's Who in California*, p. 173.

7 Kenneth C. Burt, "Latino Empowerment in Los Angeles: Postwar Dreams and Cold War Fears, 1948-1952," *Labor's Heritage*, Vol. 8, No. 1 (Summer 1996), pp. 4-25; Sanford D. Horwitt, *Let Them Call Me Rebel: Saul Alinsky — His Life and Legacy* (New York: Vintage Books, 1992), pp. 222-226.

8 Author's interview with Jaime Gonzalez Monroy, Monrovia, June 22, 1997; Author's interview with Henry Nava, Monterey Park, February 9, 1995; Henry Nava interview; Tony Rios interview; Edward Roybal interview; Margarita Duran Mendez interview.

9 Author's interview with Msgr. William J. Barry, Newport Beach, November 2, 1994; Henry Nava interview; Tony Rios interview; Hope Mendoza Schechter interview; Sanford D. Horwitt, *Let Them Call Me Rebel: Saul Alinsky — His Life and Legacy*, pp. 231-332.

10 James Mendez interview.

11 Hope Mendoza Schechter interview.

12 "Latin Vote Registration Doubled, Group Announces," *Belvedere Citizen*, April 30, 1948, p. 1. See also"X-Ray Used in Registration of Voters for Tests for TB," *Los Angeles Daily News*, March 6, 1948, p. 2; "Spanish-Speaking Group Spurs Vote Registration," *Los Angeles Times*, March 15, 1948.

13 "Tabulation of Returns, City Council District 9, City of Los Angeles, 31 May 1949," Los Angles City Archives. The precincts were plotted to a precinct map of the district to develop insights in voting patterns by neighborhood. Katherine Underwood, "Process and Politics: Multiracial Electoral Coalition Building and Representation in Los Angeles' Ninth District, 1949-1962" (Ph.D. diss., University of California, San Diego, 1992).

14 Tony Rios interview; CSO, "Highlights of the Past 20 Years," author's files; Minutes, JCRC, June 14, 1949, p. 2, in 10/CSO-1948-1949, Jewish Community Relations Council Papers, Urban Archives Center, California State University, Northridge.

15 For a fuller description of the election, see Kenneth C. Burt, "The Power of a Mobilized Citizenry and Coalition Politics: The 1949 Election of Edward Roybal to the Los Angeles City Council," *Southern California Quarterly*, Vol. 85, No. 4 (Winter 2003), pp. 413-438.

16 Kenneth C. Burt, "Tony Rios and Bloody Christmas: A Turning Point Between the Los Angeles Police Department and Latino Community," in the *Western Legal History: The Journal of the Ninth Judicial Circuit Historical Society*, Vol. 14, No. 2 (Summer/Fall 2001).

17 One of the requests that the CIO and the Catholic Church made of Tony Rios in 1952 is that he became a union organizer. See Kenneth C. Burt, "The Battle for Standard Coil: The United Electrical Workers, the Community Services Organization, and the Catholic Church in Latino East Los Angeles," in Robert W. Cherny, William Issel, and Kieran Walsh Taylor, eds., *American Labor and the Cold War: Grassroots Politics and Postwar Political Culture* (New Brunswick, NJ: Rutgers University Press, 2004), pp. 118-140.

18 Author's interview with Dan Luevano, Sacramento, June 22, 1996; Tony Rios interview; Hope Mendoza Schechter interview CSO, "Highlights of the Past 20 Years," author's files; Ralph C. Guzman, *The Political Socialization of the Mexican American People* (New York: Arno Press, 1976), p. 141.

19 Hope Mendoza Schechter interview; "Padilla Wins Council Seat in San Fernando," *People's World*, April 14, 1950, p. 12; "Spanish Vote Rallied in Los Angeles," *Christian Science Monitor*, May 29, 1950; CSO, "Highlights of the Past 20 Years," author's files; Minutes, City Council, April 18, 1950, Clerk's Office, City of San Fernando; Ralph C. Guzman, *The Political Socialization of the Mexican American People*, p. 141.

20 Margarita Duran Mendez interview.

21 Henry Nava interview; Hope Mendoza Schechter interview.

22 Author's interview with Leopoldo Sanchez, Los Angeles, January 4, 1982; Author's interview with George R. Sotelo, Pasadena, 1981-2002; "Carlos M. Teran," Martindale-Hubbell Law Directory, 1957, p. 164; John Anson Ford, *Thirty Explosive Years in Los Angeles County* (San Marino, California: The Huntington Library, 1961), p. 137.

23 Hope Mendoza and Harvey Schechter interview.

24 Tony Rios interview; CSO, "Highlights of the Past 20 Years," author's files.

25 Author's interview with Hank Lopez, Los Angeles, January 4, 1982.

26 *Ibid.*; Author's interview with Herman Sillas, Los Angeles, August 22, 2003.

27 Norris Poulson, Oral History, UCLA, p. 441.

28 "Los Angeles: Upset," *Newsweek*, June 12, 1961, p. 38.

29 George Sotelo interview; Eddie Ramirez interview; Richard Tafoya interview; Benjamin John Bridgeman Allen, *Amigos Sam? Mayor Sam Yorty and the Latino Community of Los Angeles* (Thesis, Department of History, Harvard University, March 23, 2000), p. 48. The author wishes to thank Raphael J. Sonenshein for a copy of the thesis which provides new insights into the relationship between Yorty and Latinos.

30 Kenneth C. Burt, *The History of MAPA and Chicano Politics in California* (Sacramento: MAPA), 1992, p. 7.

31 Author's interview with Philip L. Soto, Los Angeles, March 9, 1982; Author's interview with Dionicio Morales, City of Commerce, July 29, 2003; Hispanic Link News Service files.

32 *MAPA News*, May 24, 1967, p. 8, Chicano, Subject File, Southern California Library for Research and Social Studies.

33 Julian Nava, *Julian Nava: My Mexican American Journey* (Houston: Arte Público Press, 2002), p. 72.

34 Author's interview with Henry L. Lacayo, Newbury Park, January 4, 1997, and 2000-2004.
35 Statement of the Vote, 1968-1974, California State Archives.
36 "Roybal Speaks, Interview Council Candidates at Mass Meeting," n.p., n.d., Clippings, Edward Roybal Papers, Special Collections, California State University, Los Angeles.
37 *Ibid.*
38 Clippings, Edward Roybal Papers; Raphael J. Sorenshein, *Politics in Black and White: Race and Power in Los Angeles* (Princeton, New Jersey: Princeton University Press, 1993), pp. 40-46.
39 Miscellaneous Clippings, 1962, Edward Roybal Papers.
40 Author's interview with Richard Tafoya, Montebello, May 31, 1997.
41 George R. Sotelo interview; Richard Tafoya interview.
42 Peter Skerry, *Mexican Americans: The Ambivalent Minority* (New York: The Free Press, 1994).
43 James Richardson, "The Members' Speaker: How Willie Brown Held Center Stage in California, 1980-1995," in Michael B. Preston, Bruce Cain, and Sandra Bass, eds., *Racial and Ethnic Politics in California*, Volume Two (Berkeley: Institute of Governmental Studies Press, UC Berkeley, 1998), 137-158. For full disclosure, the author worked for the Speaker's Office of Majority Services for a number of years.
44 Richard A. Clacus, *Willie Brown and the California Assembly* (Berkeley: Institute of Governmental Studies Press, UC Berkeley, 1995); Fernando J. Guerra, The Career Paths of Minority Elected Politicians," in Bryan O. Jackson and Michael B. Preston, eds., *Racial and Ethnic Politics in California* (Berkeley: Institute of Governmental Studies Press, UC Berkeley, 1993), pp. 117-131; James Richardson, *Willie Brown* (Berkeley: University of California Press, 1996), p. 225; Peter Skerry, *Mexican Americans.*
45 Bruce E. Cain, *The Reapportionment Puzzle* (Berkeley: University of California Press, 1984), pp. 166-178. The U.S. Supreme Court subsequently restricted the Justice Department's interpretation: "Court Overturns Federal Rule for Voter Redistricting Plans," *Sacramento Bee*, May 13, 1997, p. A6; "High Court Again Bars Race-Based Redistricting," *Los Angeles Times*, June 30, 1997, p. A12.
46 Richard A. Clacus, *Willie Brown and the California Assembly*, p. 122; James Richardson, *Willie Brown*, p. 329; Richard Skerry, *Mexican Americans*, p. 332; Dan Walters, *The New California: Facing the 21st Century*, 2nd Edition (Sacramento, California Journal Press1992), p. 33.
47 The legal breakthrough came in a Watsonville case. See Joaquin G. Avila, *Latino Political Empowerment: A Perspective* (self published, [1990?], p. 21.
48 Richard Skerry, *Mexican Americans*, pp. 333-335, with "stole the election" quote on p. 334; Jaime Regalado, "Conflicts Over Redistricting in Los Angeles: Who Wins? Who Loses," in Byran O. Jackson and Michael B. Preston, eds., *Racial and Ethnic Politics in California*, pp. 373-394; Dan Walters, *The New California: Facing the 21st Century*, 2nd edition, p. 24.

49 Cuban-born Ileana Ros-Lechtinen was elected to Congress in 1988 from Florida and the Puerto Rican-born Nydia M. Velázquez was elected from New York in 1993.

50 Statement of the Vote, 1990-1992, California State Archives; Raymond A. Rocco, "Latino Los Angeles," in Allen J. Scott and Edward W. Soja, eds., *The City: Los Angeles and Urban Theory at the End of the Twentieth Century* (Berkeley: University of California Press, 1996), pp. 365-389.

51 Fernando J. Guerra, "The Career Paths of Minority Elected Politicians," in Michael B. Preston, Bruce Cain, and Sandra Bass, *Racial and Ethnic Politics in California*, Volume Two, pp. 450-451.

52 Dan Walters, *The New California: Facing the 21ˢᵗ Century*, 2ⁿᵈ Edition, p. 19. Richard Santillan and Federico A. Subevi-Velez, "Latino Participation in Republican Party Politics in California," in *Racial and Ethnic Politics in California*, pp. 285-319.

53 H. Eric Schockman, "California's Ethnic Experiment and the Unsolvable Immigration Issue: Proposition 187 and Beyond," and "Nativism, Partisanship, and Immigration: An Analysis of Prop. 198," both in Michael B. Preston, Bruce Cain, and Sandra Bass, *Racial and Ethnic Politics in California*, Volume Two, pp. 233-304.

54 H. Eric Schockman, "California's Ethnic Experiment and the Unsolvable Immigration Issue: Proposition 187 and Beyond," p. 269.

55 George Skelton, "Straddling the Line on Illegal Immigration," *Los Angeles Times*, August 26, 1993, p. A3; "State's Diversity Doesn't Reach Voting Booth," *Los Angeles Times*, November 10, 1994, p. A1; "Prop. 187 May Show Clergy's Political Role is Dwindling," *Los Angeles Times*, November 20, 1994, p. A3; "Despite Gains, Latino Voters Still Lack Clout," *Los Angeles Times*, December 4, 1994, p. A1.

56 "House GOP Charts California Agenda," *Los Angeles Times*, November 13, 1994, p. A1.

57 H. Eric Schockman, "California's Ethnic Experiment and the Unsolvable Immigration Issue: Proposition 187 and Beyond," in Michael B. Preston, Bruce Cain, and Sandra Bass, *Racial and Ethnic Politics in California*, p. 261.

58 See Michael B. Preston and James S. Lai, "The Symbolic Politics of Affirmative Action," Michael B. Preston, Bruce Cain, and Sandra Bass, eds., *Racial and Ethnic Politics in California*, Volume Two (Berkeley: Institute of Governmental Studies Press, UC Berkeley, 1998), pp. 161-198.

59 Bruce E. Cain and Karin Mac Donald, "Race and Party Politics in the 1997 U.S. Presidential Election," in Michael B. Preston, Bruce Cain, and Sandra Bass, *Racial and Ethnic Politics in California*, Volume Two, p. 200.

60 Harry P. Pachon, "Latino Politics in the Golden State: Ready for the 21ˢᵗ Century?" Michael B. Preston, Bruce Cain, and Sandra Bass, *Racial and Ethnic Politics in California*, Volume Two, p. 420.

61 John B. Judis and Roy Teixeira, *The Emerging Democratic Majority* (New York: Scribner, 2002), p. 29.

[62] Author's interview with Miguel Contreras, Los Angeles, 1977-1984.

[63] Miguel Contreras interview, March 28, 1977.

[64] Fernando Guerra, "Latino Politics in California: The Necessary Conditions for Success," Michael B. Preston, Bruce Cain, and Sandra Bass, *Racial and Ethnic Politics in California*, Volume Two, p. 450. The need for the three legally separate campaigns arose from a newly enacted but since discarded campaign reform law. The basic outlines of the campaign, targeted union members and newly registered immigrant voters, along with a more generalized candidate campaign would be used repeated. In terms of full disclosure, the author served on the AFL-CIO campaign during this election as the newly hired political director for the California Federation of Teachers, a post that provided a participant-observer vantagepoint for most of the subsequent events.

[65] For more on the County Federation, see Larry Frank and Kent Wong, "Dynamic Political Mobilization: The Los Angeles County Federation of Labor," *Working USA: The Journal of Labor and Society*, Vol. 8, No. 2 (December 2004), p. 154-181

[66] "A significant question, especially for political incorporation theorists, is whether the incorporation of communities of color will be more difficult to achieve, and sustain, under term limits," asked Jaime Regalado. "It seems likely that, since mass-based electoral and community coalitions have historically been difficult to maintain over time, it would be difficult to consistently create/or maintain electoral coalitions to replace 'termed' councilmembers," stated Jaime Regalado, in "Minority Political Incorporation in Los Angeles: A Broader Consideration," in Michael O, Michael B. Preston, Bruce Cain, and Sandra Bass, eds., *Racial and Ethnic Politics in California*, Volume Two, p. 393.

[67] To date, Latinos and Asians have gained from the process. In Los Angeles, Contreras has worked to ensure African American representation, helping to elect Blacks supportive of Latino and working family concerns.

[68] Harold Meyerson, "Getting to 50-Puls-1," *Los Angeles Weekly*, April 27-May 3, 2002.

[69] Cover, "Latino Power: L.A.'s New Mayor—And How Hispanics Will Change America's Politics," *Newsweek*, May 30, 2005.

[70] "Out With the Ho-Hum: L.A. Times Endorsement: Villaraigosa for Mayor," *Los Angeles Times*, May 8, 2005.

[71] "Leader Who Restored Labor's Clout in L.A. Dies," *Los Angeles Times*, May 7, 2005.

[72] "The 2005 Mayoral Election Compared to 2001," *Los Angeles Times*, May 19, 2005, p. A19.

[73] City of Los Angeles web site, November 26, 2005.

[74] John B. Judis and Roy Teixeira, *The Emerging Democratic Majority* (New York.: Scribner, 2002), p. 6. The book focuses explains the role of Latinos and California in the evolving Democratic Party coalition. Specific attention is focused on Latino Los Angeles.

Selected Bibliography

Abu-Lughod, Janet L. *New York, Chicago, Los Angeles: America's Global Cities.* Minneapolis: University of Minnesota Press, 1999.

Acuna, Rodolfo F. *Anything But Mexican: Chicanos in Contemporary Los Angeles.* New York: Verso, 1996.

Allen, James P., and Eugene Turner. *The Ethnic Quilt: Population Diversity in Southern California.* Northridge, CA: Center for Geographical Studies, California State University, Northridge, 1997.

Avila, Eric. *Popular Culture in the Age of White Flight: Fear and Fantasy in Suburban Los Angeles.* Berkeley: University of California Press, 2004.

Balderrama, Francisco E., and Raymond Rodriguez. *Decade of Betrayal: Mexican Repatriation in the 1930s.* Albuquerque: University of New Mexico Press, 1995.

Burt, Kenneth C. "The Power of a Mobilized Citizenry and Coalition Politics: The 1949 Election of Edward Roybal to the Los Angeles City Council." *Southern California Quarterly* 85 (Winter 2004): 413-38.

Cannon, Lou. *Official Negligence: How the Rodney King Riots Changed Los Angeles and the LAPD.* New York: Random House, 1997.

Chang, Edward T., and Jeannette Diaz-Veizades. *Ethnic Peace in the American City: Building Community in Los Angeles and Beyond.* New York: New York University Press, 1999.

Cole, Carolyn Kozo, and Kathy Kobayashi. *Shades of L.A.: Pictures from Ethnic Family Albums.* New York: The New Press, 1996.

Davis, Clark. "The View From Spring Street: White-Collar Men in the City of Angels." In *Metropolis in the Making: Los Angeles in the 1920s*, edited by Tom Sitton and William Deverell, 179-98. Berkeley: University of California Press, 2001.

Davis, Mike. *City Of Quartz: Excavating The Future In Los Angeles.* New York: Verso, 1990.

Deverell, William. *Whitewashed Adobe: The Rise of Los Angeles and the Remaking of its Mexican Past.* Berkeley: University of California Press, 2004.

Escobar, Edward J. *Race, Police, and the Making of a Political Identity: Mexican Americans and the Los Angeles Police Department, 1900-1945.* Berkeley: University of California Press, 1999.

Flamming, Douglas. *Bound for Freedom: Black Los Angeles in Jim Crow America.* Berkeley: University of California Press, 2005.

Gottlieb, Robert et al. *The Next Los Angeles: The Struggle for a Livable City.* Berkeley: University of California Press, 2005.

Hata, Donald Teruo, Jr. and Nadine Ishitani Hata. "Justice Delayed But Not Denied?" In *Alien Justice: Wartime Internment in Australia and North America*, edited by Kay Saunders and Roger Daniels, 221-33. Queensland, Australia: University of Queensland Press, 2000.

Hise, Greg. "Border City: Race and Social Distance in Los Angeles." In *Los Angeles and the Future of Urban Cultures*, edited by Raul Homero Villa and George J. Sanchez, 545-58. Special issue of the American Quartely 56 (September 2004).

Horne, James. *Fire This Time: The Watt Uprising and the 1960s.* Charlottesville, VA: University Press of Virginia, 1995.

Johnson, James H. Jr., and Walter C. Farrell, Jr. "The Fire This Time: The Genesis of the Los Angeles Rebellion of 1992." *North Carolina Law Review* 71 (June 1993): 1403-20.

Klein, Norman M., and Martin J. Schiesl. eds. *20th Century Los Angeles: Power, Promotion, and Social Conflict.* Claremont, CA: Regina Books, 1990.

Kurashige, Lon. *Japanese American Celebration and Conflict: A History of Ethnic Identity and Festival, 1934-1990.* Berkeley: University of California Press, 2002.

Laslett, John H. M. "Historical Perspectives: Immigration and the Rise of a Distinctive Urban Region, 1900-1970." In *Ethnic Los Angeles*, edited by Roger Waldinger and Mehdi Bozorgmehr, 39-75. New York: Russell Sage Foundation, 1996.

Leonard, Kevin Allen. "'In the Interests of All Races': African Americans and Interracial Cooperation in Los Angeles during and after World War II." In *Seeking El Dorado: African Americans in California*, edited by Lawrence B. de Graaf, Kevin Mulroy, and Quintard Taylor, 309-40. Seattle: University of Washington Press, 2001.

Lotchin, Roger W. *The Bad City in the Good War: San Francisco, Los Angeles, Oakland, and San Diego.* Bloomington, IN: Indiana University Press, 2003.

McBroome, Delores Nason. "Harvests of Gold: African American Boosterism, Agriculture, and Investment in Allensworth and Little Liberia." In *Seeking El Dorado: African Americans in California*, edited by Lawrence B. de Graaf, Kevin Mulroy, and Quintard Taylor, 149-80. Seattle: University of Washington Press, 2001.

Modarres, Ali. "Neighborhood Integration: Temporality and Social Fracture." *Journal of Urban Affairs* 26 (July 2004): 351-77.

Modarres, Ali. *The Racial and Ethnic Structure of Los Angeles County.* Los Angeles: Edmund G. "Pat" Brown Institute of Public Affairs, California State University, Los Angeles, 1994.

Monroy, Douglas. *Rebirth: Mexican Los Angeles from the Great Migration to the Great Depression.* Berkeley: University of California Press, 1999.

Nicolaides, Becky M. *My Blue Heaven: Life and Politics in the Working-Class Suburbs of Los Angeles, 1920-1965.* Chicago: University of Chicago Press, 2002.

Oliver, Melvin L., James H. Johnson, Jr., and Walter C. Farrell, Jr. "Anatomy of a Rebellion: A Political-Economic Analysis."

In *Reading Rodney King, Reading Urban Uprising,* edited by Robert Gooding-Williams, 117-41. New York: Routledge, 1993.

Ong, Paul and Evelyn Blumenberg. "Income and Racial Inequality in Los Angeles." In *The City: Los Angeles and Urban Theory at the End of the Twentieth Century,* edited by Allen J. Scott and Edward J. Soja, 311-35. Berkeley: University of California Press, 1996.

Pagan, Eduardo Obregon. *Murder at the Sleepy Lagoon: Zoot Suits, Race, and Riot in Wartime L.A.* Chapel Hill: University of North Carolina Press, 2003.

Sanchez, George J. *Becoming Mexican American: Ethnicity, Culture, and Identity in Chicano Los Angeles, 1900-1945.* New York: Oxford University Press, 1993.

Sides, Josh. *L.A. City Limits: African American Los Angeles from the Great Depression to the Present.* Berkeley: University of California Press, 2003.

Vigil, James Diego. *A Rainbow of Gangs: Street Cultures in the Mega-City.* Austin: University of Texas Press, 2002.

Wild, Mark. *Street Meeting: Multiethnic Neighborhoods in Early Twentieth-Century Los Angeles.* Berkeley: University of California Press, 2005.

CONTRIBUTORS

Kenneth C. Burt is the political director of the California Federation of Teachers and the Carey McWilliams Fellow at the University of California at Berkeley. He has published in a number of journals and anthologies, winning the Historical Society of Southern California's Doyce B. Nunis Award.

Mark Morrall Dodge, a native southern Californian, is a lecturer at California State University, Los Angeles, and adjunct assistant professor of history at Pasadena City College. He is the author of *Pasadena City College, a Seventy-fifth Anniversary History* (2001), edited *Herbert Hoover and the Historians* (1989), and has published in a number of history journals.

Donald Teruo Hata is professor emeritus of history at California State University, Dominguez Hills. He was a prisoner at the concentration camp for persons of Japanese ancestry, Gila, Arizona. He and his wife Nadine collaborated on publications on the Asian American experience, including *Japanese Americans and World War II* (1998).

Nadine Ishitani Hata was vice president for Academic Affairs and professor emeritus of history at El Camino College. She was active in the American Historical Association, the Organization of American Historians, vice chair of the California State Advisory Committee to the U.S. Commission on Civil Rights, and chair of the State Historical Resources Commission. She was the author of *The Historic Preservation Movement in California, 1940-1976* (1992), and editor of the *AHA-OAH report on Community College Historians in the United States* (1999).

Delores Nason McBroome is professor of history at Humboldt State University, California. She is the author of *Parallel Communities: African Americans in California's East Bay, 1850-1963* (1993) and contributor to *American Labor in the Era of World War II* (1995) and *Seeking El Dorado: African Americans in California* (2001).

Gloria E. Miranda is the Dean of Behavioral and Social Sciences at El Camino College and has also taught history and Chicano Studies courses during her twenty-five year career. Her publications range from pioneering work on early Hispano-Mexican family life to Mexican immigrant family experiences in the United States.

Ali Modarres is Associate Director of the Edmund G. "Pat" Brown Institute of Public Affairs at California State University, Los Angeles and a professor in the Department of Geography and Urban Analysis. He specializes in urban geography and his publication interests are society and space, identity, transnationalism, urban history, and planning. His recent publications have focused on theories of poverty, race and ethnicity, and immigration in American cities.

Martin Schiesl is professor emeritus of history at California State University, Los Angeles. He is the author of *The Politics of Efficiency: Municipal Administration and Reform in America, 1880-1920* (1977), co-editor of *20th Century Los Angeles: Power, Promotion, and Social Conflict* (1990), and editor of *Responsible Liberalism: Edmund G. "Pat" Brown and Reform Government in California, 1958-1967* (2003).

Josh Sides is the W.P. Whitsett Professor in California History at California State University, Northridge and author of *L.A. City Limits: African American Los Angeles from the Great Depression to the Present* (2003).

INDEX

Wong, Evelyn 100
Wong, Delbert Earl 100
Woo, Michael 101
Wood, James 196
Woods, Tiger 103
World War I 12, 68, 70ff
World War II 13, 14, 30, 32, 33, 49-55, 111, 113-115, 179
Wyman, Roz 184

Y

Yamagata-Noji, Audrey 101
Yamaki, Mike 103

Yamauchi, Wakako 103
Yorty, Sam 129, 141, 149, 185, 188
Yoshima, Karen 157
Young, Charles C. 150
Young Citizens for Community Action (YCCA) 148
Young Workers Liberation League 155
Younger, Evelle 151

Z

zoot suits 30
Zoot Suit riots 31-32, 175, 195